We Were 49ers!

We Were 49ers!

Chilean Accounts of the California Gold Rush

translated and edited
by
Edwin A. Beilharz and Carlos U. López

WARD RITCHIE PRESS
Pasadena, California

ACKNOWLEDGMENTS

Recognition and sincere expressions of gratitude are due to the National Endowment for the Humanities for the grant, in 1973–74, that helped finance the study of the Chileans in California; to the Sourisseau Academy for the grant that made possible the purchase of Chilean materials; and to Señor Filiú Cruz, Director of the Sala J. T. Medina, for his assistance in locating the works of Combet.

The authors wish to express their gratitude in a special way to Professor Pereira Salas for wise advice and assistance, to Donald K. Rosenberg for invaluable aid in selecting and processing many of the illustrations, and to Frieda Rosenberg for her critical reading of the manuscript and helpful suggestions.

The sketch of Pérez Rosales and the reproductions of his drawings were supplied by Editorial Francisco Aguirre. The sketch of Vicuña Mackenna was provided by *El Mercurio* of Santiago through the courtesy of Thomas McHale. The views of the Mokelumne area and the photograph of Colonel Ayres were taken from the latter's book, *Gold and Sunshine*. The sketch of Sacramento in the 1850s was taken from Louise Taber's *Gold Rush Days*, where it appeared through courtesy of the Society of California Pioneers. The other sketches of early California came from *Hutchin's California Magazine* of 1857 and from the *Century Illustrated Monthly* of 1892.

CONTENTS

ILLUSTRATIONS

INTRODUCTION

The people of Chile exhibited, almost from the beginning, a temperament, character, and attitude that set them apart from all other Hispanic peoples in the Western Hemisphere. Nations, like individuals, are products of heredity and environment; and in the case of Chile both of these influences were unique.

Chile is a long, narrow ribbon of land stretching down the west coast of South America between the 17th and 57th parallels of latitude. If transposed into equivalent latitudes in the Northern Hemisphere, it would extend from Honduras to Alaska. Yet, despite its enormous length, it is a well-defined land united by strong national feeling. It derives this sense of limits and identity from the awesome natural boundaries that fence it on every side. A Chilean was always aware that he was different from the Argentinian who lived on the other side of the Andes, and from the Peruvians and Bolivians who lived beyond the deserts to the north. Human nature being what it is, the Chilean was inclined to translate this sense of difference into a feeling of superiority—or at least into an attitude marked by consciousness of his own virtues and of the rather less admirable traits of neighboring peoples.

These characteristics did not endear the Chilean to his neighbors. The common appellation of *perro chileno* heard in Peru testifies to this. But that invidious term itself carried an overtone of respect and even of admiration. It was a recognition that Chileans were an unusually virile, enterprising, and efficient people, a people ordinarily well able to take care of themselves and one it was wiser not to antagonize needlessly. We shall see something of this same reaction to the Chilean on the part of Anglo-American miners in California.

[xi]

The character of the Chilean people was also a result of their distinctive origin and history. The land was explored in 1535 by the expedition of Diego de Almagro from Peru. He discovered that there was no civilized Indian nation in Chile whose wealth could be appropriated, but that the land was beautiful, the soil fertile, and the climate salubrious. When Pedro de Valdivia led a colony south into Chile in 1540, therefore, it was understood that its members were settlers and that they would make their living through agriculture. The Indians of the central area were primitive and few in number, so they were quickly absorbed—with the result that the Chileans developed quite early into a homogeneous racial type, predominantly European in character. The society they established took on the characteristic Hispanic form; that is, it was made up of two classes: the dominant landed *ricos,* and the landless and subservient poor. But this class division was not so markedly racial in character as that found elsewhere in the Americas.

In southern Chile the settlers found a very different Indian people, the Araucanians, so fierce and warlike they could not be subdued. The result was that Chile remained throughout the colonial period a battlefield, or, in the Spanish phrase, an *escuela de armas.* It is impossible to weigh the psychological effect of this upon the Chilean temperament, but it may well be that this constant frontier fighting bred a militant spirit in the Chilean nation.

In the period of the struggle for independence in Spanish America, Chile was fortunate in its leaders. The Liberator, Bernardo O'Higgins, was an enlightened man despite his dictatorial behavior. During his brief period of power (1818–23), he genuinely tried to lay the foundations of republican government. He began a system of public education and helped found a library in Santiago to serve the Chilean people. After a brief period of civil war (1823–29), an even more able leader appeared. He was Diego Portales. Under his tutelage Chile emerged as one of the most stable republics of Latin America. The regime he helped establish was not democratic, but it was government under law. It provided for an orderly and constitutional transfer of power from one administration to the next; and it did give the country a long period of almost uninterrupted peace. Portales has been called the Alexander Hamilton of Chile. Like Hamilton, he was a man of clear, precise ideas and gifted with a great deal of common sense. Like Hamilton, too, he was distrustful of idealists to the point of cynicism, basically conserva-

tive in his beliefs, but no tyrant. His system left all real power
to the landowners: the right to vote was limited by high property
qualifications. The president of the Republic was dominant. He
was not responsible to the Congress, and he had absolute power
to veto its enactments. He named national and provincial officials.
He controlled elections and, in effect, virtually chose his successor.

The authoritarian system of Portales would, like Hamilton's, be
reformed and democratized as time went on. But it was still essen-
tially intact in the period of the California Gold Rush when so
many Chileans left their country to share in the great bonanza
to the north; and it is against this background that the interesting
reactions of the Chileans to the political system of the United States
must be viewed.

The large-scale migration of Chileans into California during the
Gold Rush, and the significant role they played then in California
affairs may seem surprising. Their numbers, it is estimated, may
have reached seven thousand. In the early months they constituted
the second-largest foreign contingent, the first and largest being
made up of Mexicans, mainly from the bordering state of Sonora.

The first report of the gold strike in California reached Chile
on August 19, 1848, when the brig *J.R.S.* dropped anchor in Valparaíso. The ship had been engaged in the hides and tallow trade
with California and brought a cargo of these products consigned
to G. L. Hobson, a merchant of Valparaíso. The news the captain
brought should have been electrifying. It was being said in California, he reported, that the area was "all gold." The precious metal
was so abundant that all one had to do was bend over and pick
it up. He complained that half his crew had deserted to go off to
the gold fields, leaving him too few men to work the ship properly.

Apparently, though, his report was too fantastic to be believed,
and it was only after ten more days had passed and the schooner
Adelaida reached port carrying two thousand, five hundred dollars
in California gold dust that the excitement began. But, once generated, it spread rapidly up and down the coast.

The first men in Chile to react were foreign merchants, English
and North American, who had establishments in Valparaíso. They
doubtless felt their knowledge of the English language would give
them an advantage in California. At any rate, within two weeks
of the arrival of the *Adelaida*, forty-five English-speaking passengers
set out from Valparaíso, bound for California aboard the frigate

Virginia. Other men like themselves, once residents of Chile, already had gone to California. They bore such famous names as Faxon D. Atherton, William E. P. Hartnell, James Lick, and Robert Livermore—names commemorated now in well-known California towns and institutions. Some of the men on the *Virginia's* roster, Armstrong, Ellis, Hubbard, O'Neill, and Poett, were to achieve only slightly less fame and fortune.

Most of these men had Chilean wives and families, and brought them to California. They regarded themselves as Chileans and so listed themselves in the later United States census, although, of course, all in time became citizens of this country. Their knowledge of Chile, and the economic contacts they had built up there, were valuable to them in California, for Chile quickly became a major supplier of the California market. There was an enormous demand for mining equipment of all sorts: shovels, picks, gold pans, and scales; a virtually insatiable thirst for wines, brandy, and all other liquors; and a great and growing market for grain, milled flour, dried fruits, and other foodstuffs; for clothing and shoes; for frying pans, cutlery, gunpowder; for building materials—even including timber, which one would have thought was already in sufficient supply here. The explanation of this oddity was that mining tended to draw off the labor supply that would have been needed to fell the trees and to saw them into usable lumber. Chileans even brought prefabricated houses and found a ready sale for them.

This market was an unpredictable one, subject to violent changes. It could become clogged and oversupplied when too many ships came with identical cargoes. An importer could lose a fortune at such a time. At other times Californians would buy everything that was offered, and at whatever price was asked. The market was also a temporary one so far as Chileans were concerned, for merchants in the eastern part of the United States were not slow in taking advantage of the opportunity offered, and production in California itself developed, with a labor force made up of a backwash of disappointed men coming out of the mines. The truth of the matter is that, after the first years, the real opportunity for the poor man lay not in mining but in feeding and supplying the mining population.

The first wave of English-speaking argonauts from Chile bearing down on California was soon followed by a much larger one made up of men—and women—of Spanish speech. Again, not surprisingly, those who led the way in this migration were persons who possessed some special skill or aptitude they felt would be advantageous to them in the new land. Many of these were professional miners in Chile, experienced tunnel and shaft diggers, or at least men who felt they had gained some practical knowledge of mining methods through observation. Men of this sort had an important role to play, for they, with the men from Sonora, were to give the Anglo-Americans their first instruction in mining methods.

Most California mining (and all of it in the earlier years) consisted in the working of placers, that is, sands and gravels, chiefly in river beds. It was in this type of mining that Mexicans and Chileans had the greatest expertise—the very word *placer* is Spanish. Chileans had begun to reach the mines in the last months of 1848, and they were in a position therefore to demonstrate the proper procedures in placer mining. They could point out the most promising gravel formations, identify sites where gold was most apt to be concentrated because the river had changed course or was flowing more slowly, and could spot the massing of river boulders that might lead to the formation of a "glory hole." They knew how a gold pan should be manipulated, and at what point (the black sand stage) a man should cease pan-washing and add the material in his pan to his store of concentrates for further processing with quicksilver. The Chileans had a long curving knife, the *corvo*, well adapted to picking deposits from the cracks in rocks; and a dipping tool, the *poruña*, made from the horn of a cow. They knew how to use a winnowing method, the *aventamiento*, where water was not available; and they built a stone-wheel mechanism called a "Chile Mill" to grind resistant materials. These stone wheels were of enormous size, and were hewn out of solid rock by Chileans. Two Chileans are listed in the census of 1852 as "stone cutters," but it is probable there were more than that number following this trade.

The gold fever did not stop with Chileans who were more or less experienced in mining. It spread also into the general population. The bulk of these lacked the wherewithal to pay their passage, and had to beg, borrow, or steal to get together the needed funds. Some were able to get work as sailors or service personnel on the ships; others hired themselves out as mine workers to wealthier men who would pay their way.

All of them, of course, expected to make fortunes in California. If they were men, they were for the most part foredoomed to disappointment. Not so if they were women. Prostitutes from Valparaíso and Talcahuano did very well. Many of them married in California. If they were shrewd they could marry well; they had a wide choice of eager suitors in this woman-starved land. Some became founders of California families that were to play honorable roles in the history of the Golden State.

A word should be said about the effect of this excitement and activity on Chile itself. It was obviously stimulating and beneficial to the Chilean economy, especially at first. Some Chileans did make a go of it in the mines, and returned to Chile with their riches. For a time, too, Chilean products were in great demand, and Chilean ships were kept busy plying the sea lanes between their motherland and San Francisco. Profits were phenomenal and almost anything taken to California could be sold.

In early 1849, ships from the eastern ports of the United States began to make stopovers in Chile after rounding the Horn. They needed food, fuel, and water to continue their voyages northward. Talcahuano, the port for the city of Concepción, did an especially flourishing business. The sellers of rum (and this meant almost everybody) and the local prostitutes had all the clients they could handle. Valparaíso went through a similar experience. Talcahuano could berth a dozen ships in its harbor; Valparaíso could accommodate more than a hundred. They came and went constantly. A German captain reported that he had counted three hundred ships visiting Valparaíso in a single day, and that a dozen of these were from Hamburg, his home port.

It was too good to last, however. As noted above, the law of supply and demand eventually produced other sources of goods and food for California. Chilean shipowners also noted a deplorable tendency for the ships they sent north to stay there; their crews and even their captains deserted the ships to head for the Sierra, and the ships either lay rotting in San Francisco Bay or were converted into shops and housing after being run ashore. Ninety-two of the 119 ships registered in Chilean ports were derelicts at San Francisco by the end of 1849.

What added the final touch of disaster was the development of a strong anti-Chilean feeling in California itself. This hostility had many roots. Basically, of course, the Anglo-American argonauts disliked all aliens, whatever their nationality, because they regarded them as rivals. Resentment and jealousy became intensified when the Sierra streams were overpopulated by gold seekers in proportion to the number of good spots available. It is noteworthy that there was none of this rancor in 1848 when the miners were chiefly Californians and neighbors, and the placers were plentiful.

The Chileans felt that they were singled out as targets for this malevolence and ill treatment, however. This is the burden of their story in page after page of the reports that follow. The evidence on the Anglo-American side indicates that the Chilean complaints were well founded. A very marked difference can be noted, however, in the explanations each side gave for the difficulties that arose. The Chileans felt that they were especially disliked and subjected to greater cruelty and injustice than other aliens because they fought back. Men of other nationalities, they said, tended to be intimidated by the "Yankees" and to yield up their claims without a struggle. Not so with the Chilean. If he could get his hand on his knife he would resist his attackers—even at gunpoint.

Anglo-American miners, on the other hand, have a very different tale to tell. Their objections to the Chileans, they insisted, were the same ones they had to men who came to California from the southern states with slaves. The Chileans brought peons, and these in Anglo-American eyes were semislaves at best. A southerner would take out mining claims in the names of his slaves, and thus engross and monopolize a large rich area all for himself. Chileans, it was complained, did the same thing with their peons. It was a system with which freemen could not compete; and they did not intend to be forced to do so.

No conflict of this sort is ever simple. Certainly in this case the causes were complex. Both the Chileans and their adversaries were partially correct. It is no doubt true that if the Chileans had not resisted claim jumpers they would have been feared less; and if they had not employed peons to get control of huge sections of the placers they would not have been resented so hotly. But they would still have had difficulties!

Even the most obliging foreigners found themselves defrauded and elbowed aside by the miners from the eastern states. All were subjected to the Foreign Miner's Tax. Almost all were pushed out of the richer northern mines and into the poorer southern ones instead—only to be forced out of those, too, eventually by their covetous oppressors.

The abuse and violence to which the Chileans were subjected in California are horrifying to contemplate. That they actually occurred is undeniable, however, and—shocking and repulsive as they are to read about—they must be faced. It is the first law of history that it must tell the truth.

Violence is an element in the psychology of the people of the United States. It lies not far below the surface and can erupt spontaneously on occasion. Violence was especially in evidence on our frontier; so it is not surprising that it developed in California. Not only were the provocations extreme, but the gold fever had attracted to California a larger than usual proportion of the restless, rootless individuals who made up a goodly part of the first wave of population on every one of our frontiers in turn. The atrocities such men visited on the Chileans in California differed in frequency, but not in ferocity, from the kind to which the French pioneers had been subjected in their peaceful riverbank towns when these were overrun by the so-called Kentuckians in the Illinois country of the 1780s. They were not any more savage than the Mountain Meadow Massacre in the Utah of 1857, or the fighting in "bloody Kansas" that launched us into Civil War. For that matter, they were no worse than the mistreatment our Indians met everywhere the frontier spread.

Having faced these facts as we should, it is only right to point out that such detestable excesses were acts of a minority of the pioneers, that there were other pioneers who did not approve of such misconduct, that public opinion censured it and insisted on the establishment of law and order as soon as possible, and that history has attempted—even if belatedly—to render justice to those to whom it was denied.

The story of some of these atrocities, told for the first time from the Chilean point of view, will be found in the pages that follow. There are vivid descriptions of the "Hounds," a gang of ruffians made up of discharged soldiers of the New York Volunteers, who terrorized early San Francisco but vented their spleen especially on aliens in the city. If one had antagonized a Hound by resisting him, the Chileans report, the only sensible thing to do was to leave town, for the whole gang was sure to come looking for anyone who had the gall to defend himself. The most infamous deed of the Hounds was their raid on "Little Chile," a squalid settlement of men, women, and children at the foot of Telegraph Hill in an area now bounded by Montgomery, Pacific, Jackson, and Kearny

Streets. The assault, involving robbery, murder, and rape, occurred on July 15, 1849. Its perpetrators were never adequately punished.

Equally notorious was the so-called battle of Chili Gulch (an odd contemporary misspelling) in December of that same year. The attack was launched by Anglo-American miners who coveted a rich area the Chileans had occupied in a ravine of the gold country near Mokelumne Hill. The story of this incident, written by an interpreter who was present at the kangaroo court trial of the Chileans, has few parallels for poignancy, harrowing detail, or the eloquent indignation of the narrator.

Chileans in the mines were concentrated in several such areas. There was a Chili Camp and a Chili Town as well as the better known Chili Gulch. Sonora, Murphys, Hornitos, and Hangtown all had large contingents of Chileans. The bulk of these, along with other aliens, were driven out in the summer of 1850; and the largest part of the Chileans seem then to have abandoned California and returned home. But a good many remained, to be absorbed gradually into the population of California by intermarriage.

The violence visited upon the Chileans and others was in part a product of the absence of any legally constituted authority. What is most interesting is that the Chileans, with that strong dash of individualism that is part of the Hispanic heritage, very often reveal a genuine liking for the freedom they enjoyed under this kind of government—"if," as one of them put it, "it is a government."

In this same spirit many of them vigorously applauded the activities of the vigilance committees in San Francisco in stamping out disorders and punishing evildoers. Their approval was based not only on the fact that they were themselves being avenged; they also genuinely liked the direct, public-spirited "democracy in action" that, it seemed to them, the vigilantes represented.

In this connection it is worth noting, too, that the Chileans were very much impressed by the democratic ideals, the constitutional principles, and the political sophistication of the Anglo-Americans. They marveled at the ease and rapidity with which the Californians organized a constituent assembly at Monterey, drafted a constitution, and set up a new state government in 1849.

It seems needless to add that the Chileans did not, of course, hold all "Yankees" responsible for the wrongs they suffered. Many of them found friends among the Anglo-Americans; and they seem to have recognized that most of the people among whom they moved bore them no ill will, even if they were not overly friendly.

The accounts that follow are valuable historical documents that provide primary eyewitness testimony on the kaleidoscopic events and frenzies of the Gold Rush. But they are also intensely interesting human documents, as fresh and vivid as when they were written more than a century ago. They offer us a new and illuminating view of ourselves, in the persons of our ancestors, seen by perceptive, intelligent, and highly articulate observers. Through the eyes of the Chileans we can come to know and understand better the founders of the commonwealth that has grown into the California of today.

We Were 49ers!

Vicente Perez Rosales

VICENTE PÉREZ ROSALES
1807-1886

———◆———

Pérez Rosales was born in Santiago. His boyhood spanned the
period of the Chilean War of Independence. In 1825, at age eighteen, he was sent to France to complete his education. There he
came to know the leading figures in the world of art, literature,
and politics, among them the great South American Liberator, José
de San Martín. The loss of the family estate brought him back to
Chile in 1830. He vainly tried to recoup the family fortune as a
cattleman, a distiller, the operator of a brass foundry, a cooper,
a glass and pottery manufacturer, and a merchant. He then turned
to smuggling tobacco and cattle between Argentina and Chile—with
no better results.

In 1848, at Copiapó he heard about the gold strike in California
and decided to seek his fortune there. He was then forty-two years
old. With him went three of his half-brothers: Ruperto, César, and
Federico, surnamed Solar Rosales; his cousin, Felipe Ramírez; and
two peons from Las Tablas hacienda: Cipriano Avello and Juan
Urbina. To record the adventure he kept a journal, which he enlivened with drawings. This work, Diario de un Viaje a California,
is now lost, except for the first forty-six pages preserved in the
National Archives of Chile. However, in 1878, he published a memoir
based on the still intact diary, under the title Viaje a California.
He followed this with an edited and polished version, "Recuerdos
del Pasado," in the Revista Chilena of 1882.

On his return to Chile, he was sent to Europe to promote immigration to Chile; and later he was appointed a provincial administrator
in Concepción. He ended his career as an honored member of the
Senate of Chile.

The text that follows is his original diary. The story is continued
from the narrative provided in Viaje a California.

[1]

DIARY OF A JOURNEY
TO CALIFORNIA 1848-1849

What surprising changes and turnabouts life brings to men! It is foolish to say, "That is one cup I will not taste." This was the ageless truth we were considering philosophically as we sat on the poop deck of the *Stauelli* on January 1, 1849, just four days out of Valparaíso. We had embarked on December 28, 1848, a year of tragic memory.[1] If anyone had told us three months ago that today one of us would be on his way to California, how we would have hooted at him. Now, I ask myself, what would we have done if he had been bold enough to line us up in a row and say, "Step forth, sons of Zebedee. It is not just one of you who is going to California. Vicente is going, so is Ruperto, so are César and Federico, and, what is more, so is Felipe Ramírez."

December 28, 1848

There was no wind as we left port the afternoon of December 28, 1848, so we were towed by nine boats and as many oarsmen as the French naval station in Valparaíso could lend us.

The ship is so full of passengers, curiosity seekers, and a thousand other people who have come to see us off, that no one can move on deck. Luckily we have on board Orella, the port officer, who has come to straighten out the tangle and clear the ship of all but the passengers. Orella intends to stop the sailing of a buxom and portly damsel allured by the prospect of California gold. She holds a passport under the false name of Rosario Améstica, but rumor has it that her real name—the one she got at birth—is Anacleta, and that she went by the name of Juana in Concepción, Pancha when she lived at Talca, and Rosa Montalva, the name she used in Valparaíso before boarding the ship. Her magnificent rotundity has no doubt been in many tight spots before (in a life worthy of Dante's pen), but I feel sure she has never been in a

---
1. Pérez Rosales had engaged in various enterprises, including that of smuggling, none of them very profitable.

[3]

Escena de California
Dibujo de Vicente Pérez Rosales

Rosita

more bitter-sweet dilemma than now. She is torn between the six *onzas*[2] she paid as passage money and the gold of California that she evidently expected to start collecting during the voyage. She is like a lost ship herself, dashing hopelessly against the rock-like, inflexible face of the port officer. Poor Rosa complains bitterly, swears she is an honest woman of good character and that many on board will testify to this; everyone will say so who has had the good fortune to meet her, and that means most of them. She pleads with one after another, she promises, she weeps, she becomes desperate. Finally, much against our wishes, she is permitted to continue her auriferous voyage, to the applause of most of the sportive passengers.

All told, we are 148. The passengers include 90 men, plus 4 cows, 8 pigs, 12 sheep, a few dozen chickens, 3 dogs, 7 sailors, the captain, and the mate.

---

2. $124.50 in United States money of 1848.

We are a mixed lot in this little Tower of Babel: Frenchmen, Englishmen, Germans, Italians, Chileans; nabobs and beggars. One of us, Alvarez, is a very odd fellow, undersized, a complainer, and addicted to malice and quarreling. He has been declared a bastard by all on board. Castorcito Guzmán is another. The mulatto hates him more than he does seasickness. May it lay them both low as soon as possible.

It is now evening. There is no wind, so we can go neither forward nor back. We are riding at anchor, and we have been vainly peering through a telescope in the hope we could see mother in the distance and bid her goodbye again.

During the night, which we have been forced to spend within sight of Viña del Mar, we have hurled the most outraged and repeated maledictions at Julián, our shipping agent. If any of those curses had reached him he would have melted like lard. This fine gentleman, whom God confound, whisked us all on board just to get rid of us, with no regard to the weather. The first night at sea has been hell for all of us.

Friday, December 29, 1848

We hoisted anchor at sunrise, though there was no more wind than on the previous day. A little later a breeze did set in from the north, and although it was against us we were able to work away from shore after much tacking. Seasickness is widespread. Federico is the one of who has suffered the least, along with our friend, Hurtado. After them, Ruperto, the mulatto, and Felipe have been the first to recover. So far as the Dean[3] is concerned, you cannot count on him: he is vomiting his insides out. Our peons, especially the one known as Chinguillo, are in an extreme state of suffering. The sides of the ship are covered with dripping vomit, and the cabin and the ladders as well. Everywhere you see green faces and hear the sounds of men retching. But it is some consolation, at least, to have Alvarez and Guzmán on their backs.

December 30–31, 1848

Nothing much is happening. The wind is aft, but slow and at times barely moving. The seasickness is tired of pestering us.

---

3. The Dean is Vicente Pérez Rosales himself.

January 1, 1849

Thank God we have reached the new year we longed for, even if, as Adelina[4] wished, it finds us breathing other air than that of our native country. Will this year be like the past ones? Will Fate set the final seal on its malice, crushing the last hopes we have, the last golden dream after so many years of terrible nightmares? We shall see. At any rate the new year is smiling now, and as we are already at the bottom we cannot go any lower. We must be patient.

The day is magnificent. The seasickness has left us in peace. Rosita paid us a visit in the cabin after dinner. We had asked her to bring her guitar, and she regaled us with two marvelously bawdy numbers. She was strongly applauded, and responded with some French songs, and then with *La Marseillaise* and *La Chilena*, both of them badly rendered. The evening was gay enough. Everyone sang, danced, and flirted with Rosita who, though seasick, is still very pretty.

The days following New Year's have been dull and monotonous. The wind, though it gives us little headway, is nevertheless blowing in the right direction. Between this day and January 9, we would all have died of boredom if it were not for the three scenes I will now describe.

January 9, 1849

One of the three dogs that came with the passengers looks like a beast of prey. It bit one of our elegant peons, Cipriano Avello, in the calf, and when he turned his back his attacker nipped him again in the buttocks. Fortunately we remembered about Devil's Balm,[5] and so through Ruperto's application, with faith, hope, and charity, we brought about a complete recovery.

We send our thanks to Don Jorge[6] and beg him to order more of this balm from England so we can work other such miracles.

A few days afterward we had the satisfaction of seeing our dear little Guzmán tossed ignominiously out of the cabin for stealing, eating with his fingers, belching at the table, and getting drunk.

---

4. Adelina was a family friend.

5. A liniment based on *scabiosa succisa*.

6. A family friend.

On the sixth of January we had to witness, against our will, a most unpleasant and dangerous run-in between the captain and the mate. The captain accused the mate of giving too much meat to the dogs. The mate denied it and the captain jumped him and tried to throw him out of his quarters. The mate is well liked by the crew, and the captain got into a tight spot when he ordered the mate arrested. No one would obey him. Some of the passengers had to intervene in this crisis then by rushing in and separating the two struggling men. Thus an immediate stop was put to a violence that could have led us to God knows where. The captain did call the crew to the poop, though, and there relieved the mate of his duties, appointing the bosun in his place. Think what that could mean. We would have only the captain and a simple sailor in charge. The captain would have to rest sometimes; he is not made of iron. The sailor, knowing he was not being watched, might then decide to take a nap, too. As a consequence we might be ushered into Purgatory before our time. Luckily, though, we managed after some argument to compose the quarrel that same night. So all is now back as it was in the first place.

We spend every evening on the poop deck, some making plans, some singing, others showing off their strength and agility. We have had no serious quarrels among the passengers up to now.

We are worried about the possibility of fire. All of the peons have flint lighters, and also matches that are a thousand times more dangerous. We almost got burned up the day before yesterday. A box of matches suddenly caught fire in the cabin of the second-class passengers about four in the morning. We held a meeting and decided to take precautions against this dire peril. Every day the passengers will have their peons keeping a lookout under their direction and control. They will see to it that no one smokes, and they will watch for fires. Our peons set the example by acting as the first fire watchers.

January 11, 1849

Up to the present we cannot call this voyage a happy one. The wind is always from the rear, but weak; so the ship sails from four to six miles as quietly as if it were at anchor. We now have in view the second ship we have met on this voyage. The first was a frigate that appeared to be bound for Callao. This one is sailing to Valparaíso. We would like to have thrown a line on board so we could have had the pleasure of sending a letter home.

Among the strange creatures on board there is one who stands out not so much for his personality as for his build. He does not look like a man; he looks like a pair of buttocks on legs.

One cannot behold this promontory without a shudder, all the more so when one remembers that this monster haunts the least fragrant location on the ship.

The shape of this ambulatory mass kept me up all night trying to understand how Our Lord, Jesus Christ, could have formed this turtle shell of a man with His divine hands without laughing. After much meditation on the problem I have decided it must have happened in this way. You be the judge.

The Creator decided to set aside one day for making several hundred human beings. He put the dough in a pan, sprinkled and kneaded it, added the yeast, then set it off in a corner to rise. But, because the business of running heaven is not simple, and because the Lord wants to and has to be everywhere at once, He forgot about the dough. When He finally remembered and came to examine it, He found it heavy, bloated, and hard to cut. He did not think this funny, and was about to throw it all away; but before doing so He stuck His finger in it to check on its condition. Imagine His surprise when wind rushed out of the hole He had made, and the dough sagged in the middle while the sides remained high. "Why, it's a posterior!" the Creator exclaimed. He intended to make a giant out of the dough, but instead of saying, "Let it be a man," He said, "Let it be a posterior."

Because the massive rump of this rotund personage haunts us as the shade of Ninus haunted the wife who slew him,[7] and because we cannot mention him among ourselves without fear of being overheard by him, we have unanimously decided to call him *culatus* (wide rump). It is a high, sonorous, and appropriate name because he is a rump, and wide; that is to say, broad, spacious, and extensive.

Among the various gentlemen who honor us here with their good will, we should single out with special pleasure the Belgian consul,

---

7. Ninus, King of Assyria, according to the legend rooted in Orosius's *Historiae Adversum Paganos*, was killed by his wife, Semiramis.

De Boon, the chancellor of the French consulate, Pioche, and the captain of the ship. Nothing on the ship is refused us, and there is not a single passenger who does not look up to us with respect and courtesy. Even our *culatus* lifted his bulk out of a chair and offered it to me when I came on deck this morning.

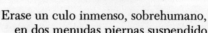

SONNET

Erase un culo inmenso, sobrehumano,
   en dos menudas piernas suspendido;
   érase un cerro a culo parecido,
culo que an un hemisferio llama enano,
y en cuyo cráter que llamamos ano
   chisporrotea el caldo embravecido
   cual en el seno del Vesubio erguido
la lava que sepulta a Herculano.

Culo estupendo; colosal pegote
   que puesto aquí se viera desde Flandes;
   culo en fin, para hablar sin embarazo,
que visto en alta mar fuera un islote,
   en Bío-Bío tetas y en los Andes
   las faldas de Orizaba o Chimborazo.[8]

January 15, 1849

Good weather so far. We are a hundred leagues from the equator. The health of the group could be better. *Culatus* is not constipated, but the rest of us are. This morning he had the kind of enormous relief in the devil's locker we would all like to have. I thought he would look like an empty bag, but instead I found him wedged so tight in the passageway ladder he could not move forward or backward. The jam he was in put me in the mood to return to the cabin and compose the following *redondilla*.

---

8. This is a parody of *A Una Nariz* by Francisco de Quevedo (1580–1645). Because Alexander Pope said poetry is untranslatable—and for other reasons—this poetic effort and the one that follows have been left in the original Spanish.

REDONDILLA

Quién podría divisarte
sin decir con disimulo:
¡vaya un culo!

Al verte erguido y turgente
con tus redondos carrillos:
dicen todos los corrillos:
este no es un culo de gente;
es más bien traste de mulo.
¡Vaya un culo!

Sale de su camarote
cual tinajón de bodega,
empuja, se queja, brega,
y al fin asoma el mogote.
Yo de risa me estrangulo.
¡Vaya un culo!

Si causa desasosiego
entre nos la falta de agua,
él como fuelle de fragua
se hincha y sopla con sosiego.
¿Si será culo de rulo?
¡Vaya un culo!

Es un culo gaditano
de formas muy abultadas:
mas se riera a carcajadas
el más popudo gitano
si viera el de aqueste chulo.
¡Vaya un culo!

El globo que en su ascención
cúpulas pisa engreído
fuera a su lado pulido
globulito de jabón.
A su lado es nulo.
¡Vaya un culo!

January 18, 1849

The monotony of the last few days is enough to make one despair. The heat is becoming more unbearable every day. The sea, always calm before, is beginning to be enlivened with fish; although up to now we have only seen blowfish, flying fish, and bonitos. We caught two of the bonito and they were served up the same day, but the flesh was tough and the flavor not good. It is so cloudy today we cannot take a sighting on the sun, so all we know is we are some eighty leagues from the equator, more or less, and to the west of the Galápagos which we will avoid for fear of being becalmed.

All the documents relating to our business are now completed, signed, and put away, but more and more difficulties seem to be coming up between the patrons and their peons. They refuse to obey now; how will they act later? Things are calm for the time being. The captain, though, knowing how hard it will be to hold on to his sailors once we have arrived, has signed a contract with them to work the ship on shares, while at the same time furnishing pay and expenses for them just as though they were still only deck hands.

January 19, 1849

Rosita is completely cured now and promenades on deck like a ship of war in a steady tail wind. Ship rumor has it that a young man on board by the name of Puelma is paying the freight.

When will we reach the equator so we can say we are half-way there? We are only fifty leagues away, but becalmed. We have made no headway since the night before last. However, the heat of the day, the appearance of the sky, and the observations of the captain all tell us we are close to the equator.

There is a ship in sight, a frigate, and she is bearing down on us. Where is she from, and where is she heading? Those are the questions that are being asked everywhere on deck.

At nine-thirty it appears certain she intends to speak to us. At ten o'clock we see with delight that the ship, a United States whaler, is putting out a boat; a moment later we see it approaching under sail and by oars. One hundred and ten of us, full of curiosity and pleasure, line the rail to await the friendly visit of the Yankees. Four rowers and the captain jump on board and are at once surrounded by a crowd that stares at them as though they were men from the moon. The captain comes into our cabin, and the oarsmen go into the crew's quarters before the mast. Rosita, the only woman among us, excites great interest in our visitors, and also considerable envy, to judge by their expressions. During lunch we find out that the ship is the *American,* and that she is bound for Talchuano and then around the Cape for home.

How pleasant it is to have this opportunity to write to the family midway in our voyage, and with what zest do we take advantage of the chance that fate has provided. All of us get busy at once on the same letter. We address it to you, [mother], and we have asked the captain of the whaler to put it into the hands of Señor Rondizzoni when he stops at Talcahuano.

The captain of the whaler is very likable. At the same time, though, he set us to thinking very seriously about the way fate affects men so differently. Many men, less well off than we, are happier despite that. This good man, looking with resigned eyes at all the many comforts we enjoyed, could nevertheless exclaim: "In the thirty-nine months I have been at sea, this is the first time I have sat down at such a table. You have plates, silverware, fresh meat, and excellent bread. I have almost forgotten how to use a knife and fork. Wormy hardtack and spoiled black-looking salt meat have been the most delicate foods I have tasted since I said goodbye to my wife and children. You are lucky to have all this, and to be going to the gold fields, too. But I do not envy you. I am going to see my children."

The day was a very full one for us. We had not even lost the ship from sight when we caught a big shark. The appetite of this dread denizen of the tropical seas is remarkable. We found a sardine can and a sailor's boot with heavy nails in his stomach when we opened him up. I set its beating heart in a soup tureen. For three continuous hours it did not stop beating, and it jumped when touched.

The heat is becoming more and more unbearable every day. Our water is turning bad, and its taste overrides all seasoning. Today we decided to shave our heads, Chinese-style. César and Ruperto, scissors in hand, have left us looking younger and more handsome.

January 21, 1849

We have already crossed the line. We did not celebrate the event lest there be disorders. Ever since leaving Valparaíso we have noticed that the passengers between decks resented the fact that we are better treated. This has reached such a pitch that we have reason to fear an uprising that would bring a host of troubles.

Our apprehensions were almost fulfilled today. At five in the afternoon we heard furious yelling from the crowd between decks. A Peruvian was especially insulting to the captain. We got ready to fight and all the peons took out their knives. Fortunately, though, we were able to quiet the disturbance, and that night I wrote out the naval rules[9] on food, and read these to the between decks crowd the following day. The rules actually worsened their condition, but the very things that should have angered them more, it seemed to us, had the opposite effect and calmed them down.

Nothing else happened worth recording during the rest of our voyage until we were near the coast of Alta California where the journey was to end.

February 13, 1849

We have had fine weather up to now, but today, when we are only two days from reaching our anchorage and getting some idea as to the outcome of our expedition, the wind for the first time is against us.

A calm followed, accompanied by fog. We had hoped for good weather but found ourselves drifting fogbound in a current instead. It is dangerous because we are not far from the rocks called the Farellones. These lie only some five leagues from the port, and it is necessary to find them to locate and enter it. It is noon and the fog has not lifted, so we cannot determine our position by solar observation. This has put the captain in a bad mood.

At four o'clock the captain orders the sails hauled in and the anchors got ready. There is no more pleasant sound during a long ocean voyage than the noise the anchor chain makes as they draw it out of the hold and prepare to heave it overboard. This evening as usual we will play chess or whist with the captain, the Belgian consul, Señor De Boon, and the chancellor of the French consulate, Señor Pioche.

---

9. These would have been in French, because the *Stauelli* was a French ship.

Before sitting down at the table, the captain told me we must be very near the rocks and that he had given strict instructions to the lookout on the bow. Then he sat down quietly to play. At nine, though, on a sudden inspiration he left his cards and ran up on deck. A moment later we heard his terrifying order, "Haul to the wind. Furl everything!" I assure you that for anyone who has travelled by sea these words mean you had better say your prayers. Hearing the noise of the rudder chain and the uproar on deck, we all made a dash for the door, knocking down chairs and smashing plates and glasses in the process. Fat *culatus* was in the lead. He forgot to turn sideways to go through the door, and got stuck. He was shot out like a cannonball by our combined efforts and trampled on by all of us. Through a clearing in the fog we beheld the black and impressive rocks of the Farellones with mixed feelings of awe, delight, and terror. A moment later we had turned the ship away by tacking, but the calm did not let us do very much, and the current was frightening.

At two in the morning the captain finally got us anchored, and we went to bed, confident that we had a lucky star in 1849. It seems we have nothing to fear.

February 16, 1849

At five in the morning, it is still calm. The rocks are so close that we can hear the cries of the sea birds and the barking of the seals. There is nothing new. The calm and the discouraging fog are still with us.

February 17, 1849

There is sun this morning and the weather is beautiful. A breeze is rising, and we have three ships in view. We hoist anchor and leave our dangerous neighbors. By noon, though, the wind had failed and the fog closed in again. How much longer are we to stay in this perverse situation? At four, unable to see, and with the wind gone, we had to anchor again.

February 18, 1849

The calm continues, now with low fog and rain. There is no hope of moving away from here. We have cast out fishing lines and are catching dogfish exactly like those at Valparaíso. How exasperating it is to keep running into insurmountable obstacles that a freakish fate throws in our way to prevent us from realizing our one hope: to see land!

February 18, 1849

Strong wind all last night and vibrations set up by the anchor robbed us of sleep. At ten in the morning the captain remarks that if it does not clear by noon we shall not be able to land today. The fog is getting thicker every instant.

The wind also is increasing. We have reason to fear that we shall either have to stay anchored or try to get across the reefs that lie all around us. The captain has just decided to hoist anchor and carry out a tacking maneuver. A brigantine loomed up on our rear like an apparition, and we could see they wanted to know if we had sighted land and, if so, where. We told them it was east on their compass, and almost at once lost sight of them in the fog.

We have been moving about two hours with a good wind, and if we are not deceived we have caught a glimpse of the continent. I will not write any more now.

It is four o'clock. The opening called the Golden Gate is in sight. We are entering it now. It is an emotional experience. How beautiful and how impressive this coast is. All its hills are covered with trees, and you can see cattle on the slopes.

We are at last in California. The bay of San Francisco is without doubt the greatest in the whole Pacific Ocean, and the loveliest in the world next to Rio de Janeiro. Its entrance, the Golden Gate, is like a throat two miles wide and three leagues long, adorned with cliffs and small islands that do not interfere with either entering or leaving. The tides alternate with mathematical regularity. For six hours the sea flows out through the Golden Gate and for the next six hours it flows in. On reaching the end of the throat, one would not imagine he was entering a bay. On the contrary, he would believe he had passed through a strait from one ocean to another. The bay is so enormous that from one side of it one can barely see the opposite shore. The coastline of this handsome body of water is very irregular and forms a series of lagoons and lesser bays. The sand and clay bottom would delight any anchor man; except for some small shallow areas, a ship could anchor in perfect safety anywhere along the shore.

Boats can be beached with ease, and on many beaches passengers can step off onto beautiful park-like areas covered with lush vegetation very similar to that of Valdivia.

The preconceptions we had formed of this city of San Francisco were certainly not favorable. We knew that it had belonged to Spain and Mexico and had gained worldwide attention only the year before. We were expecting, actually, that San Francisco would be something like Curacaví.[10] We were totally surprised when we doubled the point of the anchorage, in rapidly gathering darkness, and saw spread before our eyes there like an amphitheater a rather pretty although irregular village strewn with good-looking if rather small homes, some of them worth at least 100,000 pesos. The port was crammed with ships of all kinds and nationalities. A North American warship of three decks, with three corvettes and a transport to make up the squadron, stood guard over the harbor. We felt our way into the anchorage with anchors poised, and very cautiously, as one must do if not sure of his ground. As we crept forward we passed close to a number of ships and were bombarded with questions in various languages. They all boiled down to this: "Where are you from?" and "How long have you been at sea?" Finally we heard the longed-for order, "Heave to!"—and the clank of the anchor chains going down. We threw ourselves into one another's arms and exchanged congratulations as if we had just escaped from some awful peril. The next moment we saw lights going on in the town. We felt like prisoners waiting to hear sentence pronounced as we stood there wondering if what we had heard about this place were true or not.

A boat headed for us. To understand how we felt as we waited for it you would have to have been there to see our strained expressions. Our very souls were quivering with hope and fear. We thought the boat had come from shore, but it was only the captain of the ship *Anamakin*, wanting news from Chile. Believe it or not, this gentleman's arrival was upsetting to us. We had all run up

---

10. An insignificant village in Chile.

to him with the same question in mind, no matter how differently we would have put it. The vitally important question was this: "Is there gold here as they say?" But, strange to say, we all backed away toward the other rail before we could hear the answer. We wanted to prolong the uncertainty; no matter how painful, it was better than a disappointment. We turned quickly enough, though, when one of the questioners, unable to contain himself, ran toward us yelling, "It is all true! There is a lot of gold! A whole lot of gold!" As you can imagine, these words were enough to draw our souls back into our bodies. Once the wave of emotion passed, we gathered in a happy circle.

I wished I could read minds at that moment. There were so many things written on the very faces that had been so drawn and anxious a moment before. Even though I am not a mind reader, I fancied I could hear secret voices deep inside each one. One said, "At last my dreams have come true! I am rich! Poor Amalia is going to die broken hearted. She turned me down because she thought I was poor!" And another, "You no-good Cunigunda, I've got you now! You gave me the air, you flirt! Now scratch yourself!" A third, "If there is a lot of gold, then I am a rich man now. Panchita is a nice girl, and virtuous no doubt; but—we shall see—it seems to me that she is a little homely. Yes, she is homely, homely as a donkey!" One fellow who did not go much for the girls seemed to be saying to himself, "If there is gold there are bound to be loafers, and naturally where you find loafers you find gambling. Now for my loaded dice and marked cards!" Another looked as if he were thinking, "I'll be somebody now. No one is treated like a jackass in Chile if he is rich."

The news Captain Robinet of the *Anamakin* gave us was stunning. What we had heard in Chile was as nothing compared with this. A prodigal oaf could throw his money around like a Croesus if gold were really so plentiful all you had to do was bend over and pick it up. He also said this was the land of equality, that here it made no difference whether you were master or servant because in this land aristocrats and commoners were treated the same. I could go on listing the things he told us in the brief half-hour we were with him. Suffice it to say we believed everything he said, with the greatest willingness. When he left we seemed to be thanking him for making us all millionaires rather than bidding him goodbye.

Once we were alone, though, a flood of argument began. Each one had heard something from Robinet no one else had heard; and as we tried to sift it all out, a mass of contradictions emerged. We were going to have to cut our way through a tremendous jungle of lies before we got to the mines, and it began there on the very ship that brought us. It got to the point where we doubted ourselves and did not even trust our own ears. It seemed to us that Captain Robinet was of too responsible an age to be a liar; but we were almost ashamed that we had accepted his stories so readily.

Be that as it may, we went to bed worn out with argument and full of illusions, hopes, and fears; but by that time there was little of the night left.

February 19, 1849

It was raining by six o'clock the next morning. Each one was up and gathering his belongings and equipment to be ready to spring on shore. While that was going on, my companions and I climbed up onto the poop so we could quietly study the place where we were about to land. It is the port of Yerbas Buenas, or the port of San Francisco, one of the numberless inlets that form the irregular southern coast of the bay of San Francisco. In spite of its being inland, very strong winds blow there, strong enough to cause a good deal of trouble in fall and spring.

The city, or rather the small village at the port, lies upon the slopes of some hills. These are treeless, but covered with bushes, wild strawberries, and colorful flowers. The population of the town is rather small, about five thousand. The houses are of one-story, many of them made of adobe in the Spanish style, some of a more modern look, along with a great number of tents and cabins. At the moment they represent the beginnings of a new and unusual town.

All of it conveys the impression of a large camp. There are twenty-five ships in the port if you include the squadron.

Our ship is an object of interest to many. It has been, all of a sudden, surrounded by boats and launches, some looking for passengers, some looking for business, and some for news of Chile. All was noise and confusion. Those who had recently arrived confirmed the stories of gold. Most of them had some of the precious metal to show. Wrapped in rags were nuggets as big as walnuts, and gold dust like lentils.

What a pleasant surprise it was to be surrounded suddenly by people we knew—though one had to look hard to recognize the dandy of Valparaíso or the fashionable gentleman from Santiago in ragged pants and huge pea jacket, with calloused hands and tar-blackened face. Young Hamilton, now a sailor and the operator of a boat in partnership with a Negro who owned the solitary bed in which they slept, was waiting in oilcloth hat and soggy woolen shirt for a passenger to carry ashore. Manuel Price, fat and rosy, with pants rolled up and shoes full of mud, fired questions at us to find out what we had brought, and answered our flood of questions with tales of wonders.

Rosa's friend, Nisser, together with Sánchez, Cross, Pinet, and others called me by name, though we had never met, and swarmed into the cabin. Each of these adventurers was clad in clothing so wild and odd that Dumas, the mulatto, would have found material for ten novels just by looking at them. It was not curiosity that brought this bustling band of men on board. There is no time to waste on curiosity here. Each one had business in mind. They knew everything on the ship could be sold in California at fantastic prices, and they wanted to make deals before the passengers had time in town to discover this. Chileans are not all that stupid, but they are not accustomed to Yankee methods. Cross, who is making a lot of money here, was trying to bargain with someone for the windows of the poop when another man rushed by on another deal, collided with him, and knocked his hat into the water. Neither one noticed it. Cross kept on bargaining and the man kept on running. A little later Cross left, wearing a tattered sailor's cap as jauntily as though it was a papal tiara.

To avoid the uproar and expense, we decided not to go ashore that day. We will let the small fry go to the lie-factory while we pay our respects to the port captain who has just come on board. He is a tall Yankee, portly and bright of eye—or rather in one of them; the other is black and blue from a blow someone gave him last night. He is also rather run-down and smells of alcohol. Along with him there is a customs officer who is to stay on board until the cargo has been landed. On entering the cabin the captain hailed us in a loud jovial voice:

"Welcome, gentlemen, to the land of gold. Lots of gold. Lots of gold."

Our captain, who did not understand English, thought he wanted the passports, and immediately produced them. You should have beheld the Yankee's face when he saw the passports and the official stamps. It was as though we had insulted the stars and stripes. You remember that one of the causes of the American Revolution was the Stamp Act.

Our fine Yankee, tearing his one good eye away from the thing that disturbed him so, said to us:

"Forget all those stamps and passports. You are now in the United States, and here we don't put up with the stupid tyranny of pass-ports and the robbery of having to buy stamps for documents. I only came to congratulate you on your happy arrival in this rich land, and to give this customs official my authorization here on the ship to receive and put through the permit you need from the government to unload your cargo."

We offered him wines or liqueurs. He replied that he drank only champagne. He was given a generous dose, and wound up his visit to the satisfaction of all.

You may be surprised at the lack of curiosity we showed by remaining on board ship that way. The truth is we were a bit stunned. Besides we had to write letters to Chile to go by the *Anamakin*, which was ready to sail. As we had to write at once, we decided to content ourselves with what we had seen and heard, and with what we had been told by the port captain. He was a respectable official, even though he had not been respected by the drunkard who had struck him. They had probably been drinking together.

Rosita had outfitted herself for business with a magnificent silk dress, a cape, and a cap or hat as they call it nowadays. She had won the good will of everyone on board. I do not know what kind of card or letter of recommendation she carried, but everyone on board had had dealings with her, and she with them.

All except us, that is. We alone were virtuous, chaste; or finicky and choosy. The truth is, one would have to come to this country and spend days and nights seeing men and only men before he could find the sight of this charming siren tolerable. That is why she has the eyes and attention, now, of everyone who happens to see her.

But let us say goodbye and Godspeed to Madam Rosita. May she go conquering, and being conquered, as is the norm and custom in these calamitous times.

As soon as the captain left, our newly arrived dandies fixed and fitted themselves up as if for a ball, and went ashore looking as if they had just stepped out of a band box. You should have seen what they looked like when they got back! It was as if they had been rolled in the mud. They returned happy, but full of contradictory tales about the mines, and cursing the mud that made up the streets-to-be of this extraordinary town.

As we had been able to get no very clear idea about the mines, their distance away, the weather there, or the best way to travel, we decided to send a reconnaissance party ashore next day.

What you see and hear in California is so odd and unexpected, so different from the natural order of human affairs, and everything goes by so quickly, it is only by writing things down as they happen, and later looking at the account in your own handwriting, that you can convince yourself it was not all a dream. You remember we all had laughed derisively in Chile at the first stories we heard about California. I thought it was only natural that the account of its richness would be more and more exaggerated the farther the news travelled; and as Chile was two thousand leagues away, the increase would be on the scale of a funnel: what was the size of the spout would have grown to the size of the upper rim. I believed, though I did not say so then, that California would be only a second edition of Chile's own gold strike.[11] It would be one of those golden dreams with which a man consoles himself when he is maddened with desire for a gold that does not exist.

We came, in the end, because we could not resist the weight of so much testimony and because we felt sure only a lazy man could fail to make money, and we were willing to work hard. But little did we know what we faced. We went on shore, and, after having paid our entry fee per head and sloshing through the muddy slime of low tide, took our way to the hillside slopes that form the dry part of the town.

We had been told the day before that we should go armed, and in pairs. So, like most people in the town, we had pistols and daggers thrust under our belts.

To reach Price's house we had to pass through a good part of the town. The people look as though they are having a carnival,

11. Chile had a gold rush very similar to that of California in the previous century; but it was neither so extensive in area nor so rich.

with their strange costumes, the character of their occupations, and their tongues, which seem more multiplied than those in the Tower of Babel. Apparently, too, all the women here dress up like men, for there are no skirts to be seen anywhere. At each step we have to move aside to make way for a man in wool shirt and rolled up pants, panting under the weight of a trunk or big sack he is carrying from the beach for pay; or to make room for a more fortunate drayman with a wheelbarrow, pushing it along proudly and exciting the attention and envy of those who do not own such a marvelous vehicle.

Some men are putting up tents; others are dragging timbers. This man is rolling a barrel; that one is struggling with a post, or trying to drive it into the ground with mighty blows of a crowbar. The ones who had managed to get their tents up are already doing business. Through their tent openings you can see open trunks, and ragged clothes one would be ashamed to wear but which are on sale for fabulous prices. Liquor is unbelievably expensive here as

Escena de California
Dibujo de Vicente Pérez Rosales

"Yankee" and John Bull

compared with Chile. Brandy sells for sixty pesos an *arroba*, champagne for half an *onza* per bottle.[12] Goods have whatever value the seller wants to set; because the buyer, aware that in California time is money, will buy at sight whatever he needs, without bothering to shop around.

Gold dust is the money used, and the ease with which it is exchanged in buying and selling suggests that one has little difficulty in acquiring it. The streets are strewn with broken bottles; and among the many little buildings that have sprung up like magic—or rather like mushrooms in the first rains of May—there are many saloons and gambling houses.

Near the beach and about in the middle of the town an elegant brick and stone house is going up. It belongs to a certain Mr. Hassar, yesterday a common sailor but today a millionaire. On the plaza they are building at great expense an immense structure that will house a cafe. It belongs to another sailor as rich as the first.

Most people here speak English, good or bad. But you find, at the side of a lean Yankee in tight pants, others recognizable by their clothing or accent. There is a stocky John Bull, a Chinaman, a Hindu, a Russian, and a native Californio, all trying to converse. A Chilean and an Oregonian are watching each other suspiciously. A Frenchman and an Italian are winking at a Hawaiian girl crowned with flowers and clad in a blue dress and red shoes.

In short, you can find whatever you like in terms of oddities and extravagances in this land of promise. It is like a masquerade ball of gigantic proportions. Not the least strange are those creatures of what some call "the fair sex." Here they are called simply "shes,"[13] or, as the Yankees say, "females." What else can you call women who belong to such animals as you find here?

At the end of a slow but entertaining fifteen-minute walk we reach an attractive hotel that belongs to a gringo adventurer of the filibustering army that went down into Mexico. One of the servants (actually a young gentleman clad as a waiter) is ringing a huge Chinese gong to call those nearby to dinner. We found Price and Claro there in the dining room. Claro was making scabbards for daggers for which he was paid two dollars each. These

12. Pérez Rosales uses the peso as the equivalent of the United States dollar. An *onza* was worth $20.75.

13. The Spanish word is *hembra;* its basic meaning is a female animal, but, like the English word female, it also can be applied to human beings.

men, and other acquaintances of ours, were getting ready to sit
down at the table. It occupied the whole room, and we watched
as the most grotesque group of diners imaginable hurriedly took
their places. There were men from all countries in their national
dress. Their talk was a real gabble. You could see, sitting shoulder
to shoulder, poorly dressed men with fine manners, and boors in
fancy clothes. There were very very old men alongside burly lads
wolfing their food like so many Heliogabaluses.[14] Among them all,
however, there reigned an air of contentment as if they were partak-
ing of the finest of cuisines. The Yankee eats three times a day,
and always the same things: roast meat, salted salmon, an inferior
stew, tea or coffee, and butter. He has breakfast at seven, lunches
at noon, and has dinner at six.

Despite the fact that we talked to everyone we could reach,
none of them was able to tell us exactly what we wanted to know.
The men who had been in the mines did not want to talk about
it just for the sake of satisfying our curiosity. We had to listen
to stories by fellows who knew as little about it as we did; at the
same time we were simpleminded enough to accept as true the
tales confided to us with an air of mystery by the troop of jokers
who take advantage of newcomers.

See what you could have made out of these bits of advice:

—Don't go to Sacramento; there's no gold there. The place is
Stanislaus.

—Don't even think about Stanislaus. Sacramento is a better bet.
A guy took out several thousand dollars worth in one day.

—The mines are flooded and it's crazy to think you can go there
now. A friend of mine has just got back, and he tells me he
was wading in water up to his middle.

—What do you mean, water? That place is drier in winter than
it is in summer.

—An ox is worth one hundred dollars.

—It's worth five hundred at least.

—Don't believe anything they say. They're fooling you. There are
rich farmers around there who will rent oxen to you. Just bring
your carts.

14. Heliogabalus was a Roman Emperor, A.D. 218–222. His name became
a byword for profligacy.

—Don't try to carry a cart through those marshes and up the hills. Buy some horses, or break some wild mares that can be bought for fifty dollars.

—Forget about mares, horses, and carts. Whoever advised that has never been to the mines. Get some good boots and a leather bag. You can only find good places by walking.

This was the kind of information we got. As far as distances were concerned, the stories were even more contradictory. We were given estimates of from forty miles up to one hundred and eighty leagues.

Price took me to the house of a friend of his who had just got back from the mines. There, for the first time, I saw a solid nugget of three pounds. He told me he had picked it up while taking a walk before lunch. I also saw some sacks of gold. I returned with my head in a whirl and not knowing what to think. After this we decided to leave our future course up to fate.

February 20, 1849

We have finally found a map of this area. It is hand drawn and not very accurate, but it gives us at least a less-mistaken idea of locations. We paid six dollars for it, and as there are similarities between this area and Chile we are having some copies made to send to little Carlos.[15]

They want a thousand pesos to transport us by river boat to Sacramento. We do not have much money and we figure we will need twice that much to get started in mining, so we have borrowed one thousand, three hundred pesos at 5 percent a month from the Sánchez firm.[16]

February 21, 1849

We really need the carts that the *Julia* is bringing to us. The ship is late and this is creating difficulties.

We have decided to wait a few days more for her. If she does not arrive by then, we will go on but leave Ramírez behind. He

---

15. The half-brother of the author.

16. That is 60 percent a year! The Sánchez brothers engaged in real estate and commerce, and owned large tracts in Sacramento. One of their projects was to be called Washington City, California.

will see his brother and then come on up later with the tools and provisions we will have to leave behind for the time being.

We have also caught the general enthusiasm for physical labor, which can accomplish so much right now. Because we do not have to worry about board and room for we are living on board the ship where we get everything we need for a peso a day, with special privileges not given to the other passengers, we decided to organize ourselves into committees to carry out certain projects. The Dean will stay on board and take charge of the house and money, and the bills. Ruperto, César, Federico, Casalli, Clakston, and Hurtado will take the ship's boat and go out to transport passengers and cargo. Felipe and the peons will go on shore to work as loaders and stevedores.

The boat carries only four oars, so we have two men in reserve when the others tire. The currents of high and low tide here are very strong and therefore dangerous, and that causes me some anxiety, but our oarsmen are brave.

Once we had decided on a provisional plan of operations, the blue work shirts appeared; and, in spite of rains varying from light to heavy, everything is going happily and well.

The mission on shore entrusted to Lieutenant Ramírez has run into difficulties caused by weather and mud, so we have decided to do something else instead. We are out of clean clothes, and, as in this land you have to do everything for yourself, we have voted to transform ourselves into a laundry committee on which everyone will serve a term eventually. To put this into effect we have taken the boat to an inlet of the bay where there is running water. We have equipped ourselves with pots, soap, a big container for hot water, and a smaller one to use for cooking beans. The whole group came, each one loaded with a big sack of dirty clothes that represented the gentleman's accumulation in a two-month cruise through the tropics.

The inlet picked for our operation presents a picturesque if lonely aspect. To the east lies the open bay; on all the other sides are high cliffs of earth and sand, covered with brush and berries. The little cove is thus walled in. In its center is a pool of brackish water. It shows evidence that other men have done their washing here, too.

At this isolated spot in a far corner of the world we set up the basic equipment for our new enterprise. In a short time buckets, boiler, soap, and clothes were all in active operations. Laundry-maids Borja and Rosario have never in all their lives scrubbed so long and so vigorously as laundrymaids Ruperto and César and all the others in turn are doing to keep the project going. We ply underwear and socks with the same spirit we previously expended on oars and rudder. César says we are doing a marvelous job. Ruperto and Federico, however, complain that they are scrubbing the skin off their fingers.

For our band of rovers, the former command of "Forward charge!" and "Be brave!" has been changed into "Move it, lads!"

By evening we are all back on board the ship, and with good appetites. We recount our exploits amid general laughter. We all think of you,[17] and we all talk fondly of María Guerrero. Do not be surprised or jealous about this, for we are sure she is also thinking of us. The health of the group is excellent. Only our good peon, Chinguillo, seems to have made up his mind to remain seasick.

February 28, 1849

We keep up our impromptu labors for six days without a halt. Tomorrow we plan to go hunting in Contra Costa.

Contra Costa lies opposite this port. It looks like a handsome beach with trees down to the water's edge, surrounded by hills covered with pines. They say there are plenty of geese, partridges, hares, deer, and even bears, as well as all the other fine things that would appeal to a hunter.

It is now eleven o'clock at night. It was nine when we made up our minds to go to Contra Costa, and we have been cleaning our guns and getting our gear ready ever since. As you can well imagine, our tongues were as busy as our hands, each one of us bragging of past kills. The Dean was in his glory as he told the group around him of his steady hand, his sure eye, his stealthy stalking, his lordly bearing, and general resemblance to Apollo, god of beauty, poets, and hunters.

The night was spent in expectant dreams. "Apollo" dreamed of a battlefield strewn with bloody quail, mutilated hares, wounded deer, and of a great, great deal of flying about, my lady. I can assure you, if California had not come weeping and pleading that a few creatures be left alive for breeding, it would have been a

---

17. His mother, who was to read the diary.

bad year and a worse month for all the wandering gourmets of these golden regions.

February 30, 1849[18]

Our trip to Contra Costa was amusing enough.

We were all up at sunrise. The boat was readied and all of us climbed in, including the captain and two sailors. It is six miles to Contra Costa from San Francisco. About halfway between the two shores there is a beautiful island that is called Los Angeles.[19] The boat in which we sailed was so loaded with food, men, and weapons that we had good cause to fear there would be no room for what we would hunt. The oars of the hunters and the two sailors soon brought us to the beach of the island. The morning was cool, the sky clear, and we felt sure that we would clean out everything at this stop. The Dean seemed to be in a pensive mood, a posture conducive to setting in high relief the happy spirits of the young hunters and sailors. Why was there this contrast between men of the same disposition and circumstances? Could it be that he was meditating on the rise and fall of nations? Was he absorbed in contemplating the immensity of the most splendid bay in the world? Or could it be that some dark anxiety clouded his thoughts and happiness? It was none of those. The venerable Dean was dreaming; yes, that cupid in days of yore, that clever hunter, was dreaming, though wide awake, of some way to solve the problem of getting a bear to fly so he could shoot him on the wing. That was his preoccupation; that was his anxiety!

On a rocky point facing toward San Francisco we saw some wolves with their wild dog faces, but looked at them with disdain. To allow time for the return of the tide, which was then going out with a strong current, we rounded the point and landed. The entire coast of this beautiful island is made up of steep overhanging cliffs except for one spot. We headed for it, climbed like goats through the rocks, and in a short time dispersed ourselves all over the island.

The brush there is so dense that when we had gone only a little way we had lost contact with one another. We walked a good

---

18. This is an uncharacteristic error in dating. The context shows that he meant this to be March 1.

19. Angel Island.

way, got all scratched up and tired, but as for hunting, *nequaquam*; there was none, not a thing was sighted. Even the birds do not seem to like this island, and there is not a single human being there. There is a herd of wild goats, but they seem to have been put there just to arouse a hunter's competitive spirit and then tire him out and infuriate him. After an hour of futile clambering up and down, forward and backward, we finally reassembled with much shouting and swearing at the very point where we had landed. Not only was the hunt a disappointment, but we had then to eat lunch standing and very uncomfortable as well.

Once we had finished that frugal, or, rather, hellish meal, we took to the boat again with our oars and, more bruised than tired, ran it aground about a hundred yards from the beach; and there we were stranded. The tide, then at its ebb, was also in the conspiracy against us. And now there were plenty of game birds: great flights of duck, geese, and woodcock. Being stuck out there made us desperate. Some of the group could not bear it and jumped into the water, some of them fully dressed and with their shoes on, and others with their pants rolled up as high as possible. The Dean, shrewdly weighing the advantage of the game we might get against the disadvantage of getting wet, decided to die in the boat like a brave man rather than surrender to mud and water.

César and Ruperto leaped into the water and began to tow this barge of Nereus,[20] who, standing on the cross struts of the boat with oar in hand to push with, looked like Neptune or the Storm Spirit.

The boat was towed across the mudflats with great effort to within some six yards of the beach, but there it decided to stick fast. The towing duet were worn out by this time and decided to go hunting, abandoning, without hope of human aid, the most important member of the party and its chief ornament. It was horrible! There followed a lot of shooting here and there. There were no shouts of triumph, however—only cries of "Wounded it!" Flights of frightened birds, some of them even wounded, darted past the most accomplished of hunters and filled this extraordinary being with the most bitter grief. Faced with such a critical situation, with shooting going on in all directions, he then decided to do or die, leaving his name to future fame like a new Leander seeking

---

20. Nereus was "the Old Man of the Sea" in Greek mythology, the father of the Nereids. Pérez Rosales is, of course, referring to himself.

his beloved, and he threw himself into the water—which came up to his ankles.

When we were all gathered on the beach, action was got under way with a great deal of gunfire. "Move it, lads!" We plunged into the woods, which really were full of everything a hunter could want.

To anyone looking at Contra Costa from San Francisco, it seems that he could reach out and touch the pines on the slopes of the beautiful hills as he landed. But it is really not like that at all. There are intervening plains, and it would take a good long time to hike across them actually to reach the hills. The hills looked like a marvelous place, though, and Ruperto and I decided to go. It proved impossible. We crossed plains, circling back and forth like dogs around pretty little ponds, and finally came back to the site of the abandoned boat, dead tired and hungry. With appetites whetted by vigorous hunting we pillaged the remaining provisions to the applause of all present.

On depositing the fruits of our destructive raid on the ground, it appeared the total number of dead trophies was one perforated hat, but everything we had aimed at was still alive.

The guns, that, according to their owners' opinions the night before, could kill by themselves, had no doubt caught colds during the voyage because they had killed nothing. We all said the weapons were cheap ones, and thus saved our honor. Then, to put an end to our day of hunting, we all returned to the boat. We still had to get back across the bay, and the wind was beginning to rise.

The rowers really had to show muscle-power to get us safely back from that bedeviled expedition. César never left his oar during the whole trip. The rest took turns—all, that is, except Hurtado who, taking offense at something and acting just like Rosita, would not take the place of the mulatto.

The sea, the wind, the tide, the night that closed in all of a sudden, and general weariness of all set the Dean to reflecting more than twice on the immortality of the soul. César claims he has never behaved so well as on this occasion, and it is true. The waves were so high and the gusts of wind so strong that we were doused with water in bucketfulls. But they did bring us back to the ship after a two-hour trip, dead tired and wet to the marrow. César was so worn out when we finally did come alongside that he cannot remember climbing the ladder.

You need not ask whether we slept well that night. Today we are going to eat the few partridges and woodcock at whose death, decreed by fate, we had been lucky enough to be present, yesterday, as the agents of destiny.

Before leaving for Sacramento, the place in the interior we have chosen as our destination instead of Stanislaus, I want to tell you one of the many things that happen here daily under the farcical government of this city.

The supreme authority in San Francisco is not an alcalde as many say he is. He is only a Yankee, more or less drunk, whom they call alcalde. His only function, if two Yankees are quarreling, is to smooth things over; if the quarrel is between a Yankee and someone who speaks Spanish, his job is to declare the Spaniard guilty and make him pay the court costs; if the dispute is between two Spaniards, he sees to it that the decision goes against the one who has money enough to pay the costs and the interpreter. A short time ago there was a trial between two of the first named. The courtroom was full, and as both the litigants were Yankees the judge tried to reconcile them as best he could. But the weight of the evidence was so much against one of them that there was nothing for the alcalde to do but sentence him to twenty-five lashes, for that was the minimum sentence possible in such cases.[21] There was an immediate murmur of disapproval in the courtroom.

The alcalde thought he was a lost man because he had passed such a light sentence for such serious misdeeds, but while he was getting ready to admit his error and increase the dose, one of the spectators asked to be heard.

"Citizens," he says, "since this alcalde is so free with punishments he passes out, I propose that the fifty strongest men here drive the alcalde three miles out of town, kicking his behind all the way."

"Hooray!" shouted the crowd. The alcalde, not knowing what was happening to him, left his seat and, quicker than a run, dived out the window, followed by general booing and laughter. The culprit was then let go.

I do not know how all of this is going to end. There is a gang of ruffians in this city called the Hounds. They are young, vicious, and shameless, and seem to have sworn a mutual pact to protect one another's lives and interests. They start fights in the cafes all

---

21. The crowd's attitude represents the almost universal reaction of Anglo-Americans to the procedures and penalties of Spanish-Mexican law.

the time, and if anyone rises to the provocations of these united ruffians he is beaten up. If it happens that there is only one of them in the place, and he therefore comes out on the short end of the fight he starts, he leaves in a rage to find his comrades and they return en masse and do all the damage they can. If you have won a fight with a Hound, the safest thing to do is disappear and never show yourself again.

We have recently celebrated two festive days. One was February 21, Washington's birthday. The whole North American squadron fired off a broadside. Ours was the only French ship in the bay, so we ran up our flag and saluted the great country of the north with three hurrahs. The crews of the warships immediately took to the rigging and replied to our courteous salute with three tremendous hurrahs that resounded like thunder in the surrounding hills. Those on shore replied to the cannonade with repeated cannon shots of their own, using a swivel gun without a carriage that a number of drunken men had set up in what would be the city plaza. Liquor flowed like water in spite of its cost.

That night there were fireworks, and tar barrels were set on fire in the plaza and on the hilltops.

The other memorable event was the arrival of the steamship *California*. It had left Valparaíso before us but arrived a month later than we did. It was the first to arrive of those constructed especially for these regions, and it was welcomed with hurrahs, cannonades, tar fires, and champagne, the only means for celebrating they have around here.

When the Squella ship, *Confederación*,[22] arrived, our stevedores boarded it to see whether it had brought letters or any passengers they knew. There were no letters, and, so far as news is concerned, the only thing we were told was horrifying. It was that the bark *Stauelli* had caught fire and gone down with a full load of passengers just a few days after leaving Valparaíso. There had been no survivors. This had become known only because some half-burned ship timbers had been washed up on the beach and the name of the ship could still be made out. The poor Solares group had been lost along with a multitude of passengers.

Our young men suppressed their laughter as best they could at this sad tale, but in the end they burst out with it. The newcomers

---

22. The *Confederación* belonged to the Squella firm of Valparaíso.

were not a little astonished when they found out to whom they were speaking and saw the destroyed ship riding at anchor. Our amusement did not last long, though, because we soon realized what grief such a cruel story would have inflicted on those at home. You may be sure we shall not rest until we are certain you know the truth.

The failure of the *Julia* to arrive with our carts is costing us a great deal. We cannot delay our departure for the mines much longer. We have decided that Felipe will stay here, and when he has got together the rest of our equipment he is to come on up and join us. We must leave without taking time to gather further information, so we are getting all our things ready for the trip into the interior.

Journey to Contra Costa

March 6, 1849

We have hired a little vessel called *Dice-mi-nana*—or, in the English pronunciation, *Daice-may-nana*. It may have a capacity of twenty tons. It is actually an oversized barge with a deck and two miserable masts. Its sails are patched and dirty, and so constructed that nothing can stand on the deck, which is the only refuge for the passengers.

In this wretched boat we all embarked with the exception of Felipe, and we piled our provisions and equipment as best we could in the little storage space and on deck.

Twenty-nine passengers, including two dogs, a woman, and child, covered the little deck, already crowded to capacity with sacks, boxes, pots, shovels, guns, baskets of food, and thirty thousand bundles of all kinds that needed only a slight list to slip off into the water along with everything piled on them. There were so many passengers on deck that we could only stand or sit. You cannot imagine our discomfort.

No one could take a step without treading on his neighbor, nor could one lie down without having to use knees or elbows as pillows.

In short, we would have envied sardines or herring in barrels; at least they travel lying down, for good or ill.

A Captain Robinson commanded our ship. He was a Yankee with a lisp, undersized, a ridiculous old man and a drunkard. Serving under him as sailors were a Scottish gringo who spoke Spanish rather well, and two Yankees who were going to the placers and had hired on as sailors to pay their passage as far as Sacramento.

It would be an endless task to describe the bandit-like faces of the passengers. We resembled each other in one respect, though; we all had on huge nailed boots and carried on board rifles, daggers, and pistols that we did not leave even for an instant.

The captain of the *Stauelli* came along and helped us up to the last moment, and then, at about four o'clock in the afternoon, we moved away from the side of the bark and began the difficult task of working our way through the ships that surrounded us.

We had made the grave mistake of placing on board a demijohn of brandy and eight bottles containing what was left of a now empty wine barrel. When he caught sight of articles so precious, the captain decided to take care of them himself, and we took care of our other baggage as best we could. The current was against us, and the captain, through incompetence or malice, maneuvered so badly that instead of advancing we were blown back until we found ourselves suddenly stuck on the mud flats. The ship and passengers were as fixed and solid as a marine rock. The air was rent with curses more sacrilegious and horrifying than even a Turk could have spewed out—if you could ever find a Turk brutish and immoral enough to talk like that. In vain two oars were thrust into the water to push the ship free, but no human effort seemed to be enough to move it.

Night was falling fast, and the cold and rain seemed likely to put an end to us because we couldn't get our sleeping bags or blankets out from under the wet and grudging feet of the herd all around us. We were resigning ourselves to spending the night in those miserable conditions when the approach of a little boat suddenly restored our spirits. The rescue boat reached us, but, to our consternation, far from coming to help us it had come alongside only to bring us four more passengers! This made Robinson happy, but it terrified the rest of us. Someone then thought of lowering the flag to half-mast, and almost at once a Russian launch came up to us. The Russians were very polite and did everything they could to free us; but it was no use, merely a waste of time. Our drunkard of a captain had no intention of getting under way then. His running aground was no doubt intentional so he could smuggle passengers on board without the knowledge of the owner.

We transferred to the Russian ship without waiting any longer, leaving Caselli and the peons on the *Dice-mi-nana* to look after our things. We went ashore to complain to Brannan,[23] a rich merchant, the priest and leader of the Mormons, and the owner of the *Daice*. We told him that the captain talked about sailing at one o'clock in the morning with the high tide, a dangerous thing in view of his condition.

Brannan was in bed, but he hastily wrote on a scrap of paper an order that Robinson was not to sail before daylight. Steeling ourselves with patience we returned to the *Daice* and handed the note to Robinson. He would not take time to read it, so Clackston broke out: "It's an order from your boss telling you not to sail before daybreak."

At the word, "boss," Robinson jumped as though he had been bitten by a scorpion. "What's this about a boss? I don't have any boss. Nobody is boss around here—and if you want my opinion, of all the crooks that need hanging, that slippery Brannan is number one."

We did not sail then, however, because he fell asleep. So it was not until the dawn of the following day that we resumed the voyage so auspiciously begun.

By then the deck of the ship looked like a battlefield. Everyone was as juiced as a grape. The only barrel of water we had on board for the trip was as empty as the bottles and demijohn we brought on board yesterday. We had no oars, and we had to call to ship after ship following the current to see if they would sell us some. We had no boat either, and no ship goes on these rivers without one because there are long stretches where there is no wind and you have to tow the ship. Finally we found someone who sold us two oars, and so we managed to get started.

I am writing this after having completed that ridiculous and bedeviled trip. A fallen pine serves as my desk, and also as part of the wall of our camp during this first night in Sutterville. This is why I can remember the details of the trip so clearly.

It lasted seven days. We kept the same spot on deck day and night, and always seated because the working of the rigging and lateen sail would not permit anyone to stand up. Even though we were seated, though, the ropes raked across our faces in each one

---

23. Sam Brannan.

of the two hundred thousand tacking maneuvers the wind and tide forced us to make.

Most of us had to sit on iron pots that were tied up and always having to be opened; the rest on rows of containers for water, salt meat, and firewood.

Each one of the seated travellers kept between his legs his pots, pans, shovels, guns, and other devilish gear, which impeded even the slightest movement. In addition, we spent the nights wrapped up in blankets and ponchos that became dripping wet in the heavy dews of this area. For all these discomforts, the only thing that really marred our happiness was being continually walked on by the sailors. They never stopped coming and going from stem to stern, shod in Russian boots with cleats. These brutes never look where they are stepping; their goal is to reach a certain point, and all they do to get there is to keep their eyes fixed on it. They would step on Saint Peter's beard if it were in the way.

Poor Casali got a boot full in the face. When he let go with a curse, the only apology he was given was an expression they use all the time: "It's all right." It means "That's nothing"—and the sailor just kept right on going.

I have never in my life heard such furious cursing. Whatever expressions the English language affords that are swinish, shameless, sacrilegious, or immoral are used by these brutes in human form even on minor occasions. The orgy of the night before made them as red in the face as tomatoes. Not content with having drunk up our brandy, these scoundrels rifled our saddlebags where we had a bottle of quimagogo.[24] One of the damned gringos drank it all, thinking it was port; and I am still wondering why he did not explode.

The bottle held enough to kill three horses. When we saw they had gulped down this medicine like wine, I can assure you we would have been terrified had we not been secretly enjoying a mood of vengeance. The gringo was kept sweating, cursing, drinking all the water he could find, and vomiting over the side. It was not that he had a bad case of seasickness; it was rather that spewing from that sinful body, up, down, north, and south, there came gushes of brandy, pork, quimagogo, and bacon. This selection from Góngora fits well here.

---

24. A very bitter tonic brewed from the bark of a Chilean tree.

Salieron los elementos
de aquella concavidad
como suele por Agosto
temerosa tempestad.[25]

Everything, everything was coming out except his drunkenness. Shortly after that we ran aground. We were two days from port. Our water was all gone. Our provisions, planned for four days, also were exhausted. We kept going, though, with courage and patience. At the end of seven hungry days, bad nights, crowding, continuous damp, and all the griefs that a trip of that kind could bring, we finally arrived at a place called Sutterville. Here we say goodbye to our charming companions of the *Daice-may-nana* of unpleasant memory, to the Bacchanalian revels compounded of quimagogo and its pestiferous consequences, and to that ogre, Robinson, whom I would be glad to see on the isle of Juan Fernández.[26] He might very well have been Bacchus himself in the disguise of a sailor come to sample the *placeres* of California.[27]

If our trip had not been so brutally uncomfortable, it would not have been without charms. We crossed the beautiful bay of San Francisco. It seems to end in the north with a strait formed by two identical-looking islands called Dos Hermanos. Anyone sailing into it would think himself in the mouth of a river, and it is with some surprise that you leave the islands behind and find yourself sailing into another bay called San Pablo that stretches inland for many miles.

This bay looks like a tremendous lake without an exit. It is ringed with beautiful hills and fertile fields covered with cattle. Frigates of the first rank could navigate it without danger and find excellent anchorages everywhere.

The most notable thing in navigating here is the effect of low and high tides on the calm appearance of the water. The periodic six-hour low and high tides create moving sand bars. These are too far down in the water to be dangerous, but they do cause turbulent flows and eddies in the water. Long lines of foam cut across the traffic during high tide, and it is known that the eddies

---

25. "The elements burst forth from that hollow space like a fierce storm of August."

26. Juan Fernández is the island group that inspired the story of Robinson Crusoe. It was, in 1849, a penal colony.

27. A play on words: *placer,* in Spanish, means both a placer and pleasure.

act like small whirlpools and carry down small objects that approach the circling water.

This same situation makes the entrance to the bay dangerous. The incoming tide, dashing against the current of the Sacramento River, raises foam and causes currents that can throw ships against the rocks of the narrow channel if proper precautions are not taken. If, however, the ship enters at mid-tide and carefully stays in the center of the channel, the mouth presents not the slightest danger.

Ships sail close to the shore in San Pablo Bay, through a very calm body of water that discloses a constant succession of shelters, ports, and anchorages, and amid a host of boats and launches coming and going with full loads of passengers and cargo. One traversing the bay for the first time would not suspect there were any outlets.

However, after three hours of sailing on a favorable wind, you find yourself in a canyon. It is narrow and deep and has a strong current, but frigates of war could sail through it without trouble. This handsome strait or channel is about a league in length. On its shores they are laying the foundations of a new town to be called Benicia, after the wife of the California general, Vallejo. He is well-to-do and held in high respect here. This little town already has one house, some tents, and a warship at anchor. We can already drink the water on which we are sailing; and because we, despite our notable talent, cannot understand a word of the English the captain uses, we are happy in the belief that we have at last entered the main course of the river. The shores, adorned with greenery and full of birds, fill us with delight.

As we continued on our course, however, we suddenly discovered that the river had broadened into another beautiful bay, called Suisún. The land bordering this new body of water is very low, and therefore looks more extensive than it really is. Toward the south there is a huge conical mountain known as Mount Diablo. It is continually in sight for many leagues as you travel onward.

Suisún Bay, lying amid low lands covered with impenetrable reeds, is full of sand bars that make navigation extremely difficult. The most expert sailor can easily run aground over and over again. If he does, he will have to wait for high tide to free himself. Reeds, banks, small islands of straw and cane multiply themselves as one proceeds north until one reaches a labyrinth of channels and openings really imposing. These mark the confluence of the Sacramento and San Joaquín, which empty together into Suisún Bay.

From Benicia onward one begins to meet clouds of mosquitoes. Their bite is vicious. You find them at San Francisco as well as in the reedy marshes where the two rivers come together. Their number defies any human comparison.

It is necessary to have an experienced pilot if you wish to locate the traffic channel.

The main arm of the river that leads to the projected city of Sacramento is in the northern part of the labyrinth. At its mouth they plan to build another town called Montezuma. At the southern end of the labyrinth there is another principal channel, which goes to the city of Stockton on the San Joaquín River, and at its mouth they are planning a town to be called New York.

We took the northern route and soon found ourselves sailing on the most beautiful river I have ever seen. You could scarcely feel any current. Its surface was like a mirror, and its waters very clear. On both banks the vegetation was lush, and it became taller and richer each moment. The river makes extensive loops in its course, and these make it seem like a capricious waterway leading nowhere. Large merchant ships sail along without difficulty, past a multitude of small craft under sail or oar going in both directions.

If it is necessary to stop anywhere for the night, all you have to do is reach up from the boat and tie on to the branch of a tree. The river is not deep, but it is as deep at the sides as in the center. The largest trees along the bank stretch their branches out over the river so far that the rigging of the ships frequently get entangled in them. In the midst of the creaking and the deluge of leaves falling over the passengers, you can hear shouts and laughter: "Pull it down!" "Break the branch!" "Pull!" "Hang on!" Everyone joins in, according to his position, the job he has to do, and the discomfort he is enduring.

Birds are everywhere, and the river has salmon and turtles that will be put to good use when the population comes that this region is just begging for now.

We jumped ashore in various places and were greatly surprised to see that the impenetrable vine tangles are made up of wild grapes, roses, and berries. The ground is strewn with unfamiliar seeds and bulbs that must make this area enchanting in spring. Herds of deer came close enough for us to see them in spite of the thick brush. Myriad snakes also seem to be hiding everywhere you step, as though they were sprouting out of the ground. This is a virgin land, rich in everything. The kind of snake I saw is not venomous; it was an *Esculapio,* the most harmless snake of all.[28]

Snakes, however, inspire such dislike in everyone that we armed ourselves with clubs and barbarously slaughtered them; and not content with that we set the woods on fire, as others had done before us. There was so much wood that we could see the reflection of that fire on the horizon three nights later.

The channel in which we were sailing could not have exceeded a city block in width at its widest point; but it is only one of the branches of the Sacramento, and preferred for traffic because it is the shortest route.

This branch is separated from the main river by a narrow gorge where ships almost always scrape their keels on the channel bottom, if they do not get stuck. From that point on, though, one can sail and tack on the splendid river, and after some six hours the infant city of Sacramento appears on the south bank. There we tied up the infernal ketch that had been our purgatory for seven mortal days.

The area chosen for the town is a beautiful plain, covered with numberless handsome oaks, lying south of the confluence of the American and Sacramento Rivers. Many hollows full of dry reeds, and small hot ponds where the turtles must be boiling, would suggest that this is an unhealthy place in summertime. There are only four houses, made of makeshift lumber and with sailcloth roofs. A few others are going up, and numberless tents of all sizes and shapes are scattered aimlessly about. Our first objective on landing was to look over the camp and pick the dryest spot, near the cliff that bounds the city on the north, and there we set up our elegant tents.

Despite the fact that our chosen spot was two blocks from the river we quickly donned our battle gear and began to carry our goods up to it. Everyone who saw us cast envious glances when they noticed we had come with everything we would need—and this in a place where everything costs a fortune. Most of these people have not yet been to the mines, so we still do not know whether we will achieve the sole object of our coming.

---

28. Probably a garter snake. The original snake was *coluber longissimus,* held sacred in antiquity and associated with Aesculapius, son of Apollo and god of medicine.

—¡¡Qué me miráis, m...!!

—God dem chilian, blast you!... ¡bagre!!!!

—¡Bagre sería tu madre!!

Escena de California
Dibujo de Vicente Pérez Rosales

A Chilean and an Oregonian

Our large tent can be seen from afar, above the clutter of small tents and windbreaks that surround us. The inhabitants of this camp they call Sacramento City do not walk; they fly. Each man looks like a military storehouse carried on the shoulders of an army scout. You can pick out the South Americans by their flour, jerky, beans, shovels, crowbars, washtubs, daggers, the scarves wrapped around their middle and drawn up between their legs, and their steer-horn containers.

The mining equipment of the Yankee includes a rifle, a six-shooter, dagger, razor, powder pouch, ammunition pouch, grenadier boots, and several bottles of brandy.

There are three or four carts for hire here to carry baggage, and a fantastic sum is asked for each load. We had brought an iron cart. It had four wheels, but the front wheels did not swivel, so every time we came to a turn in the road we had to unload, lift the cart and turn it in the new direction, and then reload it. This made the other cart owners laugh, but we laughed harder when we finished our work without having to pay them a half-cent.

There is a good deal more mobility in this town than in San Francisco. Camps spring up, and then disappear with the same speed with which they were created. Six or seven boats arrived today, and the town is full of tents. Tomorrow everybody will leave for the mines, and the city will be reduced to a desert, or, better yet, to a battlefield covered with old clothes, farming tools, pots, saddles, harness, empty or half-empty sacks of biscuit, beans, dried peaches, and everything else that would encumber a man on foot. This is a result of the high cost of transportation, which is now thirty pesos per hundredweight for sixteen leagues—and this would take you only to the nearest mine, which is called El Molino.[29]

You hear shooting everywhere here. These people like to fire at targets, and they do not care what damage their carelessness may do. It is in the evening they waste most powder. They all fire off their weapons at that time, perhaps merely to show they have them, or perhaps to clean and reload them. No Yankee goes to bed without carrying out this indispensable duty.

We are settled in comfortably with a large box for a table and other boxes loaded with provisions as chairs. There we eat our beans every day with appetites better than a teamster's. We also pay tribute to the memory of the dear mother who sent along with us the delicious preserves we consume with so much appreciation and relish.

The arrival of Ramírez is the one thing still delaying us. While waiting impatiently we have been collecting what information we can from the men coming back from the mines. We looked at the gold they had and listened carefully to all the reports they could give us. The information gathered, though, when fitted together is still a mass of contradictions.

A great deal of what we heard in San Francisco was confusing enough; but the closer the mines, the more gigantic the lies.

Every hour we form new plans; and every hour some unexpected information comes along and forces us to change them. We cannot send out scouting parties because our resources are too limited. Yet to strike out blindly, taking our whole party and all our provisions, is to risk a total disaster. Nor can we simply follow the example set by others. For one thing, each man tends to go off on his own. We also realize that many if not all of them know even less than we do about how to go about things. That is why so many fail.

---

29. Sutter's mill.

When contradictory reports came in and forced us to change our plans we would write to Felipe, perhaps asking him to send something, or perhaps to countermand a previous order. Luckily the postal service is so bad that none of the letters reached him. At least I hope so.

March 16, 1849

We have decided not to wait for Felipe, but to go on up to El Molino, the site of the first gold strike, though it has been thoroughly worked over by now. From there we will go into the interior as soon as Felipe joins us and our circumstances permit. Transportation costs are monstrously high. They want thirty-five pesos per hundredweight for a distance of eighteen leagues. Oxen for our carts are unavailable at any price. We lost time in indecision. To bring order into our discussions they have formally conferred on me the title of "Dean." Once I was invested in this high position, the decision was made that the Dean and Ruperto would build a horse cart, while some went out to see if they could buy a Bucephalus and others arranged a public sale for the clothes and goods we do not absolutely need. Our poorer wine was offered and sold at five pesos a gallon; the Til-Til brandy at seven pesos a gallon. The sale of most of our clothes and some of our food raised our capital to a respectable footing and gave us more freedom and mobility.

Those who went out to find a horse came back tired and hungry after four hours. Instead of the horses they had been sent to find, though, Hurtado and Clackston brought a detailed report of a pretty Yankee girl, daughter of a man who owned horses. Only at the end did they admit they had not dared pay two hundred pesos for a skinny weather-beaten nag, the only thing of interest the farmer had besides the girl. At the word "girl," the Dean took the floor, and, after a calm and well thought-out discourse in which he stressed to his listeners the dangers to their enterprise that might come from the acquisition of any living thing other than the one they had been sent for, he wound up his emotional oration by taking on himself the responsibility for going to confront the siren and getting the horse at a lower price than the old man was asking.

Early next morning he launched himself on this campaign, at the head of the general staff and all the troops, because they were utterly opposed to sending him alone on such a perilous mission.

How beautiful the fields were! What an exuberance of lovely trees
and flowers! We walked a distance of some twenty blocks and came
to a little settlement called The Fort. This proved to be no more
than a large ruinous building, now only a residence, in spite of
thick walls that might once have been used as defences because
some pieces of artillery are still to be seen at their base. In this
place they plan to build a town and call it Sutterville in honor
of Señor Sutter, an old veteran of the Swiss Guard.[30]

This famous man had lived there eighteen years in constant battle
with the Indians. In the end he had managed to tame them and
to be recognized as their captain. It is to him we owe the discovery
of gold. As the country had many pines, he ordered a saw mill
built on the banks of the American River; and it was in the process
of digging the channel that they discovered the nuggets of gold
that were to bring ruin to so many.

We stopped there only long enough for a quick look, and then
went on to investigate a big store not far away which had Brannan
And Company painted on it. It was the same Brannan, the owner
of the damned *Dice-mi-nana* and one of the richest men in California. As has been said, he was the leader and prophet of the Mormon
sect. He had managed, with many of his followers, to monopolize
a rich area on the American River where they dug ditches and
achieved excellent results. It seems that as he grew richer he ceased
being a Mormon and decided to look out for himself. The store
we visited, shrewdly placed on the only road to the mines, was
admirably well stocked with everything needed in mining operations. I will not mention the prices. The aim is outrageous profit—from 100 to 2,000 percent.

We walked for another hour through an apparently limitless
plain. On our left we had the American River, an enormous stream
that is one of the tributaries of the Sacramento.

About fourteen leagues from here, this river is joined by three
famous streams that run through the gold fields. They are called
the North Fork, the Middle Fork, and the South Fork. All three
are very rich in gold deposits. We were curious as to whether the
gold-bearing sands come down as far as the Sacramento, so we
tried panning. We found there is gold indeed down to the junction
with the Sacramento, but not very much.

---

30. Sutter had no such background.

We did acquire, though, a good idea of what the mines in the interior were like, and we went happily on our way until we came to the buildings of a "hacienda," or, as they call it here, a "rancho," not far from the road.

The buildings were deserted, the doors open, and tools and foods were strewn in disorderly fashion through the rooms. The residents, like so many others, had abandoned everything for the placers. The road we followed was jammed with caravans of miners, some on foot and some on horseback, but all loaded to capacity with weapons and supplies, and all heading north.

At last we reached the ranch or country estate we were looking for. It was actually a miserable hut, with not a tree, a flower, or a bird: in short, just a lonesome, one-room hovel like the houses of all the lazy and worthless farmers of Alta California. We looked at the horse. What a mess! A mangy, skinny, cunning, and vicious nag, for two-hundred fifty to three hundred pesos! Our scouts had been taken in. Realizing this, we turned our attention to a small yellowish beast that they had rejected because of his size; and we settled on two hundred pesos for it. Up to this time we had seen nothing of the Yankee girl.

Fortune then relieved us of this disappointment. We had brought gold dust, not money, so of course we had to go into the house to weigh it. And, by heaven, we saw the first feminine creature worth looking at since we left Chile. It was she herself who weighed the gold, and she who then pocketed it. She poured us some milk, something we had not tasted for a long time. She was pleasant and said many nice things to us, and we would have returned the compliments a thousandfold if our spirits had not been repressed by that first visit, by the fact that we were pressed for time, and, above all, by the fact that her future husband was there.

As we were leaving, she administered the last strokes of Cupid's arrow by standing, arms akimbo. We went away, all much taken by her, and the Dean was heard to mutter between his teeth, "What a pose! What a pity!" We left that hospitable house and, driving our splendid acquisition ahead of us, we hurried back to rejoin the rest of our group who had been waiting so that we could eat together.

Our rickety dray horse gave them all a good laugh. We tried him at pulling a load, though, and he was good. We followed that by setting ourselves to making shoulder packs to save as much freight cost as possible, and we tried to eat up all the food and preserves we could so there would be less freight to pay for. We paid 450 pesos for two other sorry horses and, having loaded a little cart at about twenty-five pesos a hundredweight, we decided definitely to set out on our trek the following day.

It was decided that Hurtado and Ruperto would wait for Felipe in a small tent. On the day fixed, the get-ready signal was given early in the morning. By ten o'clock our carts were got under way in the care of two men of our band, the rest of us staying behind to load up our own van that was to haul our provisions and bedding for the trip. We had a lot of trouble with the confounded horse we hitched to it; it seems he did not like the kind of conveyance we had hooked on behind him. He acted up so much that for a few moments we feared the whole van would come apart. Finally, though, we got the nonswiveling van under way as well, but it was by then a long way behind the others. We said goodbye to the comrades who were to stay and keep an eye on the rest of our things until we could send for them.

We did not like this additional dismemberment of our party, for we were in an unknown land, living among brutal and unprincipled people; and neither Felipe, Hurtado, nor Ruperto could speak English. Still, loaded with as much as we could carry in our knapsacks, and armed with guns and daggers, we managed to catch up with the vanguard of our caravan in a half-hour or so, tired but happy.

The order of march was as follows: Casali and a fellow named Garcés led the way and took care of the carts; Cipriano drove the horse that pulled our van; César, Federico, and I brought up the rear; and Urbina was sometimes in front and sometimes behind, lending help wherever his strength was needed.

All of these men who had not come with us from Valparaíso, including Garcés and Herrera, had left jobs and joined us for just food and shelter. That is why they are included in our party as you see.

Our first day's trek was only six leagues. I do not need to tell you that we were worn out when we stopped, for we had to take time out to unload and reload our van every once in a while. Then we had to race and try to catch up with the carts that did not stop until the middle of the afternoon. The stopping place was the bank of the same river. The cart drivers told us we had to camp there because there would be no water from there on.

The road we have followed so far has been through a fine looking plain dotted with beautiful oaks and covered with grass. We passed by the ranch of our adorable tormentress, but we did not see her. Instead we visited the ruins of a mill that had cost a good deal to build but had been abandoned for the sake of the gold mines. We went on to make our night camp just below the first rapids of the American River, navigable to this point.

As soon as we had unhitched the horses we started preparing our camp. We chose the base of a large oak and arranged ourselves around it like the spokes of a wheel. In this country the dew settles down like rain, so that by morning our bedding was soaked through. Our "beds" had been reduced to the merest excuse for sleeping arrangements.

A piece of rug underneath, a blanket on top, a backpack or bag for a pillow, plus your clothing, that is all you have. The only things we took off were our boots. We ate jerky and flour cakes, and slept the sleep of the just.

At the crack of dawn we were up, getting the horses ready, and rolling up the bedding. Then with good heart and satisfaction we left the river in the same order as we had used the day before. The freshness of the morning, the beautiful appearance of the country through which we were passing, totally uncultivated and without a suggestion of a human habitation anywhere; the flowers, the birds, the trees, all new to us; all of this made us willing to overlook the difficulties we began to encounter toward noontime. It was hot, and the mud forced us to push the carts by hand at almost every step of the way.

The appearance of the country had changed completely. The soil was no longer covered with grass. Here and there were outcroppings of granite, and the farther one went the more rugged it became. We were soon climbing and descending slopes that we would have consigned to Barabbas if they had not been covered with the most spectacular flowers. Actually it seemed as though we were travelling through a garden richly cultivated, with as many wild flowers as there are cultivated ones in Chile. At the end of a march of about five leagues we ran into an arroyo or small creek. It had so little water, and that was so dispersed in a swamp, that it was possible to do but little toward satisfying our thirst.

We took a short rest there, and when we were ready to start again so as to catch up with the carts, which had gone on ahead a long way with the rest of our party, we noticed with dismay that our little dray horse was bleeding at his shoulder joint. It was due to the harness, which had certainly not been made by skilled London leather workers. It was plain we would not have a horse at all if we went on this way. The problem deserved some thought. The carts were too far ahead for us to reach them and get back again; and even if we had reached them they could not have stopped without adding a heavy expense for us. We could not stay where we were because we had no food and did not know the country. The sensible thing seemed to be to abandon the big van, but in that case we would lose our bedding and our most essential tools. We had to decide at once, so we made up our minds to pull the cart ourselves and give the horse a chance to recuperate. We tied ropes to the front and rear hooks, and César, Federico, Jorge, and I took hold of them. We sent Cipriano on ahead, and began a long climb that would not end until we reached a spot two leagues from Sutter's mill, where we were due to arrive the following day.

The road became steeper and more tortuous every moment, and we were very much afraid a wheel might break. Although the axle was iron, as were also the wheel rims, the iron was so worn it could give way any minute. The hills with their ups-and-downs followed one another endlessly and the bogs between them made the job even harder.

Our courage would have been shot all to hell by the heat, mud, and exhaustion if it had not been that we knew how we looked. Imagining how our friends in Santiago would laugh if they could see us slaving away like this kept us laughing like lunatics. So we kept on, boasting to one another of our strength and skill, and inventing reasons to explain away any missteps we made.

We soon realized that not knowing the road would have been no handicap to us. There was a trail of bottles strewn along the whole way. If you want to locate a Yankee, all you need do is follow the empty cognac bottles and you are sure to find him.

After about four hours of this we caught sight of our carts parked on a high plateau that was covered with grass. The view revived our spirits—but that did not last long, for a short distance farther on we found a swamp blocking our way. In it a troop of Yankees were swearing like frogs around a cart that had broken down, and another that was sunk deep in the mud.

Our recourse at this juncture was to take a brief rest, and then, recommending ourselves with all our hearts to our absent Dulcineas, we charged into the nasty barrier and, fighting tooth and nail, triumphantly pulled our contraption through to the other side of the muck, arriving more proud of ourselves than if we had won a battle.

There never was for anyone in this world a more laborious task than we had in covering the few hundred yards we had to cross to reach the carts. But this day was full of anticlimaxes. The carts had only stopped briefly to rest the animals, and then had gone on their insolent way, leaving us with no choice but to let them go and fall to the ground on our backs, panting like worn-out oxen.

Fifteen minutes later we were on the go again and, after two hours of travel, we came upon the carts. They were at the bottom of a valley formed by the hill we had just passed and another hill that lay ahead. They were set up for the night, and a fire was going. The place seemed to be a rendezvous for travellers because the trail forked there. The trail on the right went off toward a mining area called Dry Diggings, and the trail to the left went to Sutter's mill. Many people, some on foot, some on horseback, and some with carts, already occupied the better part of the area.

Escena de California
Dibujo de Vicente Pérez Rosales

A "Yankee"

What a friar's night of self-mortification we spent there, after filling ourselves with biscuit and rice!

Of course if we had not had in view the great difficulties we still had to overcome before reaching our third camping spot, we would have followed our course more happily.

Although the trail was awful, the hill we were climbing was very nice. The flowers and trees, changing at every step and becoming more abundant, would have made the journey enchanting for those who can travel like lords. I grew tired counting the varieties of oaks and pines—and they grow in size as you get into the Sierra. The many creeks, each with fine water, made it possible for us to enjoy frequent and plentiful flour-soup *culpeus*.[31] Inasmuch as the carts could not make so good a showing as they had the day before because the trail was so difficult, our Yankee drivers were glad to make a short day of it; and we camped in midafternoon with our disintegrating cart on the bank of the nearest fork of a stream called Weber Creek.

This Weber was one of the numberless adventurers who had reached this creek in the early days as he looked for gold; and, finding it had no name, he gave it his own.

We were just as tired as we had been the day before, but we felt happier because we had overcome the first difficulties of the trip. We spread out our ragged bedding, left Garcés to cook some rice for us, and then the rest of us seized shovels, pans, and *poruñas*[32] and began to pan the sands of the creek with much talking and enthusiasm. We immediately struck gold! Cipriano and Urbina said they would not need any more in Chile than they found. At the cry of "gold," the cooking was deserted and everyone, fully dressed and with shoes on, dashed into the water. In a moment we were all busy trying, as best we could, to learn how to operate the heavy yet delicate Chilean gold pan. All were happy to see one or two glints of accidentally trapped gold. Urbina, though, found the equivalent of a gold escudo.[33]

In spite of our pleasure in the light work and our general high spirits, we decided the prudent thing to do was to take to our beds. It made no sense to get so wet for so little, after such a

---

31. A Chilean porridge, named for a large variety of Chilean fox.
32. A mining tool for dipping up sand, made from a steer's horn.
33. A gold coin worth 100 pesos.

Escena de California
Dibujo de Vicente Pérez Rosales

California Indians

hard day. So we went back to our oak tree and our rice, triumphantly carrying the first gold the California placers had yielded to us.

At dawn of the next day every one of us took a good hot drink and, some leading the pack animals on ahead and the rest of us with our indispensable van, we set out once more to climb and descend the most intricate hills that formed the little tableland of the mountain we had climbed the day before.

The country appeared the same, but the pines grew steadily larger and the ground was a veritable garden. The third fork of the Weber Creek, the last stream we had to cross, runs through a beautiful meadow. We saw signs of life there. There was a half-house, half-inn made of logs on the other side of the stream, and it was apparently much frequented. This was shown by the presence of a number of adventurers of all nationalities, on foot and on horseback, with the look of bandits, who were seen to be entering and coming out contented. There were also piles of broken bottles adorning the approaches of this horrible tavern.

A party of Indian men and women came down the hill close by, naked and carrying bows and arrows. The Indian women, when they saw us, squatted down to make themselves as inconspicuous as possible. One man, who seemed to be more forward, came toward us to offer us some acorns, a unique and favorite food of those aborigines. We could not help laughing at his odd and unexpected appearance.

Casali and some others of our group tried to approach the Indian women, but when this was observed by them and their male companions they all took off, running like deer back up the hill.

Novoa has never been stupid, and, as we knew very well our hand cart would be in trouble on the uphill grades we were following, we said we needed some provisions from the carts, and then, when the drivers were not looking, we stuck all the heavy things in them that we could, even our backpacks and guns. Carrying them had really worn us out in the role of vicarious oxen we had been forced to assume.

After another climb of two hours we found ourselves on a beautiful high mesa. From there we could see the high snowy mountains in whose bowels, it is said, there is so much gold. We were told we had almost reached our destination, and there would be no more climbing.

It was true. We started down a smooth inclined slope and came, in good spirits, to another residence-inn, which looked better than the previous one. It was set, as in an amphitheater, in a beautiful marshy meadow. Many Indians of both sexes were at work washing gold from the mud of a small spring. We went among them to watch them work, and their extraordinary skill was surprising.

The men wore only a kind of loincloth or a shirt, or perhaps a ragged and dirty jacket, next to their skins. The women were dressed in an identical or very similar way; but they exposed completely those parts of their persons which are carefully covered in less liberal or more evil-minded lands.

None of them could speak any but his native tongue, so it was no use asking them anything. The only reply they could make was "bueno," and they accompanied this word with a stupid kind of laugh.

The division of labor they followed was this: the men dug and gave the mud to the children, who then carried it in baskets to the women. The women, lined up along the stream, then washed it in grass baskets of the most perfect construction. The gold was tied in rags, in amounts more or less equal, and they use these little parcels to trade with just as if they were money.

After spending some time, amused and half-scandalized by the carelessness and innocence of these bare-breasted Indian women, we went on our way toward the village at the mill. It is a nice looking place, not far away, and the path is downhill, easy to walk on, and shaded by very tall pine trees.

When we got there we set to work in haste and high spirits to set up our camp. Here, as in Sacramento, it attracted attention by the amount of ground it covered and by the completeness and good order of our equipment.

This place ought to be a city and not, as it is now, just an area in the wilderness with a name. It is a very small valley ringed with high hills and thick pine forest, situated on the bank of the south fork of the American River not far from the point where it flows into the main stream. This is the place where the discovery occurred that brought us here. At the southern end was a site suitable for a mill race, and it was there Mr. Sutter planned to build his saw mill. In digging the channel for it, the workers found gold dust and nuggets in such abundance they could not believe it was the real thing. It is said that before Mr. Sutter got wind of the discovery, the workers had divided the gold among themselves as a joke, making fun of the very same thing that would make them sober enough a few days later, as in fact it did. Sutter and those with him set off at full gallop for the location. The news, gathering speed, spread down the river to Sonora,[34] San José, San Francisco, and Monterey. The people there, stunned by the reports, left their homes, families, and property, and soon turned all the area around the mill upside down. Poor devils who had never owned a cent began to come down to the valley with sacks of gold and giant nuggets. Paupers, who did not have a shirt to call their own when they left for the mountains, came back with a pride that was justified because they carried indisputable proof of their nobility and worth in the fat sacks of gold dust tied tightly to their filthy belts. Then, as we know, the news flashed around the world.

There are only two wooden buildings in this place: the mill and a store. The others are all tents or lean-tos. This is no longer considered a mining area. It is just a stopping place on the road to the mines of the north and middle forks.

---

34. This is an error. Sonora had not been established at that time. The name intended may have been Sonoma.

We had barely got settled down to wait for our other comrades and the supplies they were to bring, when we decided, for good or ill, to busy ourselves with looking over and reworking the abandoned diggings. We resolved to start the following day.

We set out very early in joyous procession, each one carrying his pan, *poruña*, crow bar, and shovel, and, after walking along the river bank some distance through debris left by former miners, we started our prospecting. We worked until dark, some digging, some carrying the soil, and others washing it. Our success was not brilliant, but we felt happy when we got back to camp and weighed our gold. It turned out to be only an ounce; but that was because we did not know the terrain.

Our arrangement the following day was that one of us would stay in camp and cook. Our menu was to be rice, beans, and tea. We then scattered and started digging at several places. Later we decided to work on a layer of virgin clay. It contained a lot of gold but was hard to deal with because the clay had to be completely dissolved and each stone washed by hand to set the gold free. This kind of deposit is called in Chile a "royal mantle" because

Escena de California
Dibujo de Vicente Pérez Rosales

Chilean Gold Machine

of its formation and because it slopes up toward the hill. This aroused our hopes, but it did not yield any more than that of the day before. We had picked a bad spot.

You cannot imagine all the fantastic things we talked about at night in our tents, how we laughed at each other's appearance, at our diet of beans, and at our constant weighing and reweighing of our gold. Since they had heard me say we were working a "royal" mantle, everyone tried to think up an even more imposing adjective for it. None of the names stuck, though, until Felipe suggested one when he arrived. His was "Justinian's mantle." He told us he had read that when the emperor Justinian engaged in conjugal love he wore only his mantle.[35] We spent the days that elapsed from the time we left our companions and the time they arrived at the mill in fruitless labor. No sooner would we start working one spot than someone would get us all excited by saying he had found a better one. That sort of thing got us nowhere; but then nothing would have done any good. There was plenty of gold, but not enough for all the men in California looking for it.

We were working a new site we called the "Solar" diggings when our absent friends suddenly appeared. That made us happy, as you can well imagine. They joined in our work there because we had decided to give the rivers time to go down, and to stay at the mill until they had done so. Meanwhile we could repair the mining machine we had brought with so much difficulty.

We had begun to lose confidence in it when we saw how many men had brought mining machines, only to abandon them for the riffle boxes and cradles of California. This bothered me, because no matter how clever I think I am in designing machines, I am not so presumptuous as to believe everybody could be mistaken except me. We did finish it, though.

Next day we hauled it triumphantly in our marvelous cart to a place that looked promising.

It operated all that day with a constancy and tenacity that deserved better luck. Everyone worked in the water, either bringing the machine sacks of dirt or pouring water into the funnel—we were never able to place it properly so the water would flow in on its own. This doubly heavy labor continued until after dark. It must

---

35. Thirty years later, in his *Recuerdos del Pasado*, the author would write: "The good Casali gave the mine the name of Justinian's Mantle, remembering the golden sequins that adorned Justinian's mantle in the Municipal Theater."

have been a very poetic scene. Everyone was doing his utmost.
Some were barefoot, others were in the water with their shoes
on. All were soaking wet, sleeves rolled up all the way to our
necks: a group of valiant men, but looking more like an army of
madmen who were trying with might and main to find the philosopher's stone.[36]

All we got was a bit more than three ounces of gold, nothing
to brag about. Nevertheless we came back in our usual good spirits
to the tents where Hurtado was awaiting us with beans and rice
he had been keeping good and hot.

That night we were told of a very good spot some three miles
away on the other side of the river. It was the Don Pancho diggings.
We thought it should be investigated, and we delegated Vicente,
one of the Garcés men, Casali, and the two peons to set out for
it next day at dawn.

The south fork is a fairly large river, and cannot be crossed except
by boat. Though there are places where it looks fordable, the current is too strong. About two hundred yards from our camp there
were two rafts whose owners had got rich ferrying passengers and
baggage to the northern mines. Men were carried across dry, for
a dollar each, but the horses had to swim. As a precaution, two
ropes at each end of the raft guided the floating platform across
the river, and the operator pulled on one as he released the other,
moving the raft along without fear of its being carried away by
the current.

The following day you could have seen our bold adventurers,
wearing blouses, backpacks, and mining tools, marching in quick-
step down to the point of embarkation. We took Piti, Casali's dog,
with us; and young Hamilton, who was living nearby, joined the
expedition. When we reached the river we were delighted to see
that the owner of one of the rafts was accidentally absent. A penny
saved is a penny earned, we said, so let us board the raft and commit
ourselves to the hands of God. The whole company then boarded,
with the baggage and Piti.

Onward ho! Who could have foreseen, little girl of my dreams,
that in the middle of the river we would lose our balance. Splash!
All of a sudden we were under, and the raft on top of us; we

---

36. The philosopher's stone was fabled in the Middle Ages to have the power
to transmute base metals into gold.

had been dumped most unceremoniously into the bottom of the river: all of us, the Dean, the baggage, and Piti.

The upset was so sudden that we all went to the bottom before we could let go whatever we had in our hands. You would have thought the Dean wanted to see if there was any gold at the bottom of the river, but he, without letting go of his gun in his right hand, was trying with all his might to free himself from the thighs of Urbina, which were around his neck and carrying him down. Malicious tongues say that the Dean, caught in that watery vise, went so far as to promise that he would never drown himself, if he had any choice in the matter. Even today he cannot look at a river without his teeth hurting. However, Urbina swallowed some water, and so got over his first fright, dismounted from his unwilling mount, and lost no time in swimming to the opposite shore. Picture the terror of the amiable Dean by the time he finally got his neck free. Need I tell you how light the body of the poor devil felt to him then? After a few good strokes he was seen to appear on the surface of the water, a bald-headed old man, blowing water like a whale, and allowing himself to be carried downstream by the current. Cupid saw his father was drowning, though, and held out a rope for him to grasp—and, like a new Neptune, or, better yet, like a new Tagus, he raised his chest out of the water. Slowly, and without being seen, he climbed out onto dry land, but without his gun, his baggage, or his hat.

Some of the many spectators vowed they had recognized in him the tutelary spirit of the river. Others had thought he was a shark. And there were not lacking those who believed that if the author of Don Quixote could have seen him, he would have substituted his fascinating figure for that of the Knight of the Mournful Countenance.

Nevertheless, our baggage, guns, provisions—and Piti—had been swept away by the river. Casali wept bitter tears at the loss of his faithful retriever, whose final destination no one could guess. The whole group came back across the river on the other raft. Casali was quiet, with head hung low, and would not even think about eating for two whole days. What had happened, though, was that the poor animal had been caught under the raft, and was still there when the raft was recaptured and carried to shore. The dog looked dead, and was left lying there for two hours. Two days later the dead dog turned up alive at our camp.

News of the accident had reached our companions, who were busy as usual. The prudent Dean could do no more for a while but lie down and breathe out his thanks for his freedom; but, after shedding his dolphin scales, and before attempting any new tricks, he went to tell them what had happened and what he had seen at the bottom of the river.

Everyone quieted down then and went back to his work.

The river, swollen with melting snow, invaded more and more land, and, suddenly, cut us off from our mining machine and our carts. We thought the rise of the river was a temporary aberration and we could wait and get our things when it receded, so we took it as a joke. But it was not so funny when we saw our machine and carts start navigating down the river toward the Pacific Ocean.

We really did not care much. It is an act of folly to bring such contraptions to a country you have not seen and whose methods of operating are unknown to you. Everyone who brought a machine here has abandoned it and adopted the California cradle. It is a remarkably simple instrument, and produces excellent results.

It is a portable and easily managed apparatus. It looks like a child's crib, low at one end. In the upper part there is a can or a box with holes in it. It occupies about two-thirds of the cradle. The soil is placed there, it is filled with water, and the rocking begins. The bottom of the crib has two or three riffle boards that catch the gold as the water carries the lighter material through the strainer and away. Large rocks are left well cleaned and pounded in the box as a result of the motion back and forth. All you need do is clean it out now and then, put in more dirt, and rock the baby to sleep.

The simplicity of the thing delighted us, and we bought one for an ounce of gold, though it could not have cost more than three cents to build. It soon began to produce results.

We thought the whole group should have such equipment, and as our craftsmen were back in Chile, César and the Dean set themselves to learn carpentry. It was decided that Ruperto, Hamilton, and Cipriano would leave next day for the Middle Fork, which is the central stream; and that Federico, the negro John Leger, and Urbina would go to another mining area called Dry Diggings on a similar mission. Casali would stay and wash gold with Herrera, while Hurtado, who was sick, would mind the kitchen.

The exploring expeditions left at dawn. Both had as their goal to reconnoiter the areas and to decide to which place we should take our tents.

Ruperto was the leader of his group. It was augmented by inclusion of the elder Garcés; and, in addition, it had the yellowish horse of our lost van to carry the provisions and armament. He got across the river where we had our accident without any trouble. There we bade him Godspeed, recommending that he be very careful and that he return soon.

Federico had charge of the second division, and had another horse to carry the baggage. He did not have to cross the river. We watched him climb the nearby hills and disappear, taking with him, as had the other group, our prayers and our hopes for success.

Never was a camp more lonely than ours. We had grown so close that if even one was gone, we missed him.

While we waited for the return of our hardy scouts, we had an opportunity to get acquainted with some of the Indians. They paid us a number of visits, attracted by the red cotton handkerchiefs we had. When they saw we were after gold they brought small bundles of it, worth from four to six pesos, on several occasions, and gladly traded them for the three-penny handkerchiefs from Valparaíso. We could have developed a nice business with them, without the horrible things that happened a few days later between them and the Americans.

Our two expeditions returned without trouble, and with only a day's difference in their time of arrival. As soon as they came in we learned that Ruperto's group. . . .

At this point the diary ends abruptly.

Vicente Pérez Rosales in 1878 also published a memoir of his Gold Rush experiences, based on his complete diary, under the title *Viaje a California: Recuerdos de 1848, 1849, 1850.* We take up the story just after the departure of the expedition to find other mining areas.

My brother Federico left his work on three occasions—to look for some excitement, he said. The first two times he came back with his pockets full of bits of quartz with little specks of gold in them. On the third occasion he returned with a nugget of solid gold weighing 17 1/4 ounces that he had found at the bottom of a gully among the rocks.

In early April we were all in danger of being wiped out in a general uprising of the Indians. They wanted to get rid of the intruders, who would not leave them in peace anywhere. They had planned it so secretly that, had it not been for a traitor who sold them out, I might not be here now to tell what happened.

An immediate meeting was called. Everyone left his work, and in a few hours a body of one hundred seventy riflemen and eighteen horsemen were on their way to find the Indians. Because I had not gone to the meeting, something that really surprised them about a Frenchman (that is what they thought I was), their committee came looking for me. They found me, *naturally,* very sick but strongly desirous of accompanying them. They did not demand such a sacrifice, but were content to accept from the valiant fellow-countryman of Lafayette a contribution of gunpowder and lead.

Two days later the expedition returned with one hundred and forty captives, men, women, and children. They were made to stand for two hours on the bank of the river while an improvised jury decided their fate. Then the man who acted as commander, followed by some riflemen, addressed himself to the miserable wretches and said, "Now you have seen, one and all, what we are able to do and know how to do. If you behave from now on you have nothing to fear. I am going to show you what will happen to you if you behave badly. Then you'll be let go so you can tell your chiefs." With that they shot fifteen wretches who had been led apart previously, leaving their bodies strewn over the ground.

I have told this bloody tale as quickly as it happened, for I saw in it, translated anew in vigorous terms, the favorite maxim of the Yankees: "Time is Money!"

The impression this swift and horrifying punishment left on the minds of the hardy adventurers of Coloma lasted only two hours. We had scarcely lost sight of the Indians who had been set free and who were loudly wailing in misery as they disappeared in the pine-covered hills that surrounded the valley, when the report of another gold strike on the other side of the river took possession of all minds. Nobody could talk of anything else. The whole group of us would have pounced on the treasure if it had not been for the limited facilities we had for crossing the dangerous torrent that barred our way. There were only two ways to cross the river. One was to ford it in water up to your chest, pulling yourself along on a light cable that was stretched from bank to bank. The other was to be carried across in a shallow boat that could only hold about fifteen people. Nevertheless, as night fell, we could see by the fires burning on the other shore that a good many had got across already.

Pérez Rosales repeats at this point the story of his near-drowning when the raft overturned, an event that his diary reveals had occurred earlier.

Spring had come in all its splendor, painting the green fields of California with colorful flowers. Someone had to go to San Francisco to pay our debts and to get the letters of the loving mother in Santiago who mourned her absent sons. We decided to take a vote as to which of us would go. The choice fell on "the Frenchman," who had by this time recovered from his watery immersion and had continued to discharge his duties as Dean, accountant, and cook.

The morning of April 25 was very sad for all the brothers. It was the first time that one of us, alone and on foot, would have to travel a long distance through a country half barbarous in its abnormal way of life. We had thought but little of toils and dangers so long as we were together—but, separated, who knew what might happen? Here we were two thousand leagues from our fatherland, our relatives, and our resources, in the midst of a country that had been turned into a wild carnival by reckless adventurers. These adventurers were a mixed lot: some were decent men; but there were swarms of bandits, vagabonds, and the sort of evil-minded men the human wave constantly throws off. They had nothing in mind but the search for gold, recognized no right but that of the strongest, no court of appeal but a bullet. It was clear that any false step—sickness, an encounter with a wild beast or a poisonous snake, hunger or thirst while travelling, a simple spraining of a foot—either one or all of these—could bring a terrible and irremediable disaster for a lone man.

My brothers escorted me silently for a mile or so, but at that point we decided this conduct would be thought too sentimental for the country we were in, so we shook hands and said goodbye.

I was carrying on my back, all rolled up like a soldier's pack, a Mexican sarape and a Chilean poncho as a bed, sixteen pounds of toasted flour, and a tin cup. I had a rifle on my left shoulder, and at my belt a pistol, daggers, and a snake with seventeen pounds of gold dust.

Every once in a while I had to leave the road to avoid meeting hordes of adventurers who were on their way to the mines, some of them happy and singing, others shouting curses. When I met a man who was travelling alone, we had to greet each other very courteously. If I ran into two or more travellers, I was the only one who had to give greetings. They either did not look at me at all, or, if they did look, it was only to eye me up and down with a contemptuous grin.

When night fell I would make camp under the widest-spreading oak I could find, sweeping away with my dagger the grass and rubbish that had accumulated around the trunk. Then I barricaded the spot with some branches, and plugged with mud and tamped-down leaves any holes that might conceal insects or poisonous snakes. After that I made a fire with dry pine cones, and, dead tired, slept like a soldier in spite of guns going off in other camps all around me.

I tramped on in this fashion for four consecutive days, and on the morning of the fifth reached Sacramento without incident.

Sacramento had grown a good deal, for so short a time. It was changing from day to day. City streets had been laid out and some really expensive houses were going up. Milled lumber, the only material used in construction, sold for seventy-five cents a foot. Building lots now were not given away; they were being sold, and sold for a good deal of money. In the harbor you could see hulks of deserted ships and their rigging, besides many smaller vessels.

With all the noise and traffic I had to take some time to get oriented so I could find the house, or rather tent, of Mr. Gillespie, an honest and deliberative American gringo to whom we had sold our wine and leather flask of Til-Til when we first arrived.

This man had taken a liking to me, and we shook hands in a very cordial way. He was just setting out to go and look at some land he was thinking about buying about a mile from town, and, happy at my unexpected arrival, he proposed that I go with him so he could take advantage of my knowledge of farming land. I needed no urging to rid myself of the very heavy burdens I had brought, and it was like a relaxing rest to set out with him on foot.

The protective hand of God must have been guiding our steps on that occasion. On our way back we stopped for a few moments in the shade of a tree to escape the sun, and it was then the frightening event occurred that exposed our fellow countryman, Alvarez, to danger of death. We managed to stop the barbarous murder as I explained earlier in this work.

This story, told in an earlier section of the memoir, follows:

I was with my friend, Gillespie, under the shade of a pine tree near the ruins of Sutter's fort when we heard yells coming from a man who was being held on the top of a wagon. I thought I recognized the voice, and I jumped up in alarm and called to Gillespie, "They are killing a friend of mine. We must run over there and save him!"

Luckily we got there in time. I can still see poor Alvarez with the noose around his neck and the attached rope thrown over the branch of a tree, and with his feet tied to the cart which was ready to be driven away. He was going to be drawn and quartered! I was thought to be a Frenchman in California, and I knew the name of Lafayette was venerated by even the most uncouth American. So I invoked that magical name and declared Alvarez was the only protector the French had in Chile, that he had even saved my life, and that I would vouch for his honesty. My friend nodded emphatically to everything I said, and the hand of God intervened: Alvarez was lowered from the gallows.

The reason for this quick and barbaric justice was the character of our countryman: he was always getting his nose in everywhere. I do not know what he was doing with that group of men headed for the mines; but a shovel was lost, and as there were no other aliens among them but "this descendant of Africans," as the Yankees call the Chileans and Spaniards, they accused him of the theft. Without any further ado the barbarians became the jury. They were ready to do to Alvarez what they usually do to thieves. For five days the poor fellow was out of his mind and in the grip of convulsions and stupor. Once he recovered he left us, and I never heard of him again.

We returned to Gillespie's house, where we took care of the poor devil in whom impulses occupied the place of judgment. His amiable character had almost cost us both our lives.

The good Gillespie had been keeping a can of oysters for some occasion great enough to set the bells ringing, and as he thought my arrival had set all the bells in the world flying, he brought out the can. He and his guest sat down most joyfully to deal with this treat, so rare at that time and in that part of the world. The liquid in which they were preserved seemed to me sweetish and milky, but I only began to worry when I felt stomach pains and a great desire to vomit. My friend, who suffered the same symptoms, as I learned later, lost no time in finding a reason to leave the tent. Finding myself alone, I broke out in the most violent vomiting accompanied by faintness and heavy perspiration. Almost burning up with thirst, I dragged myself to a nearby tent where I had heard French spoken, shouting to them to give me water because I had been poisoned! They hurried to oblige me, but all the water I could drink was not enough. Finally, after the last vomits, which were bloody, I began to feel better. I asked these kind people at once to go and help Gillespie. Next day, my friend and I shared the only bed in his tent, as weak and crippled as if we had both been given a most savage beating. Water, which had brought me to the gates of death at the mill, had saved me in Sacramento.

No one has time to get sick in California, so two days of quick convalescing were enough. Then a boat of Gillespie's, stocked with all the necessities, took me down to San Francisco. I arrived there twelve days after leaving the mines, weak and crippled, it is true, but full of good humor and high resolve.

How different San Francisco was from what it had been when I left it to go into the interior. Instead of an "Araucanian" village with foundations marked off here and there on which buildings were to rise, now those buildings were finished and others were under rapid construction. The tents, huts, and windbreaks of old were now lined up beside streets in the suburbs. But, by the look of things, all these suburbs too would soon be built over and become part of a beautiful town. Building lots were already being laid out and measured in feet there, and prices had gone out of sight!

What a mistake we had made in not acquiring land in the towns at prices that would almost have made them gifts. It was depressing to me now to see how much they had increased in value in so short a time! Here I want to say something, without meaning to offend anyone: the men who made fortunes in California were gentlemen who lacked the hardihood to go prospecting for gold all out, scorning hunger, weariness, and danger. It was those who acquired valuable building sites either by just taking them or buying them at low prices; or those men who happened, without meaning to do so, to bring merchandise into the area to sell. Such men found themselves wealthy overnight.[1]

The bay was full of ships, all of them abandoned. Their passengers and crews had swelled the town's population to thirty thousand souls; and, whether permanent residents or transients, their activity was so great that the city seemed to change and expand as if by enchantment. Long piers, supported on redwood piles, were being constructed or were being further extended at the end of every street that ran down to the beach. These carried the street out over the tidal flat, and provided roadways and foundations for additional buildings. At one place a lack of ready materials for piers had been solved by piling boxes and sacks of earth across the muddy beach; at other locations, so as not to lose time, piers had been improvised by grounding ships side by side at the ends of streets and laying beams up to them; and there, too, shops and offices were built.

---

1. Among British and American residents of Chile who came to California with Chilean families were Faxon D. Atherton, James Lick, and Robert Livermore.

One of the first to transform his ship into a home ashore was a young Chilean, Wenceslao Urbistondo. He had taken advantage of an unusually high tide to beach his deserted and useless bark at the end of the last street to the north of town; then he had laid his masts and spars to form a bridge across the mud so he could get back and forth.

The sidewalks along the streets were made with bales of jerky, because it was the cheapest and most readily available material. The bales were pushed down into the mud along the front of the buildings so one could get around without sinking into mud up to the knees.

Business was at the mercy of the shifting tides in that city. Sometimes the high water invaded everything, reducing the value of the highest quality merchandise; at other times it left everything high and dry. The most provident merchant was not safe from the

San Francisco Street Scene

ruinous effects an unexpected high or low tide might produce. One man might get rich with no idea how it happened. Another would be ruined despite precautions of the most meticulous sort. I remember, for example, that because there was a shortage of housing in San Francisco, they asked that prefabricated houses be brought from Chile. When these arrived, houses were so plentiful in San Francisco that those who had ordered the houses had to pay to get them landed and then had to pay someone to accept them. I am witness and victim of what I am describing.

Nobody, however, was discouraged. Even the lowest-priced items could be given scarcity value by arranging for convenient fires. We saw such fires break out all over town day after day, posing the danger of a general conflagration.

In this theater, where the most uproarious international fair that memory records was in process, no actor played the role his lot would have assigned him in his native country. Masters were transformed into servants; a lawyer might be a freight agent; a doctor, a stevedore; sailors found themselves digging excavations; and philosophers, having abandoned the realm of the abstract, were working with the most concrete materials. I have seen, without surprise and with the just pride of a Chilean, a soft and effeminate dandy from Santiago, with the same gold vest chain he wore at dances in our capital city still hanging from the buttonhole of a sweaty wool shirt, standing in water up to his waist and carrying the baggage of a tarred and brawny sailor with a smile on his face; and then, after having got paid for that job, offering his services to some other oaf.

The most ostentatious signs had been hung up everywhere. A wooden barracks bore the name, "Hotel Frémont." One man had a sign that said "So-and-so, Physician and Surgeon" painted on the flap of his tent, though he had never been more than a gravedigger. An insurance salesman from Valparaíso had a hut that bore two signs: "So-and-so, Attorney at Law," and "So-and-so and Company, General Insurance Brokers." An arbor made of poles called itself, "French Hotel"; it belonged to an old Santiago barber. This sort of thing was done by Chileans of prominent families—few of which were not represented by family members in California.

The crowds of men—and only men, because that creature called woman was not yet in fashion there—had made it necessary to set up at least a makeshift kind of civil government in that Babylon.

They had an official they called an alcalde. He was a factotum whose duties were precisely like those of our old "subdelegates," with this difference: the orders and decrees of our subdelegates, whether just or unjust, were carried out, while those of the California or San Francisco alcalde were carried out only if convenient.

Pérez Rosales placed at this point in his memoirs the story of the trial before the alcalde in San Francisco, which his *Diary* shows had occurred earlier.

With justices and trials of this sort it is not surprising that lawsuits and appeals are often decided with pistol or dagger.

The relations between Chileans and Americans were anything but cordial. When General Persifer Smith sent a decree from Panamá to the effect that, after that date, no foreigner was to be allowed to exploit gold mines in California, that decree brought to a head all the hostility shown to peaceful and defenceless Chileans.

Merchants and traders were alarmed by this, and the authorities proposed to the aliens that they become full United States citizens; they were to be charged only ten dollars, a small sum for such an imposing title. But this safe-conduct was only halfway effective: it worked only where it was accepted. In other places it was treated as a joke. A little later on, the provisional government in San José made a ruling that an alien could work the mines on payment of twenty dollars a month in advance. A receipt would serve as sufficient authorization for the right to work. But how many clashes there were that arose from that agreement between collectors and contributors.

The ill will of the Yankee rabble against the sons of other nations, and especially Chileans, was rising by that time. They offered a simple and conclusive argument: Chileans were descended from Spaniards; Spaniards were of Moorish ancestry; therefore a Chilean was at the best something like a Hottentot, or, to put it more gently, something like the humbled but dangerous Californio. They could not stomach the fearlessness of the Chilean, who might be submissive in his own country but did not behave that way abroad. A Chilean would face up to a loaded pistol at his chest if he had his hand on the haft of his knife. For his part, the Chilean detested

The "Hounds" Attacking Little Chile

the Yankee and constantly referred to him as a coward. This mutual bad feeling explains the bloody hostilities and atrocities we witnessed every day in this land of gold and hope.

It was not long in San Francisco until an organized group of bandits appeared, called the Hounds. They were vagrants, gamblers, or drunks, drawn together in a fellowship of crime; and they had as their motto, "We can get away with it." Fear and hatred spread in advance of their appearance, and they deliberately generated these feelings by their provocations. Everywhere they went they established their control by quarrelsomeness and violence.

They did not always "get away with it," though. One morning

when they were passing by a little point of land to the north of town where a sort of Little Chile had grown up, separated from the center of the city, these vicious Hounds decided to give it a savage going over. Because in California, time is money, these merciless ruffians in large numbers charged the Chileans there with pistols and clubs. You can imagine the shouting and uproar this brutal and unprovoked attack brought on. The Chileans rallied and counterattacked by hurling stones. One respectable Chilean gentleman, not being able to escape through the front of his tent because it was jammed with a threatening band of Hounds, brought one of them down with a pistol shot as he came toward him and then, slashing with his dagger the cloth of his tent, managed to escape through that improvised exit and join his friends in safety.

Brannan, ex-Mormon owner of the unforgettable *Daice-may-nana,* informed by some Chileans of what was happening in Little Chile, climbed up on top of his own house in just indignation and shouted in a loud voice for the people to come. Then in a short but forceful speech he declared it was time to make an example of those who had perpetrated such unheard-of atrocities against the sons of a friendly country, a country that had day after day supplied the city of San Francisco with its best flour, as well as the most skillful arms in the world when it came to making *adobe bricks*! "I propose," he said, "that to take care of this once and for all, the Chileans of good will, led by citizens of the United States, go at once to the scene and arrest these disturbers of the peace!" A general "Hurrah!" was raised, and the almost instantaneous appearance of the defenders of order at the point put an end to the savagery that could have brought on the most terrible consequences.

Eighteen of the bandits were dragged from hideouts by force and were incarcerated on board the flagship of the Yankee American squadron, and with this, peace returned to the new Babylon.

Three days later while I was busily preparing to go and rejoin our company, I read with alarm in a San Francisco paper this ominous news: "North American blood shed by infamous Chileans in the placers! Citizens, be on your guard!"

By the following day the report had taken on unimaginable proportions, and by evening it was being said not only that the Chileans had been expelled violently from the banks of the San Joaquín River, but that the same band of vigilantes, seeking vengeance and plunder, was moving in upon the Chileans working the tributaries of the American River!

You can imagine my state of mind in such a fearful situation. What should I do? An acquaintance gave me a very exaggerated account of the most savage atrocities that had just been inflicted on Chileans near Sutter's mill. I confess my sin of credulity. I should have known better than to believe him. I knew the distance between Sutter's mill and San Francisco and that it was impossible for news to have covered that distance so quickly even if it flew in. It was the fact that my brothers were in the midst of the situation then that nearly drove me crazy. My brothers, my poor brothers all alone there, and I without the means to join them in their hour of peril. Without thinking, with nothing but my weapons, with no hope except for revenge, I paid two hundred pesos for a passage by boat to the beaches of Sacramento. Without listening to the voice of prudence—or not wishing to listen to it—I dedicated myself to a violent destiny.

Where was I going? What was I going to do? I had no idea. The one thing I remember is that anything seemed more feasible, anything far easier than to return to Chile without my brothers.

We pressed on day and night without rest. We arrived at Sacramento. I jumped into the water without waiting for the ship to land, and, with my heart full of anguish, I ran all the way to the residence of Señor Gillespie.

Imagine my surprise. God had not abandoned me. My brothers had arrived in Sacramento the day before. They were destitute, having been robbed of all they had; but they were safe. They had agreed with Gillespie that they should join me in San Francisco as soon as possible. To meet them, to see them, count them, and feel my anxieties drain away, was all a great experience. You would have to have been in my position to know what it was like. Desperation, hate, and the desire for vengeance, all had given my sick body a strength and vigor that, in this moment of great happiness, I could feel ebbing away.

Once we were together again, recounting our experiences to one another in a makeshift tent made of sarapes, our good spirits returned. We could see all that happened to us had been only an ugly and ridiculous nightmare. We were all safe and sound; no one was missing. What more could we want? The Yankees had not needed much force to drive us Chileans from Sutter's mill.

True, they had robbed us of everything we had; but in California that did not amount to much.

Our friends were all gone; so on that same night we organized ourselves into a committee to decide what we should do from then on. No one thought we should go back to Chile. Instead we were unanimous in feeling we should make an effort to reverse our luck, trying various plans of operation until we found one that succeeded.

Mining was not the only occupation California offered at that time to men willing to work. If prospecting was closed to foreigners, commerce was eminently within reach.

My brothers had heard me say that a man in retail trade, even if a loafer, made more than even the most industrious worker. Therefore we resolved, to a man, that we would raise altars to Mercury, the god of thieves. At the moment we did not have the money, the winged feet, or the caduceus,[2] but as for the purse, my brothers could conjure one up by combining the little sacks containing some one thousand, seven hundred pesos (a trifling sum in California) that they had tied around their waists and that, by some miracle, had been overlooked when they were robbed. The little wings I could buy in San Francisco in the form of a launch; I had already begun negotiations. As for the caduceus, we were agreed that it would be of no use to us at the moment.

Having looked over the situation there, and leaving four hundred pesos with the Solar Brothers Company to take care of warehouses and shops, on the day following our happy and unexpected reunion, the Dean was sailing down river, on the beautiful route that leads to San Francisco, with his head full of projects.

Moment by moment, it seemed, the number of Chileans we knew who landed at San Francisco was increasing. They arrived in such high spirits that they almost looked down on any Chilean who had not managed to become at least a Croesus; if he was poor or seemed disillusioned, they thought he must be either stupid or lazy. After answering the rapid-fire questions they asked me, I left them standing there and went on my way quietly, carrying to the beach some bales of musty jerky I had just bought at two pesos a bale. It is plain, I told myself, these babies do not know beans as yet. How quickly they learned! And how completely was their bravado turned into lamentation!

---

2. The caduceus was the serpent-wreathed and winged staff of Hermes or Mercury, messenger of the gods, and god of thieves and merchants.

Among the large number of acquaintances and relatives I had run into from time to time was Miguel Ramírez. He had heard me say I was going to buy a launch, and he offered to sell me one of twelve tons burden that had just been built for seven hundred dollars. He did not need it any more because he was going to become a lumberman instead of a boatman, so he would sell it to me for three hundred dollars. The deal was made.

Assisted by three young Chileans who were willing to turn sailor to pay their passage to Sacramento, the Dean, once a cook but now captain, formerly an accountant at the Sutter's mill mine but now a retail merchant and shop owner, was soon able to complete the loading of the *Infatigable*. That is what our fine little launch was called.

Her cargo consisted of eight bales of jerky, somewhat reduced through the efforts of moths; twenty hundredweight of Chanco cheese,[3] carefully squared by a knife to remove parts that had been spoiled; four sacks of dried peaches, two barrels of rum at eight gallons each; a small box of candied preserves I had received from Chile; and two sacks of toasted flour.

I was ready to embark when the devil—it could have been no one else—almost ruined the whole business. He appeared in the form of a customs agent who let me know I was not to move from that anchorage. My ship had not been manufactured in North America, and the keel was not of American wood, two indispensable requirements for boats that traded on the rivers. Furious as could be at such a frustrating situation in a land where time is money, I decided this was a case where the saying must be turned around: if time is money, I told myself, then, clearly, money is time. It is not only time; it is everything in the world! So I ran to the former insurance man from Valparaíso who had become, so his sign said, a lawyer or attorney at law. He pretended he did not know me, and did not even know Spanish—that he had been only a short time in Chile. He told me my launch was well known; I did not need to inform him where it was docked. He said my case was a difficult but not an impossible one. "Charge me whatever you please," I told him, "because if this does not come out right for me, a barrelful of demons will have me." "Well," he said gravely, "you can begin by paying half the cost of my services,

---

3. This comes from the region of the Maule River.

and we will get to work." I gave him four hundred and fifty dollars in gold. I had scarcely gone out the door when he called after me, "It is a whaleboat, right?" "No, señor," I replied with annoyance. "It is a launch, a launch of twelve tons and the name is *Infatigable*." The idiot answered that he knew it, and that he had lived only a short time in Chile—he had actually lived there so long his hair had turned grey.

Four days later (which is like a century in California), the counselor at law brought a bundle of papers all covered with scribbling. In them could be found incontestable proof that the wood in my hull had been cut in the "Eggplant" forest of the United States, and that the builder who had carved its keel was actually in San Francisco, on his way to the mines. It appeared that not only was the ship of unclouded ancestry, but so was its name. Instead of *Infatigable*, which Mexicans had called it because they could not pronounce English, its true name was *Impermeable*.

God bless him! I was now the owner, master, and captain of an American ship, having paid nine hundred dollars for a clear legal title, and I could now proceed to set sail.

The crew of the ship consisted of five persons, from captain to cabin boy. Two from Chiloé were named Velásquez; Valdivia was from Casa-Blanca; and a lad, Martínez, was from the south. Martínez, who was about twenty-two years old, was my favorite. He had good manners and a pleasant appearance. He suffered from a tertian fever, though, and when it attacked him he developed chills and fevers, became extremely weak, and then went into a coma that lasted for over an hour. I wish I had never taken him aboard.

There had been a violent ebb tide that morning and two whale boats had sunk in the swirls and eddies of the Golden Gate with all their men, including three Chileans. I decided not to start out until the high tide. While waiting I had a horrifying demonstration, with poor Martínez as the subject, of the effects such a fever can produce.

For three days in a row the proud *Impermeable* had sailed with winds and tides in her favor, exchanging hurrahs with all the ships she left behind. When we entered the waters of Suisún Bay, however, the wind and tide both turned against us at once. So, about noon, we tied up to a half-submerged tree trunk covered with turtles. The heat forced us to seek some shade ashore while we awaited the return of the tide.

Unfortunately, Martínez had just suffered one of his attacks, so we covered him as well as we could with a sailcloth and placed a jug of water near him. Then, leaving him there unconscious, we went ashore. We regretted having to abandon him that way, but we had no premonition of what we were to find on our return.

I have already described the enormous swarms of poisonous and persistent mosquitoes that infest the swampy shores of the Sacramento and San Joaquín Rivers, especially where the two rivers join.

We protected ourselves as best we could, swatting them with our handkerchiefs and, finally, taking cover under some bushes that faced a dry grassless area. This area was covered with small holes like those made by our *cururos*[4] in the dry area beyond the Maule River. We were there about an hour before we noticed little sticks, about three inches long, that were lying there, one beside each hole, in a manner that could not be accidental. I became curious then and walked out to look at them more closely—then backed up in a fright, yelling, "They are snakes!"

I have roamed through many solitary regions in the course of my life, but I cannot remember seeing anywhere a land with so many vipers and other snakes as golden California possesses. The coral snake[5] and the rattler can be found almost anywhere, along with a multitude of other ophidians of all different types and sizes. These are not all poisonous, but they are enough to frighten a traveler into making a detour whenever he finds one lying across the path sunning himself. The snakes we had found were not the dangerous sort. None of the many we killed had scales on its head. They looked rather like the Chilean snake which, instead of scales, has a shell that resembles the back of a turtle.[6]

We spent a good deal of time beating these creatures to death with clubs, and then bombarding with rocks the turtles that were lined up on tree trunks floating in the water. We were at the same time being attacked by such clouds of mosquitoes that they actually blocked our view, as well as tore us to pieces with their bites. They could not be driven off by hand waving, fanning with branches, or even by smoke. It was late in the afternoon by the time we got back to the ship.

---

4. A Chilean field rat.

5. This is an error. The coral snake is not native to this area.

6. This snake cannot be identified from the description. Pérez Rosales had probably not seen many. Snakes are rare in Chile.

There are certain sights so horrifying you can never forget them. Martínez was lying motionless, monstrously swollen, the blanket at his feet—no doubt kicked there in some convulsive movement. His whole body, including his head, was covered with a disgusting and bloody layer of mosquitoes, hovering, bloated and heavy, over their miserable victim; at least an inch thick, it seemed to us. When we saw that, we ran to him, shook him, and brushed off so many thousands of mosquitoes that our hands were covered with blood. But it was too late: Martínez was dead!

We had no tools to dig a grave for him. There was no point in carrying him on to Sacramento. And the thought of leaving him ashore was, of course, unendurable to us, for he would be eaten by coyotes. After a sad night, the waters of the Sacramento River received, along with our tears, the lifeless body of the unhappy young man who only the day before had been friend and companion.

The life of a California miner closely resembled that of a soldier on a campaign. A tear may sometimes moisten the bronzed face of a soldier as he grimly shakes the hand of a dead comrade for the last time; but that tear quickly dries when he is faced with new dangers, or elated by the enthusiasm victory brings.

The cool breeze of morning, the disappearance of the mosquitoes swept away by the wind, the impressive vision of the tranquil waters of Suisún Bay, the gracious hills and forest of its faraway shore, the screeching of birds, the continuous passing parade of boats filled with happy passengers—and, perhaps, also the thought that tears are useless when shed over misfortunes that cannot be altered—all of these things reawakened in our sad spirits their dormant energies.

Two days later we arrived at Sacramento. I showed my bills of lading to my brothers, and they, full of enthusiasm for the merchandise I had managed to buy during one of those periods of low prices that are so surprising to everyone in California, proceeded immediately to unload the goods and stow them away.

We no longer had a field tent; that luxury had disappeared. A small strip of cotton suspended from stakes formed the roof of our home and warehouse. The walls were made of branches set in a semicircle to protect us from the wind. A box, placed upside down in the opening where the door should be, served us as a counter; and since the merchandise did not all fit inside the shelter, we piled some of it in an open space next to it, and called that our storehouse.

Some curious patrons approached soon after they saw we had set up a scale needed to weigh the gold. Next to it we placed a slice of cheese, a small pile of dried peaches, and a bottle with two fine glasses. The bottle was the first supply we had drawn from the barrels of brandy we were keeping inside as a reserve.

Everything was selling marvellously except the jerky, which could not be exposed to the light of day without some shame. We did not know what to do with it. In addition to everything else, the moths were still in competition with us. So the Board of Directors decided the moth holes had to be filled with lard or tallow to restore the jerky to its original appearance.

The bales were broken open, and the jerky (the pieces of which really looked like sieves) was shaken out and spread on the grass after having been given a coating of hot lard. We let it dry in the sun there. On the day before, Federico had brought us a sack of peppers some Chileans had discarded by a tree trunk, and, since there is nothing human ingenuity cannot accomplish, we took advantage of this. We piled up the sun-heated jerky in an artistic Egyptian pyramid and poured over it a devilishly hot pepper sauce.

The smell wafted away from this exotic offering attracted two wealthy Mexicans from Sonora who asked what in the world this aromatic dish could be. We told them it was the most select jerky, the kind served to the aristocracy in Santiago. We added that we had never offered it before because California people, in spite of their wealth, seemed to buy cheap inferior things rather than good things that were more expensive. We lied like experienced merchants who assure a trusting female customer that they are losing money on an item, and would not sell it at such a low price to anyone but her; she must tell no one else and keep it as a secret, and so on. The accursed shreds were sold at a peso a pound; and, what is more, it was all bought up. The brandy was sold at six *reales*[7] a glass, because "it was of the quality that the Duke of Orleans drank." And so it went with the other items.

The town of Sacramento was already filling up with Chileans who had fled from the northern goldfields because of the lack of security they felt in that area. As if the hate of the Yankees and the new laws were not enough to complete the ruin of my poor compatriots, the climate also began to add to their miseries.

The scorching heat on the swamps at the junction of the Sacra-

---

7. This would amount to about seventy-five cents in United States money.

mento and American Rivers contaminated the air so much with putrid smells that in a short time terrible epidemics of tertian fever broke out, very debilitating for some and fatal for others. My brother, César, almost lost his life. Our flourishing business on three occasions had to close down so we could become gravediggers, taking charge of three unhappy cases and opening graves at the foot of trees to bury them.

We decided to leave Sacramento as soon as possible, so we sold our launch. We had to deliver it in San Francisco, so we moved there, with some five thousand pesos in our belts.

We had been miners, and had failed at that despite our best efforts to avoid it. Then we had become merchants, and although we gave commerce the full measure of deceit that is usual, that too, as they say, came tumbling down. We had begun to think that, with our luck, if we started a hat factory we could expect men would be born without heads! Then the sight of all the money cafes took in suggested to us the idea of starting one of those.

In California there was so little difference between planning and carrying out a project that not even a line of the compass could measure it. We joined with two sons of General Lastra in organizing a company; they had tried out various ways of getting ahead, just as we had. We bought a lot on Dupont Street for three thousand pesos, equipped ourselves with lumber and carpenters' tools, and set to work. A Yankee day-laborer helped us. We sawed, planed, and chiseled with such energy that in a few days (months are like centuries there) we had put up a handsome coffin-like structure with a parlor and three rooms on the first floor and four on the second. We also built a private, intimate convenience that looked like a sentry box and set it a prudent distance away from the building; this was a luxury in San Francisco at that time. I mention this little room because many Chileans, among them our fine countryman, J.M.I.,[8] spent many nights sitting in it because they did not have a better place to sleep; and slept there as well as the Prince of the Asturias could have done in a soft bed.

A well was dug for drinking water, and the job was assigned to the miner, Juan Nepomuceno Espejo. He had exchanged the manipulation of his graceful and illustrious pen for the handling of a heavy crowbar, but he did better than the strongest rustic.[9]

---

8. Possibly José María Izquierdo.
9. A well-known Chilean journalist.

He dug at the bottom of the shaft, filling a bucket, which I lowered to him, with soil and stones, and getting his head covered with the cascades of mud that dropped as I drew it up. I remember that when the water got up to his knees he called up to me in a sepulchral voice, "Vicente, it's deep enough. Look, I'm being swept away by the—" I broke in to say, "Just go on working, my friend. I'm not paying you for doing nothing!"

We hired a famous French cook called Monsieur Michel, who got, besides board and room that was worth two hundred dollars a month, a salary of five hundred dollars; that is to say, eighty-four hundred dollars a year. That is a good deal more than the Secretary of State earns in Chile. We hung over the door of our cafe a large sign, "Citizen's Restaurant," and got under way with a full force in the summer of 1849.

In the beginning, needless to say, the business went well—everything went well at first in California; it was only when things reached the middle that they collapsed. We were, at one and the same time, the masters and the servants of the restaurant. Barring some lapses of memory, excusable because we were new at the work, we did not do badly as servants.

We had a mulatto among our customers who had recently taken on the status of a gentleman but still had a good deal of the cow pasture about him. He shouted his orders in an arrogant way, and his whole manner was unpleasant. Milk had been up to that time an exotic luxury in San Francisco. I had not had any since that which was given us with so much amiability and good will by the siren of the horse we bought in Sacramento. I was tempted by Satan one morning and almost finished in two swallows the milk reserved for the lunch of our gentlemanly customer. I replaced what I had drunk with water, and went about my usual duties.

I was serving a cocktail to a customer, when I had to drop everything and run to my brother Federico because of the vile oaths and imprecations being heaped on him by our loud-mouthed friend because of the kind of milk served him. The mood and behavior of the man made Federico forget his role as waiter, and he was doubling up his fist. I intervened just in time to save the good name of our restaurant. I applied the most exaggerated and polished courtesies, took away the modified water that had been served as milk. I took it out to the kitchen, poured it into another mug and brought it back to the customer immediately. The grandson of Africa, mollified by this, then exclaimed, "At last; this is more like

it, waiter!" A cat can be passed off as a rabbit with many customers
if it is done properly.

When the restaurant was closed late at night, we all sat on the
floor and did the dishes. Then one of us was designated to sprinkle
and sweep the floor, and get everything ready for next day, while
the rest of us went happily to bed like any other innkeepers.

That is what our life was like during the brief time we ran the
restaurant. As the business did not need all of us to manage it,
and I could not forget the trick I had pulled with regard to the
milk, I gave the excuse that I wanted to enlarge our sphere of
activity and got from my comrades the permission to make a trip
to Monterey.

I admit my real object was to get down to that town so I could
drink all the milk I wanted.

On a cool and lovely July morning, rifle on shoulder, pistols and
a slender snake of gold at my waist, wearing a dirty cloth hat,
a sarape, and a beard down to my chest, I set out on foot through
the hills around San Francisco toward the old capital of Alta
California.

I crossed the first slopes of what is called the Coast Range, accompanied by a number of men from Sonora who were returning disillusioned to their homes, and entered a wide valley covered with

Escena de California
Dibujo de Vicente Pérez Rosales

My God!!! A Bear!!!

grass and flowers. Birds and squirrels were so abundant it seemed
as though they sprouted from the ground about our feet. Herds
of deer acted like our guanacos: they would come close, scamper
away at the least movement—only to stop all of a sudden and
come toward us again. The height and value as lumber of the trees
surprise one here in this valley as they do in all areas of this privi-
leged land. Oaks, pines, and birches seem inexhaustible in number.
The coast opposite San Francisco is covered with redwoods; they
are similar to our "alerce."[10] These trees certainly do not yield
in size to the giants of our southern forest. In my earlier wanderings
I had occasion to view admiringly the marvelous conifers that grow
in the Mariposa mining area. There I saw trees that measured from
two hundred to two hundred twenty feet in height, and from sixty
to sixty-five feet in circumference at the base. What is more surprising is that lateral branches some one hundred feet from the ground
were more than six feet through. This portentous representative
of the vegetable kingdom is called by scientists the "Sequoia Gigan-
tea."[11] But it has many names in California, so many that a visitor
does not know which one to use. Some call it "the Grizzly Giant";
others the "redwood." English gringos call it "The Wellington";
Yankees, "The Washington." Perhaps we ought to call it "The San
Martín."[12]

We slept in the shelter of an oak tree, and all night long we
were bothered by the visits of coyotes. This is a variety of wolf
that, although smaller than the European wolf, is as ravenous and
vicious. It was fear of coyotes that drove Señor O.A. from California.[13] He was a recognized Argentinian socialite, well known in
Santiago. He set out to do what everyone else was doing, going
out prospecting on his own, and the coyotes chased him without
a pause until they had driven him screaming into camp. These
accursed animals did not even leave us any breakfast the next morning, for they got away with what was left of the deer we had shot
for food, even though it was lying right beside us.

In this, as in my previous encounters with Mexicans and Spanish
Californians, I had to marvel at the candor with which these poor

---

10. The alerce is a larch.

11. It is unlikely he saw this grove. He may have seen the Calaveras grove
and confused the names.

12. The great Argentinian who played a part in the liberation of Chile.

13. Octavio Alvear is probably the man referred to here.

people talked about the invasion and take-over of their country
by the Yankees. They were sure they could not by themselves drive
out "the tyrants," as they, with justice, referred to the Yankees.
But they firmly believed, having seen the vigorous resistance Chileans put up to the brutality and strength of the Yankees, that
we Chileans could drive them out! They seemed to feel safe from
being molested while traveling in my company—almost as if they
were being guarded by the devil himself. But when the time came
for us to part I confess the devil was as uneasy as they were at
finding himself alone.

On the afternoon of the third day of my journey (which I had
begun to regret undertaking) I saw the white tower of Monterey
and made up my mind to reach it before nightfall.

Monterey, the port, is one of the best on the coast. Monterey,
the town, considered up to that time as the capital of California,
was a village rather similar to our Casa Blanca in 1840, with a
total population of not more than two thousand. However, the
nature of the countryside around it and, in general, of the whole
district together with that of Santa Cruz, makes it the best and
most fertile area I have found as yet in the state of California.

The setting of this charming town was made more cheerful by
many small orchards full of beautiful trees; and although the buildings were of the sort that our heavy country houses were a half-cen-
tury ago, still, their wide-arched porticoes facing the street demonstrated the characteristic hospitality of the Spanish race.

Night was falling fast, and as neither my appearance nor my
dress was respectable enough to enable me to ask for lodgings,
I decided to take shelter in one of those porticoes. I chose a house
with windows closed and the door slightly ajar, because I thought
these conditions were evidence that the family was away. But as
I approached the house the door slammed noisily. "Bad," I said
to myself; "It's impossible to think they hadn't seen me. What did
that slamming mean?" I went into the corridor nevertheless and
knocked with three light raps in the Spanish manner on the door.
No one answered, and, remembering I was in California, I then
used the butt of my rifle on the unresponsive door. Two blows
secured an immediate reaction. Someone within said, "Who is it?"
It was the voice of an old and frail woman. "*Deo gratias,* señora,"
I replied, "I am a man of peace who only asks permission to spread
my sarape on the floor of your corridor for one night, nothing
more." Then I heard some quick movements of several persons

inside, and a woman's voice said, "It is not a Yankee; it's a Spaniard." I answered, "For ever," very slowly; and cautiously opened the door. I was met by a gentleman of about forty-five, simply and decently dressed. He greeted me and asked what he could do for me. When he heard me speak, he burst out with an expression of the most complete joy, "May God forgive you, my friend, for the fright you gave us. When we saw you coming we thought you were one of those scoundrels who infest our roads and towns ever since peace brought us a change of masters. Enter, señor, enter."

He was right to have taken precautions. Only a Californio house owner could know how many wrongs they had been forced to endure without hope of appeal since the invasion of the "barbarians of the north," as they called the Yankees.

You should have seen the general contentment that awakened in that amiable and hospitable family—made up of a gentleman, his lovely wife, and two sisters-in-law who would have been thought beautiful by any man but seemed like angels to me—when they realized they were dealing not only with a decent man but actually with a Chilean.

A Chilean who had been at the diggings in the high mountains was a guarantee of personal security, a scarecrow to frighten off Yankees and their misdeeds, and a brother to whom one should always extend one's hand.

Confidence and good will were not long in settling over these kind people and the recent arrival whom they bombarded with innumerable questions: about Chile, about the Chileans in San Francisco, about my misadventures, and about my reason for coming to Monterey. I thought they would die laughing when I told the ladies my chief reason for coming to Monterey was to gorge myself on milk.

The master of the house, Don Juan Alvarado,[14] taking me by the hand, led me to his private room; and, making me promise I would stay with him as long as I could, he then begged me strongly and even violently to accept a linen shirt and a coat from him. He did not want to be constantly reminded by my appearance of the intruders he disliked so much. He left me alone then, and I was like a new Don Quixote, changing my clothes in the palace of the duke. After a marvelous bath and a clean shave, I enjoyed

---

14. This is fiction. It is improbable the two ever met. Alvarado's residence does not match the description given.

the indescribable sense of well-being a fine, freshly ironed shirt gives a man, especially if his skin has been chafed for a good long time by wearing wool.

I actually slept that night in a bed with sheets and pillows! And on the following day, what did I find waiting for me beside the arcade that opened out into a fine patio filled with flowers?—two beautiful cows! I had all the milk I could drink, glass after glass, passed to me in my insatiable thirst by the delicate hands of the two sisters-in-law. If, as they say, there is a "seventh heaven," then I was in it! Really to know what rest is, you have to be tired first; in the same way, really to appreciate comfort, you should be a California prospector.

Through Don Juan I arranged with a ranchero to deliver twelve milk cows and eight oxen in San Francisco. I decided a relaxing vacation of eight days was enough self-indulgence for me, and I told the family I would leave the next day. I was met by protests such as only those of the Latin race know how to make to guests, so I stayed for one more day for a party they arranged for me. The day after that I got ready to leave with all my gear in good shape. The entire hospitable family saw me out to the corridor facing the street, and there a fine mule was waiting for me. It had a rich saddle of velvet embroidered with gold; the pommel was an eagle's head of solid silver of the sort so much admired by those who have visited Mexico. It was impossible to resist the insistence of Don Juan that I accept this souvenir—this trinket, as he called it. After protestations and a very affectionate goodbye, I set out with real reluctance from this oasis in my journey through the deserts of selfishness and indifference, and, full of hope and resolution, directed my steps toward new adventures.

On my arrival at San Francisco, I found the town full of new Chilean arrivals. As I have said, there were no well-known Chilean families that did not have a legitimate representative in California. These were somewhat lost when they first landed. An activity that brought invariable success yesterday would yield only failure today. In the midst of these disillusionments and lamentations, my companions and I were trying vainly to swim against a tidal wave of discouragement that carried everything before it.

I sold my mule for six hundred pesos and my elegant saddle for seven hundred. Felipe Ramírez was put in charge of selling milk to the hotels, while my brother, César, did the milking and took charge of street sales. Federico was to go back to Chile to provide company for our excellent mother. The rest of us, including myself, would attend to the restaurant.

Then, everything in San Francisco took on a new aspect.

Up to that time, as has been said, we had engaged in dealings only with men because no women were to be found on the streets.

The mercantile spirit that speculates even with immorality did not lose much time in seeking out substitutes for the fair sex. Paintings of women totally nude and very badly drawn were hung in the best cafes of the city. These nauseating pictures that covered the walls of the saloons would have put the most wanton satyr to flight in any other place; but here, offered along with gambling tables and liquor, they filled the pockets of their lucky owners with gold. With such a precedent to go on, it was only to be expected that the mercantile spirit would not lose much time in producing the real thing, of flesh and blood, as repulsive as are the painted representations.

The passenger ship from Panamá on its first voyage brought two daughters of Eve of the sort called "liberated." Those who went down to watch the steamer come in at the western headland, when they saw the hats and sunshades of women, became so enthusiastic and ran down to the pier so fast that they drew in everyone they passed; so a thousand men were waiting on the beach. No sooner had the anchor been dropped than there broke out a noisy quarrel between the two damsels and the purser. They wanted to come ashore at once; the purser said the arrangement had been that they would pay their passage as soon as they reached this city. The more spirited of the two Yankee girls, acting on the principle that "time is money," said the purser would be held responsible for damages and losses, plus interest, caused by the delay. Whereupon two of the waiting crowd, tired of marking time, clambered on board the ship, and, throwing a bag of gold at the feet of the greedy purser, came back to land with the girls to a general "Hooray!" from the crowd.

The joyful crowd opened a path, and the girls on the arms of their two deliverers, waving greetings and receiving "hurrahs" in turn, quickly disappeared into the crossroads that led to the cribs, followed at a distance by the lascivious and envious eyes of those who had not given the maxim, time is money, its legitimate importance.

It was to be expected that shipowners, noting the high passage rate feminine merchandise could command on arrival at San

Francisco, set out to procure and did procure the embarkation of as much of this kind of merchandise as they could find. On the next voyage seven more arrived, and were received with the same gallantry.

The cafe owners were alarmed by the competition that their badly painted monstrosities had to meet from these real monstrosities who kept on arriving. They planned and carried out the most incredible and obscene projects that human shamelessness can improvise in such situations. They hired these creatures, at a gold peso each, to pose in plastic displays in the cafe dining halls. They set up platforms on both sides of the room, and on them placed, totally nude and assuming indecent poses, these exemplifications of California modesty and decency.

The doors of the exhibition were opened at eight in the evening to the sound of music. The curious men, who had left a good part of their gold dust at the door, were pushed rapidly through to the exits by those coming on behind them, before they had time to look. They came tumbling out the rear door, cursing like fiends. I remember that a Chilean of good family, Don J.E., whose name I will not further clarify, said to me, "My friend, the devil tempted me, and then cleaned me out of all the gold I had in my purse, a half-pound! I was pouring onto the scale enough to pay for my entrance when a shove from behind made me dump it all; and then I was pushed on forward so I couldn't get back to recover the extra gold."

This enterprise could be kept going only for a month, though, because the steamers began coming not with a few but with whole cargoes of women on board, all under agreement to pay for their passage before disembarking, or, at least, the next day afterward.

If the scenes described to this point are repugnant, those I will sketch next, before closing this page of my notes, are no less to be wondered at.

At the door of the room each one of these first Messalinas had on arrival, fights with clubs and pistols broke out every night between those who wanted to get in first to meet them. The women knew very well there was no profit to be had from men who were beaten up or dead, so they would rush out to pacify the combatants, using kinds of arguments that shame prevents me from revealing.

The demand for women had slackened somewhat because the ships were bringing in so many; so, to keep profits up, the captains decided to sell the unpaid passage bills at auction. The highest

San Francisco Waterfront

bidder got to carry off his prize, and the captain pocketed whatever he got over the cost of the passage.

The strangest, coarsest scenes developed as a result of this.

The objects to be auctioned off were assembled in the cabin of the poop deck with all their meretricious ornaments. The man who was to conduct the auction would take one of these shameless creatures by the hand, and, after praising her figure, her youth, and beauty, he would call out in a loud voice, "Gentlemen, what are you willing to pay, any one of you, right now, to have this pretty dame, fresh from New York, pay you a very special visit?" The bidding began at once, and the highest bidder, as soon as the hammer fell, handed over the gold dust and carried away his property.

But it is time now to turn this page. May the enchanting sex, who make up the more agreeable half of the human race, forgive me if I have had to give to these abject females in skirts the same name with which we designate the angels in our homes. Among the chosen angels of God there was also a Lucifer.

This kind of vice was not, however, the only miry basis upon which a new, rich, and sovereign state would rise in time. Robbery, murder, arson, and gambling also bore a good deal of the load.

Every day the sound of music in some gambling hall, or the beat of a drum or Chinese gong in others, called the compulsive gamblers to the tables amid the intoxication that dancing and drinking produce. And every night someone was wounded, clubbed, or beaten up; and from each gambling hall the losers would sally forth and try to recoup their losses by robbery and assault.

I had occasion to observe a gambling scene in which a crafty Oregonian played a role. He approached the table and without saying a word placed a little sack containing about a pound of gold on one card of the deck. He lost. With the same silence and gravity, he set down another of the same size, and lost again. Then, without losing his calm manner he took from his belt a snake that must have contained about six pounds of gold. He stacked it on a card, took out his gun, cocked it, and pointed it at the dealer as he waited silently for the result. He won! "With that I won," he remarked sarcastically, gathering up his winnings without a change of expression, "That's certainly lucky." And with that he disappeared. He won because the sensible dealer knew very well *that* card might cost him his life.

In all fairness, however, it must be said that not everything in San Francisco was chaotic. Some thought was also given to the future political status of the area in the midst of all the hurly-burly. The strong spirit of liberty incarnate in every one of the adventurers who intended to make his home permanently in California had long before led to the rejection of military government. These people wanted the new territory elevated immediately to the rank of a sovereign state. Overt steps were already being taken in Washington to bring this about. To add weight to this just aspiration, which was being expressed more and more strongly, it was proposed to elect the members of the legislature to meet in San José; where, instead of Monterey as in the past, the capital was to be located and the governor was to reside.

Meetings were held everywhere in connection with this, and men who wanted to be elected soon had their campaigns under way. Big parades with musical bands and banners marched down the streets, each one accompanying the candidate of its choice. The aspirant, carrying a portfolio on whose first page he had written out a statement of his political beliefs, went from door to door collecting signatures. The prospective voter, if he liked the candidate, wrote down his name; if he did not, he simply said he had already promised his support elsewhere. In the first case the crowd gave three hurrahs accompanied by music and the firing of some shots in the air. In the second case the candidate merely said, "I'm sorry; perhaps another day." The group then went on to the next house.

Each candidate would choose a certain color of ribbon for his supporters to wear in their hats on election day, and the saloons and hotels that carried that same color would give free food and drinks to anyone who came in wearing it.

When the voting tables were set up they were watched and guarded by as many differently beribboned groups as there were candidates. These candidates, well mounted and accompanied by some friends, would go at a trot through all the streets of the city to call out their supporters; and they would visit the polling places, where they were greeted by their followers with hurrahs. There you could hear the speeches of the various candidates, delivered from horseback, as well as the arguments and retorts of those who supported other candidates. Barrels and tables were set up and men would climb up on them so they could hear better. One could watch circles form around men who were arguing their preferences with their bare fists; and one could see these circles dissolve. But there was no pistol shooting, and no wounds. Arms on that day were silent. How different it all was from the way these things are handled in other countries. Not only that, but once the election was over all the voters accepted the man elected and his color. They dropped the private preferences to hail the majority's choice, and showed as much enthusiasm in shouting as if they had contributed to his triumph themselves.

California had by this time lost almost all its attractiveness for venturesome foreigners, concerning the opportunities that had drawn so many people of such different types to her shores. This followed the wavering policy of support or lack of support by Gov-

ernor Smith. What was needed there now was not foreigners striv-
ing to achieve success by their own labor and for their own profit,
but rather men who would work for salaries and wages. It is not
surprising, then, that those who had considerable capital at their
disposal either lost it or resigned themselves to leaving the country
in disillusionment. We were thinking of doing the same thing, when
fate, which had treated us so badly, gave us the *coup de grace*.
What drove us out of this ex–land of promise with so harsh a dismiss-
al was one of those terrible fires, wiping out everything, that broke
out in the last months of 1850.

We had been in bed about two hours, after having made up
our minds to go back to Chile, when a flickering red light coming
through the windowpanes threw a glow into the room where we
were sleeping. The fire had been set deliberately, as so many were,
in the hotel already mentioned as having the infamous display of
living nudes. We never would have imagined that a fire more than
three blocks away from our building could have brought us any
damage. We were rejoicing over the evil end being put to all that
ugliness, and calculating the increase in price of our building as
a result of the shortage that was to follow, when, about an hour
and a half later, fate demonstrated to us that shining thoughts of
profit may continue to be shining but cease to be profitable. The
fire spread in all directions with the same reckless speed that we
have seen it spread through our wheat fields in Chile at harvest
time. In the midst of that immense and roaring bonfire enlivened
by exploding gunpowder casks in the stores, with the air filled with
sparks and burning bits of wood, and the blazing walls fanned by
the wind, the whole region was involved. We were hemmed in
by flames on every side, and we, like everyone else, owed our escape
solely to the swiftness of our flight.

❖   ❖   ❖

Two and a half months later, in the garb of seamen, we were
in peaceful Chile tenderly embracing our mother, poor as ever,
but satisfied that we had not abandoned the fort before the last
shot was fired.

AFTERTHOUGHTS

Before closing this brief glimpse of California, I believe that I should try to give you some idea of its government and of the critical and abnormal conditions that Chileans were facing in that country at the time of my departure.

There is certainly much to admire and much to criticize in the behavior of the new owners of California. However, much as we may feel tempted to present them at one extreme as models worthy of imitation, or at the other as deserving condemnation by all civilized peoples, we will limit ourselves simply to the facts and leave it to our readers to draw their own conclusions.

There were no more than five hundred North Americans in California in the summer of 1845. The country was under military law. This was administered by Colonel Mason, the acting Provisional Governor. California was a sorry spectacle: it was being regenerated in spite of itself, setting the inert force of its old customs against the innovative spirit that had invaded it. The people of California, considerably increased by immigration, presented a heterogeneous mass of usages and customs, of languages and religions; they would require, it seemed, a good many years of living together, and much wisdom, to reach the stage one finds there today. The men in authority there were unfamiliar with Spanish law. The Californios were equally ignorant of North American law. They did not know what rules they were to observe, nor how to defend their rights and make their just claims prevail. Interpreters were paid a gold dollar, and almost always tipped the scales on the side of the new masters. These rulers wanted to rectify things and put an end to the difficulties arbitrary rule brought, but the only solution they could think of was to call the magistrate in the towns by the title of alcalde. The North American laws remained in force, though, even if masked and obscured with certain Spanish procedures. This system satisfied neither the Californios nor the North Americans. The latter were disoriented, and all transactions were conducted in an atmosphere of uncertainty and suspicion.

The arbitrary nature of the taxes, and the military duties on trade that were put into force in October of 1847, tended to absorb all profits and fatten the military treasury uselessly, while drawing all the coinage out of circulation. This imposed the greatest difficulties on trade. Because gold dust was not acceptable for payment of taxes, it lost value and brought only about six dollars an ounce.

Such a state of affairs could not last. Everywhere it was felt that the highest need of the area was for a provisional government. The heavy labor in the gold fields of 1848 had scarcely ended when the people who were concentrated in the towns, who possessed a good deal of gold but were without any form of civil government that would protect their property, decided to act. Without halting their material constructions, which were astonishing in their enormous extent, the people began to hold repeated meetings for the election of deputies to a constitutional convention. The difficulties in carrying out so important an object as this were enough to frighten a people less used to governing themselves.

Nevertheless, on September 1, 1849, to the amazement of all, the memorable assembly opened in Monterey, and in only one and a half months it bequeathed to the country a government, a constitution, and a national representation. Its achievement was received with general approval. The city of San José was named the state capital. Peter H. Burnett was named governor, and the legislature met on December 15 of that very year.

On December 20, General Riley, the provisional governor named by the government in Washington, showed that he respected the will of the people who had been entrusted to his care. He issued a proclamation to his fellow citizens that he was turning over all the civil authority that had been conferred upon him to the new state government that they had organized.

From that time on, the administration, regularized and complete in all its parts, began to exercise its powers in conformity with what was laid down in the constitution. It also asked that the government in Washington admit this most beautiful of its territories as an independent state of the Union.

The state is divided into counties. In each one there is a judge of first instance; he has the same functions as the provincial intendant in Chile. There is a county sheriff who carries out the duties of a police officer, and also acts as executioner. Each county has its treasurer, a district attorney, a county clerk who keeps a register of mortgages, a county tax collector, a surveyor, a road commissioner, and assessors.

The people elect all their officials from first to last, as well as all deputies to the state legislature. The supreme court hears appeals at the capital, and also goes on circuit through the counties. It sets up in them all the machinery needed for dealing with cases that arise there. There is no army; the only men you see in uniform day by day in California are the firemen and policemen.

Such is the organization of this government, improvised amid the most pressing and inadequate circumstances, at a time when the gold fever might well have forced postponement.

The following is an official letter sent by Governor Burnett to the Consul of Chile in response to a request for information from the governor that would give an insight into the organic structure of the new California government:

San Jose, Mar., 1850

Señor D. Pedro Cueto, Consul of Chile

Dear Sir:

I have the honor to reply to your letter received on the 15th of the present month in which you informed me of the death of Don Roberto Sosa.

Under our system of government the judges are independent of the governors, and neither one can issue orders to the other. This is also true of the President of the United States. If a judge errs, the only remedy one has is an appeal to a higher court. When there is a difference between the courts and the executive power of a state or of the United States, the parties always have recourse to the Supreme Court of the United States which decides the question.

In the affair you have called to my attention, I, as the Governor of California, can do nothing. Our system of government is so different from that of other countries that even the most intelligent foreigners can seldom form a clear idea of it. Yet, both in theory and in practice, our system is the best in the world. The government of the United States and of the several states are all set up on the basis that the powers of government should be kept separate.

The Federal Government has the power to handle our affairs with other nations, to make war and peace, negotiate agreements and treaties. All other powers belong to the governments of the separate states, however. The states are independent of one another, of the central government, and of the whole world. If a dispute arises between the authorities of two states, the case has to be submitted to the Supreme Court of the United States.

If Judge Thomas has denied to you the possession of the property and testament of the deceased, the recourse you have is to the courts. You should get an attorney who can present your case to the Supreme Court of California, requesting that it order the judge to do his duty. If this court does not give you full justice, you should appeal your case to the Supreme Court of the United States. But I believe it impossible that you will not get justice.

I know Judge Thomas well, and I assure you he is one of the finest men I have had dealings with. I feel certain that he is incapable of intentionally doing wrong to anyone.

With all respect, I am,

PETER H. BURNETT

While the tireless North American was laboring to acquire riches, and building a government for his adopted state that would create security through the strength of its institutions, what were the foreigners doing in California?

Escena de California
Dibujo de Vicente Pérez Rosales

Melting Pot Types

They had arrived from all parts of the world, flocking to the great fair nature had opened up for the human race. They had come to a land where, it was said, the generous immigration laws had removed the word stranger from the vocabulary. None of them was destitute, as were thousands of North Americans, and all of them believed they could make their fortunes because wealth was so easy to acquire.

To raw and empty California their imports and industry ought to have been as beneficial and as welcome as gifts from heaven. But, needless to say, they were not viewed in that light. Foreigners had to conclude that either North Americans had changed their nature in California or it was a lie to say immigrants got a fraternal welcome on the Atlantic coast.

I will deal only with Chileans because they made a very major contribution, because they came to California in great numbers, and because the kinds of mistreatment they suffered caught the attention of the whole world. What caused the conquerors of California to pick the Chileans as the target of their hatred and brutal violence is to me, even today, an incomprehensible mystery. The beginning of San Francisco's economic development was entirely attributable to the sons of Chile. It was Chileans from Concepción and Valparaíso who built the first houses there. Prior to the great fire that destroyed a large part of the city, you could count all the buildings that were not made of Chilean lumber. Because there was not enough wood, Chileans were hired to manufacture adobes, as they were the only persons skilled at this and willing to work at reasonable wages. There is scarcely a well in the city Chileans did not dig. Chile also supplied the necessities of ready-made clothing, shoes, and bread, along with a host of other goods to that land, which was inhospitable to them alone.

Many Chileans took jobs on the promise of wages, but got only blows and insults. If they had the effrontery to complain to those in authority, they found there such weighted injustice and such extortion on the part of the interpreters that it would have been better for them to have swallowed their indignation. From the early months of 1849 on, the Chilean was looked upon as a pariah; he was viewed by most Yankees very much the way a Jew was by a Knight Templar in the Middle Ages. This inexplicable prejudice was not restricted to the cities. Outrages of a lighter or a more serious nature were also perpetrated against them in the gold fields.

Wherever the Chileans were outnumbered by their enemies they were dispossessed and driven out with the most fearful threats.

The decree of General Persifer Smith, governor of the area, issued during his passage through Panamá and denying all foreigners a right to mine gold in California, broke down the last barrier separating threats from action. Chilean blood was the first fruit of this ill-considered decree. Smith was uninformed: he did not know the region he was to govern or the character of its invading population, so he could not have foreseen the effects of his sudden declaration. He was surprised himself, when he reached California, at the imprudence he had been guilty of, and he tried to retrace his steps; but it was too late. His efforts were disregarded. It was impossible to calm the high feelings that brutal outrages and the resistance of those being attacked had already stirred up. Bandit hordes, relying on their numbers, encouraged by impunity, threw themselves with rifles and pistols on the peaceful and defenseless Chileans, robbing and treating them with cruelty. Where Chileans were numerous or brave enough to fight back there were bloody battles. It was these that set the seal of implacable hatred from that time on between men of Spanish and men of English speech.

Scattered and persecuted Chileans trickled down into Sacramento and Stockton every day. They had no one they could call upon for help, no money to continue their journey, and nothing to sell but their labor—for which they were paid little or nothing. Exposed in their need to the disease-ridden climate of summer, many caught yellow fever. Chile lost many of her sons there.

All outcry was useless. The interpreters, the collectors of customs, the freight handlers, and the merchants all wanted immigration to continue so it would keep on providing them with victims they could exploit. So they played down the malignity of the situation and called attention instead to the continuing richness and great number of strikes being made in the mining areas.

The defense the unfortunate Chileans put up to save their own hides intensified the rancor of their tormentors to such a pitch that they decided to wipe out the rest of the outlawed race once and for all. The city of San Francisco was a witness to that incredible undertaking on the part of the Hounds. They attacked with banner and drums and were guilty of horrible excesses. What is most strange, some of them spoke Spanish they had picked up in Chile, where they had been treated with a cordial and fraternal hospitality.

May I say in passing for the benefit of those who applaud the efforts of the Union authorities in San Francisco, that the least of the crimes that gang committed included robbery, arson, and murder. Any one of these by itself was a capital crime. Despite that, the heaviest penalty given to them was a mock trial and an order to leave the city; and most of the perpetrators of those outrages walked the streets of San Francisco unpunished and without fear.

After that event, the only things Chileans had to fear in San Francisco were the exactions of the police, the dishonesty of the interpreters and customs collectors, and the constant bias of the judges. In the mines, however, there continued to be an endless succession of violent dispossessions and murders. Men were whipped, cruelly mutilated, and hung.

NOTE: At Sutter's mill I saw them hang an Indian by the neck on a rope, and afterward let him fall so they could force him to make a statement. The same thing was done to a poor Chilean in San Francisco, and to Senõr D. José María Alvarez. After he had been shamefully robbed, the same bandits placed him in a gallows they had agreed to set up in a meeting in order to terrify him. The penalty of flogging is found in other parts of the world, but the arbitrary infliction of it as a punishment and, above all, the atrocity of cutting off a man's ears—criminals daring to mark another man as a criminal—that is something which can be found only in California.

The authorities were not able to stop these crimes perpetrated against the peaceful sons of a friendly nation, but they could at least have disavowed them in the newspapers, which provide a sure means there to reach the ears of the public. But Chile was not favored by even this disavowal by either the authorities of the United States or those of the state, though it would have been politically wise, courteous, and would have cost little.

The press itself, a major force in North America, and one surely not controlled by mobsters, disregarded both the interests of trade and the duties of humanity on a false point of honor, and fed the flames of discord by setting off their atrocities with the alarming headline: "North American Blood Shed By Chileans!" As if the conduct of a mere handful of valiant men, exasperated by atrocities, in fighting off a group of bandits, reflected the least dishonor upon their compatriots! As if it were not natural for a single man to defend himself and win a fight with two cowards in full daylight!

But why demand from the North Americans in California that protection which the Law of Nations secures to the citizens of a friendly nation within the territory of another, when our own government, aware of the great number of Chileans and their property then in California, knowing the ire and hatred the North Americans showed for them and the disorder that existed in a land without laws and a regular administration, seemed to care little about its own citizens?

Every other nation had a representative there. Peru, in spite of the paucity of its people and the small amount of Peruvian property in California, not only sent a consul but even dispatched a warship with a complete array of sailors and provisions. It had the laudable aim of restoring its maltreated nationals to the bosoms of their families. Peru also provided naval personnel to man Peruvian ships abandoned in the bay of San Francisco. France and England did the same things; only Chilean ships, it seemed, were destined to lie there and rot away.

Señor D. Pedro Cueto was named Chilean Consul in California only after the troubles were over, when there was no longer any remedy for the disease. Dismay, brought on by the outrages, had already dispersed most of the Chileans, who had gone home beggars after having lost everything. Our government must have had very poor information about California, for it gave the consul no funds. If there was any land where our national representatives needed generous funds, it was there!

Time is money in California, and you cannot take a single step that will not cost a good deal. This was especially true for our consulate because it was set up so late. The activities with which it had to deal were so pressing, and absorbed the attention of the consul to such an extent that it was impossible for him to carry out the ordinary duties of his office. In such a situation a consul has to either neglect his duties or face the prospect of personal ruin. The Chileans in California owe Señor Cueto their heartfelt thanks. His undertaking this assignment all alone was a service that ought to be remembered. More than that, he was not content to devote all his time to San Francisco. He undertook expensive journeys as well, to present his representations on the treatment of Chileans to local authorities.

When he was recalled, without any consideration being shown him for his efforts, and returned to his country, on his own initiative he gave free passage home to a number of unfortunate Chileans who otherwise might have died of hunger and sickness. The gentleman whose blameless and beneficent conduct were worthy of the highest praise did not deserve to be appointed and dismissed from service in such a summary fashion, nor did he merit routine thanks that governments generally give in such a situation to their ruined agents.

The consulate in California, on the footing it has today, can do nothing to better the condition of the Chileans who live in that land, nor is it reasonable to demand that it apply itself to these extra duties when it has been given barely enough resources to cope with its primary responsibilities.

METODO CHILENO

RAMON JIL NAVARRO
[n. d.]

———◆———

*Jil Navarro de Segura was born in Argentina of Catalan ancestry.
Before coming to Chile he had lived for some time in the Argentinian
Province of Catamarca where his brother was governor. He married
his cousin, Malvina Ocampo, the daughter of General Francisco
Ortiz de Ocampo, and this marriage established the present Navarro
Ocampo family of Chile.*

*He left Catamarca, crossing the Andes to settle in the Chilean
city of Concepción; and it was there in 1849 that he answered the
call to adventure in the California Gold Rush. His command of
the English language, an unusual accomplishment then, equipped
him to act as court interpreter in California courts when persons
of Spanish speech were involved in legal difficulties. It may well
be that his facility in English helped him to escape the mistreatment
to which so many of his fellow immigrants from Hispanic America
were subjected.*

*On his return to Chile in the early 1850s he again took up his
residence in Concepción, and undertook a career in journalism. One
of his works,* A Treatise on Humanity, *published in 1856, merited
a translation into French.*

*His account of the rabid anti-Chilean violence in California, in-
cluding an extraordinarily vivid description of the affair at Chili
Gulch, will be found in the pages that follow. This work first appeared in a series of articles, published in* El Correo del Sur *between
January 1, 1853 and January 27, 1854.*

[101]

CALIFORNIA IN 1849

Everyone has heard about the hatred and savage mistreatment visited on foreigners in California during the years 1849 and 1850. This irrational hostility on the part of the Americans was especially directed against the Chileans. It is curious that among the thousands of aliens there, the Chileans seem to have been singled out for a very special animosity on the part of the Yankees. In the course of events I am about to relate I will attempt to make clear the reasons for this odd and unrelenting bias.

To begin with, it is revealing to notice that this peculiar dislike was tinged not only with respect but with admiration. Yankees felt a very strong antagonism toward all outsiders whether they were Frenchmen, Englishmen, Spaniards, Italians, Argentinians, Peruvians, or Mexicans. They had enough hate to go around. Their malice tended to be concentrated on the Chilean from the start because he alone resisted and showed a disposition to stand up for his rights. He was confident of his own ability, unimpressed by the blustering pose of the Americans and their assertion that they alone had legal rights and authority in California. He refused to feel handicapped by his inability to understand the language of the country to which he had come or its strange laws and customs. If he was frightened he did not show it. He held his ground.

Other nationalities tended to feel isolated and insecure in the unfriendly and dangerous environment and gave in to their own fears. It was notorious in California—and anyone who stayed there longer than a day will testify to this—that the Mexicans, and especially those from Sonora, acquired a reputation for pusillanimity. Many who were in the California mines in 1849 and 1850 were witnesses to scenes in which Mexicans allowed themselves to be treated like cowards by the Americans. The immigration from Sonora preceded all the others, and it presented the Americans with their first problem. The Sonorans were skilled in both placer and quartz mining, and they occupied the richest "diggins." The Yankees began to burn with anger and greed on noticing that in those placers the gold seemed to flow out in a stream as if it had been purposely stored there; and in no time they were starting to put pressure on the Sonorans to force them out. The Sonorans are not cowards; they are only a simple peaceful folk who do not like quarrels.

Because they did not speak English they had no way even to put up an argument. That is why they yielded to the abusive arrogance of the Americans. A Yankee would invade the claim of a Sonoran with his revolver in hand. He would watch the Mexican panning gold for a while until he was sure it was a good claim. Then he would go up to the poor Mexican, put the pistol to his head and order him off in language that was half-English, half-Spanish: *"You largo de aquí, mi quiere you Sonoreim. Vamos de rancho."* The Sonoran did not even take time or trouble to ask in sign language why he was being attacked and his claim taken away. Instead he would shoulder his tools and leave the place, fully confident that he could find an even richer location. Naturally, he was considered a coward. That is why the Americans came to think of themselves as braver than others—though, in fact, Americans are no braver than anyone else.

But it did not work that way with the Chileans. Few if any of them had the skill of the Sonorans in locating rich claims, or the luck in making them pay as well. If they did have the good fortune to locate a promising spot they thought of it as their only chance to win the wealth they sought. Whether this desperation was the reason why a Chilean displayed bravery, or whether bravery was simply inborn in him, the fact was that he would not submit to abuse from the Yankees. There is not a single example of a Chilean letting himself be forced off his claim without a struggle. A challenge to his rights meant death either for his attacker or himself, and even after he had been shot or stabbed he would still hold his ground. That is the real reason, the only true one, why the Chileans were hated so: they were feared. The very name evoked feelings of alarm.

An American put it in these terms: "The Sonorans are good and humble people, but the Chileans are the worst on earth, all rascals!"

Could it be stated any more plainly? To the Yankees, Chileans were not good because they were not humble; they were too proud

to let themselves be pushed around. They were rascals because
they answered threat for threat, blow for blow, and injury for injury.
This response of force to force fixed that character so strongly on the
Chilean, that, even when it was Frenchmen, Spaniards, or Mexicans who were the causes of a commotion, it was the Chileans
who were blamed for it.

I was an eyewitness and at times a participant in almost all
of the events I am going to relate. I have religiously kept my notes
taken at the scene of these happenings while the guns were still
smoking and the bodies still strewn on the ground, lifeless testimo-
nials to the injustice of the Yankees.

For an example of how far this injustice might be carried one
could do no better than to examine the affair at the Calaveras
River in which a number of young men from Concepción were
involved. The jury system was misused to give a false color of
legality to the affair. The Yankees were unable to defeat the Chileans in a fair fight, and displayed cowardice by resorting to dishon-
orable falsehoods and betrayal to capture them. The sentences they
passed were horrifying: some were shot to death by firing squads
as target practice; some were hung; a number had to bear the
endless shame of having their ears cut off; and another group were
flogged like thieves and had their heads shaved. Because these acts
of injustice and cruelty were never punished, and never will be,
Chileans at least should know about them so that each one may,
if he wishes, try to vindicate those martyred fellow countrymen.

The death of one brave and generous young man, José del Car-
men Terán, is the story of a hero and martyr; it is a story of such
tragic self-sacrifice that it might well be the subject of a novel.

I was the official translator at the court when the judge and
deputy issued orders to arrest those accused of the crime, and I
served as interpreter between the Chileans and the Yankees. I took
notes at the times these solemn events were in process. I did not
intend these notes to be published, but I will give them just as
they were written. They are simple, with no pretence to literary
style. They will possess interest, however, for those who seek truth,
for those who admire bravery, for those who want to know the
full story of Yankee viciousness, and the sufferings of our countrymen. They will also provide, if in a highly summarized form,
something of the story of Chilean immigration into California during the years 1849 and 1850.

First attacks on the Chileans. Appearance of the Society of Forty under the name of the Hounds. The violence at Alegría's inn and at the house of the Italian fathers. Death of one of the Hound leaders. Declaration of war against Chileans.

Chileans could relate a long history of Yankee oppression and malice. Many of them could not understand it. Where, they asked, were the liberty, the just laws, the good will for which this country was so renowned and for which it was held up as a model all over the world in terms of the liberty and protection it extended to foreigners. In the eastern part of the United States one acquired the rights of citizens to such protection just by stepping ashore. In California, though, where even greater guarantees should have been given to immigrants because the country was virtually a desert and needed population, this was not true. In California, two years of residence were required before you could become a citizen and have the legal right to own a handful of soil. Heavy fees were demanded, and a thousand other obstacles were raised. Not only was immigration made so difficult it was virtually forbidden, however, it was also made clear that foreigners already in California were to be subjected to discrimination. There were even shouted demands in meetings that all those who were not born in the United States should be expelled.

It was during these early difficulties that Chileans had to face the problem of "squatters." Squatters operated under a law that allows a man to seize land that is not occupied or fenced. The squatter acquires legal title to the land if he plants trees or does something else to improve it.[1] No doubt, if properly used, this is a wise law, but to a foreigner who did not understand it, the squatter merely seemed a kind of thief. Many Chileans, both those engaged in business and those who took groups of workers with them to the mines, were victims of squatters. It is likely they suffered more than other aliens did, because of the special dislike felt toward them. What happened was that Chileans would buy a lot with

---

1. This is an error. Squatters was the term applied to those who settled on *public* land after it had been surveyed but before it was offered at the periodic auctions at the land office. The squatter's right entitled him to buy the land he had settled on at the base price, for no one was allowed to bid against him. This did not apply in cities.

the intention of holding it for an increase in value, and go away with the belief their title was secure. Upon their return, they would find the land staked by the land commissioner, and a building on it. The building might be a house, a hotel, or a business establishment, and, to all appearances, it might seem as if it had been standing there for years. When the incredulous Chilean wanted his property back, the new owner would just laugh at him. What was the defrauded man to do? Should he take it to the courts? You would have to possess the wealth of a sultan in those years to do that—and even then you could be sure in advance that you would lose your case.

It is interesting that squatters did not do this to you if you had the property bought for you by a Yankee.

This was not the only way Chileans lost property in land. In some cases the land was sold for taxes to the city, the county, or the state. Again, what could the foreigner do? Ignorance of the law was no excuse. Ignorance was no protection, and no exceptions were made.

The first violence in California was directed against Chileans, and the first crime committed had them as its victims. This was the attack on both persons and property carried out on June 26, 1849. Twelve men invaded an inn run by Mr. Alegría, in the same fashion as bandits attacking a stage coach on the camino real. Bullets were flying everywhere; many were wounded and some were robbed. Despite his age, Mr. Alegría was able to escape with his family and servants. To the cry of "Down with the Chileans!" the invaders then proceeded to sack the inn and the nearby tents, and set them all on fire, still shouting "Death to the Chileans!" Some Chileans got away to the hills; others sought safety on ships in the bay.

From that time on, Chileans felt a genuine and well-founded distrust. Each one of them, it would seem, took a private oath that he would never again let himself be demeaned; he would resist injustices directed at him because of his nationality.

On that same night, June 26, these twelve men marched down the streets of San Francisco blowing trumpets and shouting "Death to all the foreigners!" They came to a house where some Italian priests lived, and tried to reenact the terrorism and robbery they had perpetrated at the inn of Mr. Alegría shortly before. But the good priests did not have the patience of Job. One of them could handle a stiletto as well as the best fisherman of Italy. Three or

four shots were fired at close range, and the leader of the bandits
had his head blown open and fell to the floor with brains splattered
out. The bandits were actually winning, but at that they turned
and fled. By the time the smoke cleared the priests and Chileans
had also vanished without a trace.

It was through these crimes that the people of San Francisco
for the first time learned of the existence of the group of forty
men called the Hounds. It was said then, and in fact there are
some who still say, that most of these Hounds were Irishmen, or
deserters from the British navy, or convicts who had escaped from
prison ships. However, when lynch law [courts] were established
[by the vigilantes] they were all found to be Americans.[2]

The movement spread all over the state, and the events of the
26th were repeated in the other cities. In Stockton as in San Francisco, the same cry, "Down with the Chileans," was raised by some
fifteen men who marched down the street with drum and bugle.
They raided the more prosperous looking places, just as they had
in San Francisco. Lucien's, one of these, was probably the best
restaurant in town. They attacked the residence of a Chilean who
was in the business of hauling supplies to the mines. They shot
and killed the man who took care of the mules, slit open the sacks
of flour, broke the crates and scattered the merchandise over the
ground, and then smashed the wagons. They acted, in short, the
way a bunch of savages would if they were turned loose in a community. I was a witness to these events, along with ten other men
who lived there. We all ran to answer the pleas for help from
the wounded man, but could not save him. He told us what had
happened—things we had already seen—and died three or four
hours later.

The same story came from Sacramento. On the night of the 26th
an attempt was made to set the town on fire; and, as we shall
see, these scenes occurred almost daily from then on. Some of the
criminals were arrested and tried—only to be set free—and the
same thing happened to the two men apprehended in Stockton.
It should be added, though, that, when Chileans united for their
own protection, peace-loving people did stand up for justice. They
did not condemn the Chileans. They approved the instinct for self-
preservation, and applauded the strength that it produced.

---

2. They were members of the disbanded New York Volunteers.

Expulsion of the Chileans from Sacramento. Murders in Moke-
lumne and Jesús María. The sad case of the Chilean, Contreras.
The first misunderstanding between Chileans and Yankees at
Calaveras.

Many of my readers may think that when I say justice was on
the side of the Chileans, I am simply being guilty of partiality.
Let me give a few facts here that should change their opinion.
I was not born in Chile, and I am a Chilean only in the sense
that I lived there for several years. I do not regard the friendships
I have as any reason to change the story of what actually happened.
In the second place, I do not have any enmity toward Californians;
some of them were very dear friends. I am a Yankee myself in
the sense that I cherish freedom and am in favor of new economic
development and improvement; far from feeling any rancor against
Americans, I feel nothing but respect and admiration for them.
Thirdly, the California of 1849 and 1850 is not at all like the California of 1852. Those earlier years were abnormal in almost every
aspect, and what happened then has little or no significance in
terms of the excellent relations that exist today between Chileans
and Americans. I say this to assure you that the unhappy scenes
of those days are not being revived for the sake of stirring up
animosity. They are past; and the present gives no basis for partiality. Fourthly, California in those years was without government,
without fixed laws, without society and without established tradi-
tions. It had no predominant religion. It possessed none then of
those things that have made it one of the greatest states in the
world today in terms of its laws, civilization, and commerce. The
tragic conditions were very difficult, but they lasted only a short
time; and so did these scenes of savagery and injustice. Today we
can look back on this story as we would any other story of the
past, with an interest only in the truth, and with no desire to stir
up old enmities.

The violence against Chileans rose to such a crisis in June and
July both in the mines and in the towns that it brought on a reaction
meant to put an end to the disorder. In the middle of August all
Chileans living in Sacramento and the nearby mines were ordered
to leave the area. The order was issued by a meeting of the American
miners. The same decree was then acted on in Stockton and San
Francisco, although over protest by the good citizens.

Once they had been ordered out, however, those who remained could be considered outlaws by Americans, so the decree actually provided a justification for even greater violence and cruelty. A man who killed a Chilean was not really considered a criminal; if arrested there was a mere travesty of justice: a jury of his friends was formed, and he was promptly declared not guilty. I saw this done in the case of a man named James Wilson who had murdered Benegas, a Chilean, along with a Mexican from Sonora.

It was in that period, too, that the following news item appeared in the *Stockton Journal:*

> A Chilean was dancing the cueca in a hotel at the request of his friends and a group of Americans. His partner was a Chilean woman, the owner of the hotel. An American entered and walked up to the dancer. "Are you a Chilean?" he demanded. "yes." "Well, take this then," and the brains of the Chilean flew all over the woman and the guitar player. The American remained in Mokelumne without anyone ever bothering him.

On September 24, that same year, just a few days after the above incident, I was traveling through the diggins. A placer had been found near Mokelumne at that time, and it was called the Jesús María. I was on my way there about noon when I met a Frenchman and a Mexican. They told me not to go any farther because there was a party of Americans there who were killing all the Chileans. I thought this was false or exaggerated, so I continued on my way. About two miles farther on I came upon the bodies of two men. Blood was still flowing from these bodies, so they could not have been dead very long. One had his head shattered, not by a shot but by a blow. The other had been shot. They proved to be a Chilean and a Peruvian.

There were different kinds of abuses. I recall the one that was inflicted on a Chilean named Contreras. He was a poor man, robbed of six mules he used to transport supplies from Stockton to the mines. Contreras found the thief and asked me to act as his translator at the court of Judge M. Were. The guilt of the thief was clearly established, so it was easy to arrive at a decision; the decision was that the mules should be returned and the thief should pay damages to Contreras as well as the court costs. The Yankee, however, did not have a penny, so then the judge told Contreras he would have to pay the court costs. "But sir," I argued, "Contreras won the case; the loser should pay the costs." "Yes," said the judge, "but he has no money, and somebody has to pay." The poor Contreras then had to sell one of his mules to raise the money. My client had a kind of Don Quixote for a judge, and perhaps he should be thankful he did not end up in jail. Incidentally, the thief was not arrested.

On December 10 began the chain of events that culminated in the tragic affair at Calaveras. A group of Chileans had found a gulch full of gold on the banks of the river; naturally it was called Chile Gulch. They were joined by others who brought supplies for a year, bought at very high prices and at great sacrifice. Each group built a house to winter in. It was hard work, but they had to do it because the weather was turning cold. It was at that point that they were told to leave the area within ten days.

I will describe the law, the judge who signed the order, and the response of the Chileans.

Reactions of the Chileans to the order to leave their camp and not to stay within 20 leagues of it. The authority that expelled them, and the reasons behind the expulsion rule. Preparations of the Chileans for defending themselves, and the trick the Americans used to make them prisoners. Stealing of the Chileans' goods and destruction of their houses. Mistreatment Chileans endured as prisoners.

You would have to have been in California, buried in the recesses of the Sierra, to know what sacrifices had to be borne to get into those mountains, how severe the winters were, or how much it cost to get freight and supplies over those trails, or rather footpaths. You would have to know all that, I repeat, before you could form any idea of the cruelty, injustice, and brutality of the order of expulsion given to the Chileans. It was passed to them on December 10, two months after winter had set in. The old Californios said they had not seen so severe a winter as that of 1849 in the past fifty years. The trails, which were no more than tracks made by the miners who first entered the placers, were impassable even for saddle animals. It was better for a man to travel on foot, because horses and riders were sometimes both lost in the bogs. Freight to the mines from Stockton cost eighty to one hundred dollars per hundredweight. Flour cost sixty to seventy dollars per hundredweight, and frejoles, hardtack, jerky, and other foodstuffs were in proportion. The Chileans had provided themselves with all these things because they planned to winter over in the Sierra.

Imagine the toil and difficulty they had overcome. The Chilean companies relied on the freedom extended to foreigners by the government when they settled in Chile Gulch. They built houses there with their own hands, although they were young men not accustomed to such labor and took a great deal more time then they should. Remember, too, how much they had spent in Stockton to buy tools, food, and equipment, and the heavy prices they had to pay to get all of this up to the mines in quantity sufficient to last them a year. Consider, too, the impossibility of transporting all of this to another site, once winter had set in. That winter, 1849, they had not seen the sky clear of clouds for fifteen to twenty days; and there had not been an hour when it had not rained in bucketfulls, making the trails unusable and turning the rivers and even the smallest creeks into torrents. Think for a moment of this mountain of difficulties, and how they affected each individual

The Mokelumne River
A Rare Old Cut of a "River Mining" Scene in 1849

Much sickness and many deaths resulted from thus working in the cold rivers
with upper portions of the body exposed to the intense heat of the summer sun.

in each group, and then you can judge the impression it made
on the Chileans when they were told to abandon their houses, their
food, their equipment, their tools and, in a word, all they possessed
and all they had to live on and hope for—they had to leave behind
even their shoes because it was all a man could do to get himself
alone through those trails. Where were they to go if they were
forbidden to be within fifty miles in any direction? What were
they to do if they had no food and no tools to work with? Were
they to beg? From whom, in wintertime, when even the man who
had a bag of gold was not sure that he could buy a crust of bread
with it? The weight of those considerations is enough to make
anyone understand the kind of reply the Chileans had to make
to the threat that they must abandon their camp.

The Chileans' reply was that "they did not recognize the authority of those who ordered them to leave; that the recognized judge
of the county of Calaveras, in which Chile Gulch was located, had
not given them any such order; that no such order had been issued
anywhere in the area around Stockton; that such an order ought
to come from the state governor, or from his deputy, or at least
from an official judge from the county of Calaveras; that to expel

them in the middle of winter was the same thing as to kill them, and if they had to die they would rather die gun in hand and defending themselves; the gold discovery they had made belonged to them, first by the laws of the state than in force, which permitted all aliens to exploit any mines and placers they found, and second by the right of possession, which was even more sacred in California; that, because of all this, their reply was that they would not leave until they were all dead.

This was more or less the unanimous reply given by the Chileans then at Chile Gulch; there were more than one hundred of them. The companies that were there were those of Señor Orangui, and those of the Señores Terán, Ruis, Herrera, Montiel, Peres, Oyarson, Gutiérrez, Sisternas, M. Maturano and J. Concha. They did not even need to take a vote to come to a decision. They were like a community with the same views, the same hopes, the same thoughts and ideas; they were, in a word, like brothers sprung from the same soil and united in common defense for mutual protection, and with the same resolve to stand up to outsiders.

The Americans were camped some two or three miles away. They tacked notices on pine and oak trees on December 11, the day after the oral notices were given, repeating the order that the Chileans at once abandon their camp. Anyone failing to obey the order would be arrested and fined six ounces of gold. The Chileans remained firm in their decision not to leave the area alive, and set about preparing to fight with the peace of conscience men feel when they know they are in the right, and doing as well as they could in view of their small numbers and the scarcity of their arms as compared with the more than two hundred very well-armed Americans.

The Americans had been drawn together by envy and hatred not long after the Chileans had settled down. They had held a "meeting" to decide how to go about taking over the Chilean claim, and their decision was to act as an authority independent of Calaveras County, the state of California, or even the United States itself. They would impose their own laws, codes, and religion (one of the thousand and one that they have in the United States) and, in short, they would act like a government independent of any other authority. They denied the authority of the government of California and that of any of its officials in Stockton as well as that of the county of Calaveras to which they belonged—though those authorities were repudiated at that time by this horde alone.

They declared nonexistent the jurisdiction of the Calaveras judge, B. Scoll, and appointed a M. W. Coller in his place with power *ut fiat qua voluerit* [to do whatever he pleased].

The first step taken by the dictator of that nation (which was improvised on the model of those Montenegrans of the east who ordered the emperor, Napoleon, impeached), was to order the Chileans and all the other aliens to leave the area, giving as the justification of that order the fact that the region belonged to the United States, and therefore to them as citizens of the United States; that the Chileans and other foreigners were exploiting the mines without paying any fee, yet they had come from the [eastern part of the] United States, enduring in an overland journey of three thousand leagues all of the hardships of such travel. Consequently, they said, it was not right that Chileans, as foreigners, not paying any fees, should exploit the mines at the expense of themselves who were citizens of the United States and who had come by land with so much toil and privation and who were rightful owners of mines bought from Mexico with Yankee blood.

These and other reasons of that sort were alleged to justify their illegal and criminal conduct. They thought the Chileans would act like the Sonorans and abandon their claim at a simple order from their new judge. On December 12, two days after the order had been issued at Chile Gulch, three or four Yankees walked into Chile Gulch to take possession of the camp. Before they got to the center of the camp they ran into Terán and two of his companions who were working a placer, and, assuming an air of majesty and authority they thought suitable for the occasion, they warned him to leave with the words, "You, Chileno, largo de aquí." Terán had to laugh at that, and instead of acting terrified he adopted the same pose of haughtiness and arrogance and said to them, adopting their language, "You, Yankees, largo de aquí." More words and gestures were exchanged, but when the Yankees saw in the attitude of Terán and his companions that they were prepared to use force on them if they did not leave of their own free will, they picked up their rifles and tools and left the gulch, hurling curses and threats in English at the Chileans.

This defiance made the Americans as mad as hell. They had not expected such boldness and fearlessness from foreigners. They decided the Chileans must be punished for their attitude in such a way as to terrify all other aliens and make them respect the "I want," and "I order," of the Americans.

From that moment on the Chileans did not feel safe for a single instant and they ran to man their defenses. But they made one primary and fatal mistake: they overlooked a most essential precaution. Incapable of treachery and baseness themselves, they expected the Yankees to come in a frontal attack with blazing guns and that there would be a battle with men dead and wounded. They thought the question would be settled by valor, and therefore that they would remain masters of the battlefield. A vain hope! That was their ruin. A day passed, then another, and another, but nobody came to attack the camp where they were dug in to throw back an assault. All the time it was raining in torrents, washing out the trails and turning the streams into impassible barriers, cutting them off from their supplies and from contact with California towns such as Stockton, Sacramento, and Sonora. That was the position of the Chileans before they were treacherously taken prisoner by the Yankees.

Capture of the Chileans by "Judge" Coller and his men, and the treatment they were subjected to as prisoners.

Five or six days had passed since the Chileans were given the first order to abandon their camp, and three or four days since the scene between Terán and the Yankees. The Chileans had remained on the alert all this time, ever since the first trouble on December 11, expecting to settle the question by a battle. Now they began to think that the Americans had given up their attempt to dispossess them, and that in the end they could reach some sort of reasonable and friendly settlement. Convinced of this, the workers began to resume their mining, and some Chileans went off to hunt. This left only the company leaders in charge of the houses and the camp. None of them expected trouble, much less treachery, from the Yankees, who, though they were actually bandits, still seemed to be acting in an orderly fashion under the direction of a judge and as though in obedience to certain forms of governmental procedure—behaving that way all the more because, basically, they were lawless men.

There is much that is incredible in the lamentable series of events that took place at Calaveras. I only wish those who committed the crimes were actually bandits, without principles, without religion, without belief in anything, and under no law or government. If that were so, the spilt blood, robbery, and nameless horrors could not be blamed on anyone. They say that no nation has to answer for the crimes that this gang pulled off there in the depth of the woods, that no government is responsible for those vandals because they did not recognize any law. But I must ask in my turn, how is it, if those Americans at Calaveras were mere bandits, that they had a judge, Mister Coller, with them, a man with a reputable name, a considerable fortune, and a legitimate right to the title of judge in Double Springs? How can it be that that man, who denied the authority of Stockton, of the state of California, and even that of the American Union, who condemned and arbitrarily hanged three honorable young men, how is it that he enjoys freedom and wealth and is regarded as a respectable man in the eyes of the county authorities? How can Mister Nickleson, called "Four Eyes" by the Chileans, who was one of the executioners of Terán and his companions, be permitted to live tranquilly in the city of Marysville and practice his profession as a doctor, without being troubled by anyone—unless it be by the memories of his horrifying crimes?

But let us leave each person free to make his own judgment about these matters, lest I be accused of partiality.

The fifteenth of December dawned serene after twenty days of stormy weather. All the workers in the Chilean camp had gone to the river and were dispersed here and there as they labored, enjoying the heat of the sun that tempered the chill of the water in which they had to go more or less deeply to get at the deposits. There were very few at the center of the camp because most of the placers were from four hundred to six hundred yards away. This was the day the Americans had chosen to fall upon the Chileans, not like proud and brave bandits but like cowards incapable of fighting openly. On the way to the Chilean camp they caught two workers in the river. Ten or twelve of them dragged the miserable wretches out and took away their gold. After inflicting a thousand outrages on them, they tied them to the trunk of a pine, leaving a guard in view with rifle in hand who was ordered to shoot them if the other Chileans they were going to seize offered the least sign of resistance. As they approached the Chilean camp, twenty or thirty armed men hid themselves among the trees while Judge Coller together with four to six men went on in an outwardly

friendly manner toward the houses. They came with a smile on
their lips, with great politeness, taking off their hats as a sign of
friendship and respect, and mouthing such Spanish words as they
knew to rid their victims of any suspicion that they hid a base
and hostile intent under these lying appearances: "You mucho
bueno aquí. Mucho rico esta cañada. Nosotros muy amigo. No malo."
Such, more or less, were the words with which they gained the
confidence of the Chileans.

The workers who saw from afar their leaders in such intimacy
with the Americans suspected nothing and went on working, highly
pleased that peace had been established between the Yankees and
the Chileans. Concha, Maturano, and some other company leaders
who were there—the others were away—hurried to welcome their
guests as well as they could. They served them coffee and a light
lunch and showed every hospitable attention a guest could have
desired. The conversation turned to weapons, and all of the Chileans were quick to show theirs, handing them to the Americans
with the trustfulness of friends. This confidence showed their generosity of heart, and should have proved to the Americans, whom
they judged to be like themselves, that they harbored no thought
of malice in their generous souls, nor even the slightest suspicion.
Who would have said then, hearing the words of fellowship and
friendliness, that they were all Yankee lies along with the gestures
of respect and deference, and like the Yankees themselves! Who
could have warned them that these same men whom they were entertaining and to whom they were extending the hospitality of their
houses would be—a few moments later—their cruel masters!

Some tutelary spirit must have helped the Americans then, and
led the Chileans to fall victim to their perfidy and dissimulation.

When the Americans had got their hands on all the Chilean
weapons in the way I have described, they gave a signal to the
twenty or thirty men hidden in the woods, and within two minutes,
Maturano, Concha, and some of the other leaders were surrounded
by about fifty Yankees. When Maturano realized the treachery,
he drew a dagger he had kept without the knowledge of anyone
and at one bound reached Judge Coller, whom he took by the neck
and shook as if he were a child. When Coller made a move to
resist, Maturano brandished his dagger, prepared to plunge it into
the heart of the man. Concha, seeing the peril the judge was in,
leaped on Maturano, grabbed his arm, warning him that he would

make the situation worse if he shed blood; and that he still believed they could settle matters peacefully. If Concha had not done that the judge would have been killed without a doubt; and once their chief was dead, and the Chileans reunited, even though they were few, I am sure the affair would have ended with a victory for the Chileans, fighting there in their own houses in defense of their rights and their lives. We shall see how, in later encounters, a single fatal dagger thrust put eight or ten of the Americans into flight; so I do not think it an exaggeration to say that once Coller was dead the American cause would have been lost.

When the judge was free from Maturano's claws, instead of acting with the same generosity Concha had shown him, his first command was that they should tie the Chileans' hands behind their backs and make them suffer. They quickly seized the workers they found nearby, and, without exception, treated them the same way they had the leaders. Those who were farther off, including some leaders, escaped the outrages inflicted on the captives, but not the robbery and destruction of their homes.

After the Chileans were securely tied, the judge, Coller, in person, demanded the purse of each of the prisoners, exactly like the chief of a band of highwaymen would do with travelers who fell into his hands. At the least resistance in handing over his purse, Coller put a pistol to the head of the helpless prisoner, who then indicated where his purse was, because he could not speak English or use his hands. Thus the purses of the hard-working Chileans passed into the hands of the judge. After they had despoiled every man of everything of value he had on his person, all of the Yankees began to gather whatever they could find in the houses: food, tools, clothing, etc. Then in the sight of their victims they went through the pockets and boots, and everything, great or small, they divided among themselves as loot. I call on all who those who escaped this Saint Bartholomew's affair to testify to what I am saying: men who are now in Concepción or in other parts of the Republic of Chile. All of the houses were treated the same way exactly, not even excepting the old abandoned ones or those used for the sick. A group of Americans were sent to their camp by the judge, and they came back with mules to carry all the food to the Yankee camp. Each company had a lot of food, more than enough for a year, so you can imagine how much there was to carry away from the eight or ten companies that were there; it took two or three

days to transport it all down to Judge Coller's storerooms. Then
they demolished each house, not leaving a single wall standing,
but taking care to steal the canvas that covered the roofs.

Then each one, loaded down with all he could carry, set off
for the American camp, laughing and making jokes about their
success. The Chileans were driven along behind, with their hands
tied behind them, some without hats because Americans had taken
them to wear themselves. They were marched along like convicts
captured red-handed and being herded into jail by the police. When
they reached the house of the judge, the stronger were released
so they could help the Americans stow the stolen food. The booty
was not to be divided, it seems, until it had all been transported
from the Chilean to the American camp.

Can anyone say this was not a robbery? Can anyone deny that
these bandits were the lowest, meanest, and most villainous of their
type—because even bandits have classes and hierarchies, and these
were as vile and infamous as the worst of them.

*How the illegality of the American was regarded. The Chileans
and the authorities at Stockton. The subprefect, Mr. T. Dickenson,
and justice of the peace, Mr. G. Belt. Arrest ordered for the Yankees at Calaveras.*

These robberies and outrages perpetrated against the defenseless
Chileans, and the cowardly and treacherous method of capturing
them, made clear the character of those men. If the capture of
the Chileans had been made in an open manner, or, if that were
not possible, if the Chileans had been seized in some other manner,
but without being robbed so basely and without being mistreated
so violently after they were prisoners and helpless, there would
have appeared to be some semblance of rightful authority in the
action of the judge or chief of that suddenly gathered band. But
the acts that took place and continued were the crimes of bandits
and vicious bandits without the least trace of generosity.

Gangs of that type the world over have at least enough interest
in the good name of their vile calling to take their victims, gun
in hand, without resorting to ignoble means; and they treat them
as generously as they can once they have taken their gold and
jewels and have them helpless in their hands. Even in California

itself there were bands of highwaymen from Guadalajara in whom we have seen a thousand acts of generosity; and the same is true of the bands of Apaches and Quilches who raid down into Mexican territory to rob the stagecoaches and the mule teams that carry gold and silver bars to Mexico City; these Indians carry their respect for individuals so far that they do not touch their bodies or even so much as the hair on their heads, nor do them any personal injury once they have taken their purses. But these demonstrations of gallantry rigorously observed by savage raiders like the Apaches were completely unknown by the Yankee bandits who captured our men. Six or seven of them would gang up on one man, and if he fell down helpless they would kick him in the face with their boots.

This sort of thing was done by Yankees in California a thousand times. Ask anyone who was there even a single day, and he will tell you that in those twenty-four hours he himself saw things that prove what I say. Could it be that the Yankees of 1849 and 1850 were insane men who had been turned into wild beasts by greed for gold? Is it possible that the Yankees there today are not the same breed of men? Whichever of these is true, what is certain is that you do not see any of that kind of behavior in California today: there is not even a trace of that arbitrary action, that concentrated hatred of foreigners, and especially of Chileans.

In California today, without any sign of arms and troops, with no vigilantes or even street patrols at night by uniformed men, the cities are the best policed in the world. You never know on the streets when a man is being arrested. The sheriff and policemen wear coats and jackets like well-dressed citizens. Instead of being armed with rifle and saber they carry only a six-shooter hanging from the belt under their coats. A man charged with a minor offense there does not have to undergo the shame of being marched along the street to jail or to court by a guard wearing cape and spurs and calling attention to himself by clinking his saber as he goes along so everyone will notice he is conducting a prisoner. An alien in California is treated with respect now, just as he is in other parts of the United States; and since they introduced lynch law there, there has been nothing remotely like the things that happened at Calaveras. The animosity against Chileans is only a memory. Today there is complete harmony between Yankees and Chileans.

The events we have been describing that took place in Calaveras happened in the early days of the Gold Rush. They exemplify the hatred and abuse of aliens, and are the very things that brought about lynch law. We will say something about that law in its proper place. It is one of the wisest and most effective steps a people can take when they are being wronged and deceived by the authorities. The people reasserted the right of sovereignty properly theirs when they established lynch law and set up the vigilance committee.

Lynch law may have purged California of its bandits, but it did nothing about those of Calaveras. Judge Coller and Dr. Nickleson are both still living, rich and respected by everyone—while many of the unhappy men they robbed of fortune and future have to beg their food in California; while in Chile there are widows, and mothers without sons; and men who bear the eternal shame of having had their ears cut off—at least in the eyes of those who do not know the injustice with which this was done. All the Chileans remained captives in the power of the Yankees for two days, and were subjected to the same mistreatment as in the beginning. Terán and some of the other leaders escaped the cruelties inflicted on their comrades, and the grief of witnessing their suffering, because they had not been at the camp when the Yankees came.

On December 15, after the events described, the Chileans showed up at the camp of another foreigner who had his storehouse and troop of workers some three or four miles away. They got there at ten o'clock in the night, dying of hunger and worn out by their exertions, for they had walked on foot all the way from the camp to the Calaveras River, over the worst kind of trail. They were looking for the legitimate judge, Mister B. Scollen, so they could register their complaint against the men who had committed the crime. Luckily the aforesaid foreigner, in addition to being a friend of the judge, also knew English and was able to help them in every respect as an interpreter as well as in taking care of their needs. That same night, December 15, the foreigner and the Chileans went to the residence of Judge Scollen. He received them with the most lively expressions of sympathy and interest. They explained the entire situation to him without omitting the slightest detail, from the first order they had got to leave their camp to the latest outrage of the Yankees to their persons and property.

Judge Scollen was by nature a calm and peaceful man. He was very angry at the account of the shameless behavior by that gang.

He wanted to go that very instant to punish those brigands—but would they respect his authority? Could he control that rebellious crowd who had already denied his jurisdiction over them and even threatened his own personal security? Because of these doubts, his advice was that the Chileans go to Stockton to lay their case before the subprefect, from whom they would undoubtedly receive justice. Stockton was some twenty to thirty leagues away, and this was in the most severe winter month. How could the Chileans make so long a journey on foot and without any resources? The Yankees had not left them a cent; they had even taken their warm clothing and their shoes, and both would be needed on such a journey. How were they to pay for ferrying across the rivers, and how were they to buy food, which cost four dollars a day at the inns along the way? It is a very different thing to tell about these things than to undergo them. It required a truly strong character, an enterprising spirit, and a will of iron to triumph over poverty and often misery, in a land where you were cursed to your face if you were an alien, where you could not ask for help because you did not know the language, where, in short, you had to live as the Chileans did, virtual outlaws.

Maturano and Concha, who headed the Chileans, preferred to endure all the toil and suffering the journey down to Stockton would mean rather than allow those crimes to go unpunished because of any lack of caring or failure to act on their part. For them it was a question of honor more than one of money. Although they had been robbed of everything, even of the means of seeking their fortune there or in any other part of California, their only thought then was to take legitimate vengeance for the injuries they had suffered from the Yankees, and to see to it that the perfidy and unexampled villany were punished. The Chileans one and all said, "Let's go to Stockton to get justice even if we die on the road." Among them were boys of eight or ten years who showed the same enthusiasm and the same desire for justice.

Having agreed to this, the Chileans slept that night in the house of the friendly foreigner, and on the morning of the sixteenth started off for Stockton, taking with them the most necessary things only. All of them were afoot, pants rolled up to their knees; a poncho over the shoulders and a tree branch lopped off as a walking stick formed all their equipment for the journey. Only a few of them had shoes: those who had escaped with their boots because they

had them on when captured. The others were barefoot. They had
to wade through mud up to their knees. They carried letters of
recommendation from the foreigner to his partner in Stockton, and
another letter of introduction from Judge Scollen to Dickenson,
the subprefect. This letter certified the truthfulness of the complaint as to the crimes committed against the property and persons
of the Chileans, and asked that a warrant be issued for the arrest
of the offenders.

We will pass over in silence the toils and miseries the Chileans
went through in the trip to Stockton, so as not to weary the readers.
The news they brought created feelings of horror in that city. All
of the residents joined in asking justice, just as if the wrongs had
been done to themselves. The Chileans were properly received by
the subprefect, and by Mr. Belt, the justice of the peace. Almost
all of the merchants held a meeting to decide on the best way
to handle the difficult matter. They passed a resolution that the
leading men of the city, Messrs. Sparrow, Young, Macpherson, Belt,
and others should lead a force large enough to capture those bandits
and hang them in Stockton. Some of the older ones said, however,
that they were not in favor of this procedure, on the grounds that
such an armed force would certainly cause bloodshed; so, in place
of that, an order was signed by the authorities in Stockton to the
effect that the judge of the district in question should arrest the
men. The Chileans themselves were to take the order to all the
justices of the area to demand their help and assistance for Judge
Scollen to the extent that such help was needed. The arrest of
the malefactors was to be carried out peacefully, without endanger-
ing the lives of respectable citizens. This proposal was adopted
as the most prudent one—to the displeasure of almost all the citizens named, who were already mounted and ready to undertake
the journey. We will include an exact copy of the arrest order
issued for the Calaveras criminals.

*The arrest order of the Stockton subprefect for the Americans
at Calaveras. Combat, and the death of one Chilean and four
Americans. Arrest of the criminals and the success of the Chileans.*

After ten days of toil and suffering of all sorts, the Chileans got
back to Calaveras with an order for the arrest of the Americans;
it must not be forgotten that this was in the worst part of winter,

and that the Chileans made the trip down to Stockton and back
on foot. They were so impoverished as a result of the looting on
the 15th that they even had to sell some of their clothing to buy
food and other essentials. Often they were refused admission to
wayside inns when it was discovered that they were the Chileans
in the affair at Calaveras, and on these nights they had to sleep
in the open, or, at best, under the cover of an oak tree to get
refuge from the cold and the winter rain. I wish that some of those
who suspect me of partiality in recounting these things could have
seen this band of decent young men walking hundreds of miles,
with insufficient food and clothing, often begging for shelter and
suffering humiliation in being turned away by innkeepers as suspi-
cious characters once it was known that they were the Chileans
driven out at Calaveras. I wish they could have seen these youths
lodged under the trees at night, ringed with fire so they could
endure the cold. Would they then be able to recognize them as
the beloved and pampered sons of families, unused to any kind
of privation and suffering in their own country, now plunged into
frightful misfortunes, leading the lives of savages, persecuted as
if they were outlaws or ciminals without any rights? There would
not be one reader then who would think I was being too harsh
or that I was exaggerating.

On December 26 the Chileans got back to the home of Judge
Scollen with the arrest order given them in Stockton. I translated
this order for them in the presence of the judge, and I will set
it down here exactly:

> By these presents, Messrs. Concha and Maturano are authorized to
> arrest and bring to Stockton either freely or by force all of the individu-
> als residing in Calaveras who have defied the legal authority of this
> subprefecturate and who have recognized Mr. Coller as a judge. They
> are authorized likewise to arrest and bring to Stockton all individuals
> who took part in the robbery, violence, and expulsion carried out against
> the aliens living in Chile Gulch. By this same order, judges and all
> of the loyal citizens of Calaveras are required to give to the aforesaid
> Messrs. Concha and Maturano whatever help they need to effect the
> arrest of the rebels. The lawful judge of Calaveras, Mr. Scollen, will
> authorize the execution of this order by his presence. The rebels will
> be brought to Stockton for trial by a jury with competent authority.

> Given in Stockton, December 22, 1849.
> W. DICKENSON, G. BELT

After the judge had read this order and it had been translated for the information of the Chileans, Judge Scollen raised some small difficulties about its execution. First and foremost, he lacked the prestige and force needed to arrest those rebels in case they refused to come peacefully in response to the authority of Stockton. Secondly, it seemed to him contrary to the law of the United States to empower aliens to arrest citizens. These and other reasons that Mr. Scollen alleged all reduced themselves, we saw later, to this one alone: 'I cannot arrest one hundred American rebels with twenty Chileans." In the end, though, because the order from Stockton was definitive, he could do nothing but submit and obey; so he agreed to go next day and execute the order for the arrest of the rebels.

At twelve, noon, on December 27, Judge Scollen set out in the company of Concha, Maturano, James Necker, and two or three other Americans, for the camp of Judge Coller. It seemed to him that it would be better to communicate the order peacefully and without any display of force so as to avoid the shedding of blood. Actually, it should be said, he did not have the slightest desire to go into battle against those ruffians, who were armed with rifles, six-shooters, hunting knives, and other things. Judge Scollen arrived at the camp of Coller and found all the Americans united and armed. The lawful Calaveras judge with all the dignity of his office displayed the paper containing the order from the subprefect, and then read it in a clear voice. When the reading was over Coller answered the judge that he had tolerated the insolence of the subprefect because Stockton was far away, but if the Calaveras judge and his men did not want to be hung on the spot they had better leave at once. "The people are sovereign in the United States," he said, "and we are the people; and as such we have elected our own government or judge, and we recognize only his authority."

The judge did not wait for Coller's words to be repeated. He got on his horse and left, making a signal to Maturano and Concha that they should follow him; they had watched everything without understanding a word of what was going on around them. When he got back to his residence Judge Scollen described through an interpreter the reply Coller had given, adding that he had neither the ability nor the wish to carry the execution of the order any further. The rebels were too numerous compared with the Chileans and the other men at his disposal for effecting the arrest.

You can imagine the disappointment of the Chileans when the judge they had counted on took this attitude. They suddenly saw all of the sacrifices and toil that had undergone in the past ten days, going all the way down to Stockton for justice, and they felt their last hopes for getting back their stolen property vanishing. More than ever, in that moment of crisis, this small band of Chileans revealed their determined and tenacious character: they felt an imperious necessity to avenge their outraged honor and the insults they had been subjected to so unjustly. Almost certain they were going to their deaths, they decided vehemently to go and arrest the Americans themselves or die in the attempt. Their courage and fervor in their cause seemed to be rekindled at finding they were alone and without the protection on which they had counted. They agreed on the spot that Concha should set out along the banks of the river with twenty men and all the arms they could find, while Maturano would go by the main trail with his men. The two parties would meet at the camp, and attack it from two different points. Terán and Ruiz joined Maturano as leaders of the second party, with most of the other company leaders we have named. In this party there were boys only twelve years old, but they followed their leaders and made common cause with them. Not many besides the leaders had firearms; the others were armed with hunting knives and machetes, and some had clubs made from oak branches as their only offensive and defensive equipment. Maturano arrived at Coller's camp with some twenty men armed as I have described them. It was on a Thursday, December 27, 1849.

It was about nine or ten o'clock on a winter night as black as the conscience of the men they were going to seize. The Chileans had stripped twice to swim the Calaveras River, which meandered twice across the trail. This and the wretched sleep of the last three or four nights in the open all weighted the scales against the Chileans, along with hunger, cold, weariness, and the superior numbers of their enemies whom they would have to attack in their own houses and who were supplied with all kinds of arms. The Chileans had little more in their favor but the justice of their cause and their zeal. It must be admitted that it took more than valor to have the audacity to go and seize more than a hundred men lodged in their pine-walled cabins, made of trunks placed horizontally over each other and forming a solid barrier not even light could enter, with only machetes as your weapons. The only way you could attack these cabins was through the doors. These were mainly made of cowhide with a bar of wood at the bottom for weight. Maturano and his men got to Coller's camp undetected in the darkness of the night, in spite of the fact that they were watching in almost all the cabins.

What was Maturano's surprise then, to find that Concha, instead of being there to help, had set out for Stockton with all the Chileans he could find. This was the last and heaviest blow that awaited the Chileans in their desperate situation. Now valor became heroism. Terán said to the others, "If you are willing to go on, I will be the first to enter and set an example. If we can take one or two cabins the rest will give in." The enthusiasm of that brief speech ran through all the Chileans like an electric spark, and they answered with one voice, "Let's go!"

Because they had no interpreter to make themselves understood by the Yankees, the Chileans had adopted a phrase that would be clear and intelligible to anyone: "Subprefecto orden, vamos for Stockton." It would make it clear the Chileans were acting under the authority of the order in arresting them, and that they were not mere brigands as the Americans had been a few days before. Terán, Maturano, Ruiz, and a man of Santiago whose name I do not remember charged into a cabin where there were seven Americans, the chief men of the camp. The other company leaders, Herrera, Hermosilla, etc., each with two or three followers, burst into the other cabins. Terán and his men stopped in the doorway and shouted the agreed-upon words in a loud voice, and at once heard noise and movement within caused by the startled grasping for weapons. They supposed therefore the Americans had rifles, pistols, and daggers in their hands—although they never used the last-named weapon. They called a second time, and got no answer. "Down with the door!" said Terán, springing for it at the same moment. The door came down in pieces and at the same time they saw the flame of pistol shots. The man from Santiago fell dead on the door sill with his brains blown out, and another ball knocked Maturano's pistol out of his hand. Terán, seeing his comrade fall, let out an oath and buried his dagger to the hilt in the chest of the Yankee who had killed the man from Santiago, and who tried to fire a second shot at Terán but failed when his pistol misfired.

Ruiz also had killed an American, and Maturano was struggling at close grips with a huge man and finally threw him across a cot. While he was engaged with him another American came up from behind and was about to knife Maturano from the rear, but an unexpected help came just in time to save Maturano. A ten-year-old boy from Maturano's company, disobeying orders, had followed his leader silently and arrived just at the right moment. The Yankee had his knife poised to strike Maturano, who had no idea that he was in danger, when the boy jumped and struck the knife in mid air—at the cost of his hands, which were sliced in two. Maturano had finished with his man, and Ruiz stabbed the American who had tried to attack Maturano from the rear. Meanwhile Terán had two Americans down on their knees begging for their lives; and once they had surrendered he did not harm a hair of their heads. All the others still alive, including one who was dying, also surrendered, repeating the words of Terán: "Vamos for Stockton."

The same thing happened in the other cabins attacked by the Chileans; in some, they did not get off more than one or two shots. Terror had overcome the Americans, and all those who were not able to escape surrendered. The Chileans, now masters of the battle-field, first gathered up all the weapons they could find, then dragged the dead men out of the cabins, which were drenched with blood, especially the one where the Chilean and three Americans had died. Then they sealed up the cabins, without taking from them even a drop of water to quench their thirst. Terán, Maturano, and the other Chilean leaders ordered that they should take nothing from the cabins except the weapons. The Chileans' own property was there, the very things they had been robbed of a few days before, but they did not even examine them for fear their behavior would be confused with that of the Yankees—although in all justice they were entitled to take back their own things. They took the weapons and nothing more. They behaved with the same scrupulous care in dealing with the prisoners that they had observed toward their cabins.

When the fighting was over, Terán found that the prisoners outnumbered the Chileans two to one, so, though he did not like to do it, he ordered that the most vicious of the Americans be tied up with cloth strips for security's sake so that they could be taken to the residence of the judge. All of these things reveal their generos-

ity of character and their good hearts. We shall see other acts of
generosity performed, even at the risk of those who performed
them, which show the high principles of those Chileans in forgetting
the outrages inflicted on them as soon as they had been able to
avenge them.

*Calumnies spread by the Americans about the Chileans who car-
ried out the order of the subprefect of Stockton. They are prosecu-
ted as a consequence and imprisoned in the vicinity of Stockton,
then taken back to Calaveras.*

After they had gained control of the American camp, the Chileans did not neglect any jot of formality to comply in an honorable
and proper manner with the order of the superior judge in Stockton.
Because all the Americans who had not been taken prisoner had
fled from the camp and left their cabins, the first thing the Chileans
did was to free three or four of the Americans under their control
so they could take care of the cabins and goods. As has been said,
the leaders took care, after the fight was over, to observe most
scrupulously the inviolability of the persons and the property of
the Americans—which means, of course, the property of which
the Chileans themselves had been robbed in their own houses a
few days before, and which now belonged to them also as the spoils
of battle by a double title.

Once they had arranged everything in this fashion, they returned
with their prisoners to the house of the judge about one or two
in the morning of the twenty-eighth. Their object in not going
directly to Stockton but returning to the residence of the judge,
losing eight to ten miles by so doing, was to present themselves
to the proper authorities in Calaveras, to remove even the slightest
suspicion of arbitrariness in what they had done. It was admirable
to see those few Chileans bringing in twice their number of prisoners, and bearing up with remarkable determination against rough
weather and their inadequate food and clothing. Their trip to Stockton on foot and across the mountains to save distance, and their
return the same way, had left some without boots and others with
their feet cut and bloody. Eight or ten night hours of sleepless
toil, however, had not dampened the courage of a single one of

them. They had fought, one against five, on the night of the twenty-seventh, despite the fatigues of the previous day. Now they returned to the judge with their prisoners, with the wounded men on the only two mules they had to carry their blankets; and after all that, they were ready to set out for Stockton without allowing themselves a minute of rest.

When they got to the judge's residence, before taking care of themselves, their first act was to go to the house of the friendly foreigner mentioned before and to ask him for lint and brandy to treat the wounded men. Could anything be more noble and generous than to see those Chileans, who had been treated so cruelly a few days before, now binding up the wounds of their attackers with their own hands and giving them every kind of consideration and counsel. Could there be anything finer than to see those youths in whom, before, there had burned desires for vengeance, now shedding tears for the wounded and sharing in their grief. You would have had to see those sad scenes to give due value to those acts of kindness on the part of the Chileans. We will see later how they were repaid.

After tending the wounded, the Chileans put them back on the mules and set out for Stockton at three o'clock in the morning. But what a commotion the news of what had happened spread through the whole district of Calaveras. Judge Coller, whom no one had seen during the fighting, had been the first to flee; but now at the head of the other runaways he was going from place to place in the farms and mines thereabouts calling the people to arms and painting in the blackest colors imaginable the story of the capture. He said a horde of Chilean robbers had attacked the cabins in the middle of the night, and after killing six or eight Americans had pillaged everything without the least shame, shouting "Down with the American Government! Long live Mexico! Long live Chile!" He could not have found lies and calumnies more effective in alarming Americans and filling them with indignation. The cry, "Down with the American Government," was enough to make the case appear to be a matter of life and death. For a month or so rumors had been circulating in California that the Mexicans were planning to retake the state they had ceded to the Americans; and that seemed to give credence to what Coller and his men were saying.

A cry went up as a result, asking in the name of the indignant
American people that a force be raised to go in pursuit of the
bandits who, in addition to the crimes they had committed, were
taking thirty American citizens to be hanged in Stockton. On the
same day that followed the fight at the Calaveras, a party of more
than one hundred Americans set out to catch the Chileans, spreading the alarm in all the villages through which they passed. The
same Chileans who were at Judge Scollen's residence on the morning of the twenty-eighth to bury the dead came back with the
news that Coller had ordered a second Saint Bartholomew's against
all foreigners without regard to persons, sex, or rank, and that at
the same time an order of arrest had been issued for the arrest
of Judge Scollen and the other Americans with him who had authorized the crimes of the previous night.

Meanwhile the Chileans, ignorant of the slanders and maledictions hurled against them, were continuing with their prisoners on
the journey to Stockton on December 28. They had been traveling
through the night hours after leaving the residence of the judge.
At about eight or nine in the morning they stopped at the house
of a Mr. Frederick, an American who lived in Chillán for many
years. He can testify to much of what happened because he was
there and saw it himself. The Chileans asked for breakfast for themselves and the prisoners, and all sat down together at the same
table without any ceremony and in perfect harmony, and had their
breakfast. A kind of intimacy had grown up among them since
the night before, and even the memories of the unfortunate scenes
had receded into the back of their minds. The Chileans had given
their sarapes and other bits of clothing to the Americans who had
little on, and had made proper stops on the trip more for the
comfort of the prisoners than their own. They went on, after leaving
the residence of Mr. Frederick, in the same order as before, with
nothing remarkable happening except that the number of Chileans
was reduced at each inn they passed as those who were sick or
too worn out to continue walking shoeless on torn feet decided to
stay behind. This started happening at Mr. Frederick's house, and
occurred again and again at every inn they came to on the trip.

At twelve o'clock the next day, December 29, the Chileans
reached the inn of Mr. Bingham, eleven miles from Stockton. Aware
of the small number to which they had been reduced, they began

to fear that the Americans they met at the inns where they stopped for coffee or food might take the side of the prisoners. So they decided that Señor Lara should go on ahead into town and tell the authorities that the Chileans were coming with a large number of prisoners and needed help in case other Americans tried to set them free. Lara set off, and the Americans and Chileans sat down at the table, while Ruiz took advantage of the opportunity to catch a few winks of sleep under an oak tree. They had just finished the meal and were paying the bill for everyone, as they had at every stop, when they suddenly heard the noise of about one hundred armed Americans dismounting and pounding on the door of the inn. In a moment the Chileans were surrounded by Americans and had pistols at their heads. Weapons were given to the prisoners, and some of them jammed pistols into the faces of the Chileans and threatened to blow their brains out at the least resistance.

With this first ingratitude, the Americans began to repay the many kindnesses of the Chileans. Terán and Maturano had clasped their weapons and were ready to resist, but the others saw they could do nothing against odds of ten to one, and so all of them surrendered to the Yankees. The Chileans were all tied up, without exception, in hemp ropes, so tightly that the ropes broke the skin and stopped the circulation. The captors followed this first black deed by robbing them of everything they had, and by new outrages and threats. They showed them a noose and made signs that they were going to hang them from an oak tree. The thing that distressed the Chileans most was the vile ingratitude with which their good treatment of their prisoners was requited; for they were receiving the same tortures and abuse they had gotten before.

A party of twenty-five or thirty men took charge of them to take them back to Calaveras, and the other Americans went on to Stockton to seize the subprefect and the other authorities. Luckily, or perhaps disgracefully, the subprefect took ship for San Francisco and so saved himself, letting the full fury of the Yankees fall on the Chileans of Stockton. There robberies and assaults were committed by the same men who had been shortly before in the power of the Chileans. Señor Don Enrique Green can testify to this Sicilian Vespers. Though he had played no part in anything that had gone before, he was on the point of being hanged twice in the same day with two other Chileans, and escaped the first time by turning over his purse full of gold and on the second occasion through the intervention of honorable Americans. Señor Green, without any fault at all, had almost been put to death ignominiously by hanging. He saw the vile deeds done to other Chileans in Stockton, and he can say whether there is any exaggeration in my account, or whether it does not deserve darker colors than I have given it in these pages.

You will have greater reason to note the injustice and the fierce animosity of the Americans against all foreigners, and the Chileans most of all, in the years 1849 and 1850 when you see in black and white the report of the jury that judged and sentenced to death the Chileans who executed the order of the subprefect of Stockton. By escaping to San Francisco he turned all the fury of the Yankees upon the unhappy aliens; they paid with their lives for his fault—if it was a fault.

How the Chileans were treated in their days of captivity. The convoking of the jury to try them, and the presiding of Coller. The sentence pronounced, and the discussion on the method of executing it.

The Chileans may have thought that, once they were prisoners and tied up, the Americans would use them with the same generosity they had received themselves when they were made prisoners on the night of the twenty-seventh. They may have hoped they would be allotted a few of the plentiful horses, out of compassion for the wretched state they were in after having spent ten days going on foot back and forth over the worst kind of trails. But how mistaken they were if they expected that! Not only did the Yankees give them no help in their miserable condition, but they were forced to walk all the way back without a minute to rest. All of them with their arms bound tightly behind them were forced pell-mell out onto the road and driven along like a herd of sheep or something similar. The Americans, well mounted, went at a trot, forcing the Chileans to keep pace under pain of being trampled on any minute or receiving the sting of a whip. The American prisoners, liberated a few moments before, instead of being the kindest in their treatment of the Chileans, were in fact the most ferocious and villainous. Thus, maltreated, vexed in every fashion, tortured in body and soul, the Chileans were driven along without truce, without rest, without a hope of any relief or consolation except death. When they came to the rivers and creeks, filled from bank to bank with the winter rains, even if there was a footbridge the Americans forced the Chileans to jump into the water without caring whether they drowned there because of the deepness of the water and the impossibility of swimming with their hands manacled. They crossed the rivers in this fashion, in water up to their chests, completely dressed, in rain and in snow; and they had to sleep that way—or, rather, lie awake all night in freezing wet garments while the American slept. If the Americans had not needed sleep themselves, they would not have allowed the Chileans even that much rest. Even that rest cost the Chileans dearly because, on reaching an inn the prisoners' hands and feet were tied together. In addition there was a sentinel in view with a loaded gun. It is almost incredible that civilized men could have been so barbarous and savage at heart.

At 11:00 P.M. on the twenty-ninth, the day the Chileans were captured, the Americans stopped with their prisoners at the house of Mr. Davis on the bank of the Calaveras River. After doubling the ropes and leaving a sentry in view of the captives, the Americans went to sleep in their respective cots. The night was black and nothing broke the silence except the roar of the river some twelve or fifteen feet away. The waters were high because it had been raining for fifteen days, so the river formed a barrier on that side of the house. At about twelve o'clock that night one of the Chileans noticed the guard was asleep and told his comrades that this was the chance to get away. How were they to do this tied hand and foot and without arms? This did not dismay them. Each one began to work at his bonds with his teeth. That was the one part of his body that remained free. Finally, after a half-hour or so of effort, Señor Hermosilla liberated himself from his bonds before anyone else. Instead of yielding to the instinctive desire to flee, he started helping the others to get loose, telling them to keep up their courage and hold on to their hopes for success in getting away. But fate decreed that his heroism, his devotion to his brothers in peril, should end badly. Before he had gotten a single other man loose, the sentinel noticed and raised a shout.

Hermosilla then with the speed of lightning leaped down from the floor where the Chileans were, tore down the canvas wall, and threw himself into the river, determined to die rather than go on enduring the tortures to which he and his comrades had been subjected ever since they were made prisoners.

His star seemed disposed to protect him. When he leaped into the river, the current carried him some three hundred feet or more and lodged him under some branches and brush that had wedged in a narrow spot of the river. There he caught his breath and was able to reconnoiter the situation. He did not dare leave the river in the blackness of the night to expose the life regained so miraculously. The water rushed by so furiously that within an hour it had torn his clothes away. At the first light of day he saw he was not far from the bank, and he reached it without difficulty but almost numb from his cold six-hour bath. He looked like Adam in his nakedness, and he continued that way for two or three days, not daring to go near a populated place where he might be recognized. He was wandering without clothing and without food except for what he could find.

But the fate of those who remained captive was made doubly hard. The Yankees started them off almost immediately to rob them of any further hope of escape. Suffering the same or worse treatment, they were brought to the camp of Coller on December 30.

It was there the Chileans had to drain the last bitter drops of their ordeal. Every one of the Americans in turn struck them or inflicted some other indignity on them while they were helpless. They were jammed into a corner of a cold room, still roped up, and treated exactly the way captains of slaving ships treated the unfortunate Negroes who fell into their hands. Most of the Chileans had not been given a bite to eat since the day before when they were seized—though they themselves had seated their prisoners at table with them and had paid for their food.

I escaped the Saint Bartholomew's that Coller proclaimed against all aliens and I did not know what had happened. I'd started for Stockton at midnight, December 30. That is how it happened that I was seized by twelve men with rifles as I entered the house where the Chileans were held. My captors, I learned later, were the guards who had custody of the prisoners. When they shouted to me, "Who is there?" I answered in English that I was coming from Sonora and going down to Stockton. They held me a quarter of an hour, and during that time I saw the Chilean prisoners though they did not see me. All of them were bound, some hand and foot. A few of them, worn out with fatigue, were sleeping on the floor; the others, including Terán, were sitting watchfully on the floor in the only position possible for them as their arms were tied behind them. None of these young men, conscious that they were to die the following day, showed any sign of desperation or depression. Terán, Maturano, Herrera, Yáñez and others all showed the most perfect tranquillity—yet how much agony must they be going through internally. Two or three times I heard Terán say something to the others, with his eyes fixed on the door, but I could not hear what he was saying. Perhaps he had recognized my voice and was afraid another victim was to be added to the many who were to be sacrificed later on.

On the following day, December 31, the jury was convoked. It was actually composed of the same men who had been released two days before from the hands of the Chileans. Judge Coller presided. The whole procedure was a cynical farce, for those men had not the slightest scruple about violating the most sacred rights of the individual; they showed none of the consideration one man owes to another. The prosecutor was one of those wounded on the twenty-eighth, and the defense attorney was—nobody! They would have no help unless Divine Providence came to their aid. The interpreter was a Negro who spoke very little Spanish; every phrase he translated in the statements of the Chileans made things worse for them.

What the reader of these pages may find even more amazing, though, was the role a woman played in this tragedy. The reader might expect that this lady, wife of one of the jurymen, would act in keeping with the mission of her sex and lavish consolation and kind sympathy on our unfortunate young men; that our heroine would go to the judges begging, pleading, persuading with tears in her eyes on behalf of these unhappy ones. Nothing of the sort! She was an endless torment to the Chileans and without pity. She would stand in the doorway of the room that held the jury, showing the Chileans a noose to hang them with and pointing to the tree that would be used. At times she would show the horrible facial expressions they would have in their last agonies. That woman, from whom they could get no relief except for the times when she stopped to drink, added to the bitterness of the Chileans' last hour—which she illustrated for them in all its details. Everything, everything was against them in the last desolate perils of life. All their statements were drawn from them by loaded questions and twisted to their detriment and became new items in the articles of accusation designed to bring upon them at last the sentence of death.

Thus passed the first day of the trial and the third day of imprisonment for the Chileans. If they had known on December 31, after the trial, that on the next day, January 1, according to the custom in the United States, old enmities were forgotten, injuries forgiven, offenders pardoned, and the past wiped out and friendships renewed—if, I said, the Chileans knew such a custom was observed by good Americans, they might have felt some hope as December 31 ebbed and the New Year approached; but, unfortunately, January 1 was their last day of life!

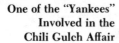

**One of the "Yankees"
Involved in the
Chili Gulch Affair**

Colonel James J. Ayers

The second day of the trial. Sentence of death against the Chileans. The Americans at Mokelumne and the discussion over the way the Chileans were to be executed. Outrages and killings elsewhere.

The illegal proceedings of the trial have been described—if that arbitrary and inquisitorial affair can be called a trial. The jury was packed with men full of prejudice and hatred toward the accused. The fact that Judge Coller presided was enough in its self to guarantee there would be a death sentence. Lacking the basic requirement of impartiality on the part of all members of the jury, what hope was there in the court process except for a decision dictated by the envenomed rage of the jury against the Chileans? Practically all the things of which they were accused would have been dismissed at a glance by anyone who was impartial. They were charged with rebellion against the legal government of the United States. That was false and absurd. We have seen how this crime was imputed to them the day after the skirmish; but how could the Chileans be acting against American authority in arresting bandits who had denied and outraged that very authority? The Chileans were accused of having broken into houses of defenceless citizens, to rob them and to commit murder against Americans. Again, this was false, as false as could be. The Chileans were carrying an order for the arrest of those Americans, given to them by the one and only legitimate authority in the country. Robbers do not notify those they intend to rob, but the Chileans did inform the Americans in advance of the order they carried on the morning of the twenty-seventh, and it was the clear refusal to surrender to the authority they represented that led them to make prisoners of the Americans that night.

And where was the booty taken by the Chileans after the fight? As has been said, it was their chief care not to leave themselves open to any such charge. Where were the gold and the goods taken from the Chileans, which would really prove who had been the robbers? They were in the possession of the jurymen and their friends, thousands of dollars worth of goods that had been stolen a few days before from the men now charged as thieves. Finally, what fault did the Chileans commit in receiving and carrying out an order issued by higher authority everyone recognized as legitimate? If anyone committed a fault in that matter it was the subprefect who did so when he ordered the arrest of the Americans. He alone ought to have been proceeded against, and not the unhappy Chileans, ignorant of the law of the land and simple executors of a superior order. The subprefect ought to have taken some action to back up his authority in simple justice to the poor men who were to be doomed to perish in serving him. But he fled from Stockton and left the Chileans to the ferocity and vengeance of the rebels.

On the night of December 31, at ten o'clock, the trial ended and the following sentence was pronounced:

> José del Carmen Terán, Damián Urzúa, and Francisco Cárdenas are to suffer the extreme penalty. The three named individuals are to be taken at ten o'clock the following morning to Mokelumne hill, taken to the top, and thrown down the cliff toward the river.

Mokelumne hill is one of the highest in the California mining area. The cliff to which the sentence referred is more than six hundred feet high, rising from inaccessible rocks. There the condemned men were to be flung from the top down the whole face of the cliff, bound hand and foot. It would truly take more than the disposition of a cannibal to devise a method of execution more cruel, and enjoy its most gruesome details. Terán and the other two listened to their sentence being translated with stoicism. Terán wanted to make some reply, but the interpreter refused to relay his words.

Ignacio Yáñez and two companions were sentenced to receive thirty lashes, to have their heads shaved ignominiously, and then finally to have their ears cut off, to their agony and eternal disgrace. No such penalty has ever been imposed in any part of the modern world—even among the Chinese, who are notoriously cruel in the treatment of prisoners. I have before me a book, *The Mysteries of the Inquisition,* that contains one thousand or more engravings of different tortures imposed by that tribunal; and whether they are real or imaginary, I do not find in any of them the sort of torture inflicted on the wretched Chileans by the bandits of Calaveras. From four to six of the other boys were sentenced to be tied to the branches of a tree, given fifty lashes, and have their heads shaved.

Both those sentenced to lose their ears and the ones sentenced to be whipped asked, as a favor, that they be shot instead of being

Chileans as Their Enemies Saw Them

made to undergo a punishment applicable to robbers and criminals of a different sort. But this petition was refused. The Yankees wanted to torture and humiliate the Chileans more than they did to kill them. All of these penalties were more deserved by those who imposed them than they were by their innocent victims. The Americans wanted the mutilated Chileans to serve as a horrendous warning to all their compatriots in California, and to have the threat of such punishment carried all the way back to their mother country. The Yankees intended, when they harshly sentenced our young men to be whipped, to make them suffer shame (in addition to pain) as honorable young men would on seeing themselves subjected to such punishment as was usually applied only to the basest of criminals. The Americans' studied hatred and insatiable desire for vengeance made them determined to outrage the dignity and gentlemanly feelings that they themselves lacked, but which their captives had, and thus subject their victims to mental as well as physical suffering. Such was the condition of the Chileans in captivity on the night of December 31.

Chileans and other aliens in the rest of the area had no better luck. While preparations were being made to welcome in the New Year at Calaveras with a bloody sacrifice of these condemned men, similar things were going on in Stockton, in Sonora, in Dry Diggins, in Sacramento, and in San Francisco to celebrate the holiday by mass violence against aliens. In Stockton, control was still in the hands of those who seized power in the excitement that was generated by the capture of the Chileans and the spreading of calumnies against them. The same things that had happened months before on the Fourth of July (a holiday well remembered by all the foreigners) threatened to break out again with the coming of the New Year. The Yankees seemed to choose festive days when they wanted to renew their Sicilian Vespers. In Stockton, armed parades led by a trumpet and drum roamed the streets, carrying out all sorts of hostilities against aliens. Twice in one night, between ten and one o'clock, they attacked the residence of a Mr. Sparrow, one of the most respected Americans, who was guilty of protecting the Chileans and of trying to hide some of those who had escaped the second seizure of the Chileans near Stockton. Many foreigners were wounded that night, and two Mexicans were killed at a dance held at the edge of town. The Americans had heard that there were to be many Chileans, Peruvians, and Mexicans gathered there.

There was another disturbance on the Sacramento River at the Mormon camp on December 31, which involved Yankees and Frenchmen. The San Francisco newspapers on January 2 carried reports of this, in which more than twenty persons were said to have died. The coincidence of these events makes one feel certain that the perpetrators of these crimes had arranged the day and even the hour for launching these attacks.

A deed of horrifying barbarism took place at about the same day at Dry Diggins. The Yankees found a Mexican and two Chileans in a state of intoxication; they were at a tavern trying to buy more of the liquor they had got earlier in the day. It was eight o'clock at night and the tavern keeper had closed up so he could have his dinner. The Chileans and the Mexican were good friends of the man who was away, and relying on this they opened the door, which was not locked, and took the bottles they were after. Some Americans saw them come out with the bottles in their hands and, not seeing the owner about, they seized them as thieves. Next day a trial with six or eight jurymen, all Yankees, was held, and fifteen minutes later the three unhappy men were marched off to be hanged, each carrying his own rope with the noose already about his neck. In vain the three men, now sober, promised to pay whatever was asked for the bottles they had taken, not as robbers but in confidence and as a joke. Equally unavailing were the pleas of the tavern owner who backed up what the men were saying, declared he had every confidence in them, declared they had done the same thing before many times and had always paid him later. All was in vain. The three unfortunate men were hung without mercy, and their bodies were left hanging for many days afterward from the oak tree where they had been executed. Let the reader decide—even granting that the taking of the four bottles was wrong—whether it was a crime bad enough to merit the death penalty.

At Judge Coller's camp, some few minutes after the Chileans had been informed of the sentence of mutilation and death imposed on them, a party of four to six Americans trooped in from the Mokelumne placer. They were told about the sentence the jury had just given, and about the plan to carry it out the following day. Almost with one voice they broke out in violent protest, condemning the imposition of a sentence so cruel it would shock any sane man's conscience, and declaring such a procedure null and void. We shall see what this opposition by honest Americans from Mokelumne led to, and how the tragedy ended.

Death of Terán, Ursúa, and Cárdenas. Torment and memorable behavior of Terán. The mutilation of Yáñez and his companions. The cruel execution of the sentence of lashing upon the other young men.

Even after organized government had been set up in California, the authorities still did nothing to punish the men who carried out the crimes committed at Calaveras. They ought at least tried to repair the grievous damage done to respect for law and order when those men were allowed to do such monstrous deeds with impunity. Later, by invoking lynch law, Californians would reestablish the secure order and peace the entire state enjoys today. Inexorable vigilante justice took care of all crimes, even the smallest. It put an end to the incendiaries who had devastated cities so often in the past, to the many bands of robbers whose insolence rose to such a level that hordes and gangs of burglars took on the guise of respectable business establishments with managers, departments, bookkeepers, treasurers, etc. There at the foot of the gallows, and facing six thousand spectators, Jenkins confessed the way he had set up his own organization during the six preceding months, how his dependents were paid, and how useful bookkeepers and treasurers were in his nefarious business. Lynch law established control over all criminal elements, the incendiaries, thieves, murderers, rapists, crooked judges, corrupt tax collectors—they were all treated without pity. Only the crimes at Calaveras, performed by men inured to robbery and murder, by the most scandalous bandits, were permitted to mock that inexorable tribunal.

It cannot be said that the Vigilance Committee was unable to deal with the perpetrators of those deeds, or that it did not know about them; for the papers had described all those deeds in detail. In its heavy and multifarious labors it might not have concerned itself with the crimes of three or four bandits, but it is incomprehensible how it could have overlooked the fact that the Yankees of Calaveras had set themselves up as a separate government, had denied the legal authority of California and even that of the United States, had confiscated property and money, and had stained itself with blood. Public dignity demanded just satisfaction for those who were wronged at Calaveras more than it did for anything else that outraged it, because those criminals had mocked the rightful authorities and violated the rights guaranteed to every alien or immigrant to the country.

The arrival of the Americans from Mokelumne stirred up a genuine storm at Coller's camp. If they did not succeed in saving the lives of the Chileans, at least they got the sentence passed on Terán and his comrades changed into something less cruel and barbarous. In defending the rights of the Chileans they almost came to blows. Their attitude did influence some members of the jury. "Four Eyes," for example, let Maturano live, in a show of generosity and gratitude for kindnesses he said he had been shown himself when he was a prisoner at Stockton. No one else, though, was let off and no change was made except that in the mode of execution; all else went on as planned. The first thing they did was to administer the whippings. They lashed the Chileans with all the ferocity of savages with victims to torture. Our young men pleaded vainly to be shot rather than dishonored; the Yankees were indifferent or pretended they did not understand. One fourth of them were absolute sadists. After the victim was in position they applied the lash without caring whether they cut the flesh or shattered the skull of the poor devil. One by one the Chileans had their hands tied up to an overhanging branch so that their feet barely touched the ground, and then they were whipped so that blood spurted from their lungs. The woman, of whom we spoke earlier, watched the spectacle in as cold blooded a manner as the worst of the Yankees.

Thus did the Americans greet the New Year, in a presentation that even they themselves would have to admit was half-tragic, half-comic. Men would have to be both wild beasts and cowards to have staged such a farcical trial and followed it by such merciless sadism. "Listen to the brave fellows," they shouted when, in the midst of the torture the Chileans were suffering, one of them let a cry of pain escape his lips. After the whippings, carried out to the very letter, Ignacio Yáñez was to undergo the third penalty, that of losing his ears; to be followed in turn by his two fellow sufferers—after they had been whipped and had their heads shaved. I still shudder, remembering the screams of those poor men as they were so barbarously mutilated. An American armed with a huge

knife came to carry out the sentence. The condemned men begged
on their knees as a last supreme favor that they be shot, but pleading
was useless with those bandits and they did not even bother to
listen. Three or four of them held the first victim and the executioner cut off his ears. The cutting was followed by a cry of pain
such as one might hear in the last agony of a martyr. The ear
with a part of the cheek was in the hand of the executioner who,
after a moment, threw it aside and went after the other ear with
the coldest insensitivity. A sea of blood inundated the face and
clothing of the poor fellow, giving him a look more horrible than
you can imagine. The horror of losing the second ear was not so
great because the victim had fainted. But what must have been
the torture and terror of those who were waiting their turn as they
watched the monstrous act!

It is not possible to dwell on the account of those exquisite cruelties by the Americans. The fate that awaited Terán and his friends
was even worse because they had to undergo many tortures before
death, and all without the comforts of religion; religion which alone
can make such sufferings bearable, and help a man rise above mar-
tyrdom and any physical or moral evils. One of the Chileans who
was to die with Terán had his son with him, a boy of eight or
ten; but the sobbing pleas of the innocent boy could not soften
or inspire pity for his father in such men as they were. Just one
glimpse of that scene of sorrow between a son and his father should
have affected the most barbarous and pitiless of executioners. What
would become of the boy, left an orphan among such men? Who
would be a father to him, direct him away from a life of infamy
and crime, when he had been exposed to the perverse example
of those men and watched his own father die? This thought must
have tortured the last hour of the poor father. Nevertheless the
son had to be present at the execution of his own father.

The three condemned men were brought out to an open space
with fifty armed riflemen standing around. The Chileans were to
be shot but the firing squad had not been picked. All of them were
to demonstrate their marksmanship with the chests of the Chileans
as targets. It was as though the Americans intended to spare no
suffering whatsoever to their victims until they were dead. The
spot picked for the execution was a mile, more or less, from the
house of the judge, and the prisoners were made to walk there
after all the torment they had been put through during the last

Mokelumne Hill from "Our Inland Towns"

twelve days. Terán spoke briefly to the others during the march to encourage them; he never lost his calm, even when one of his comrades collapsed; he bent over and helped him up before anyone else could do so. Oddly the prisoners were not bound, probably so they could get through the difficult places they had to cross. Three or four of those who had been whipped had to witness the execution of their comrades so they could report on it to other Chileans in all its details.

When the execution site was reached, Terán in his own name and in that of his comrades offered money if they were let go, and promised to leave Calaveras and even California and go back to his own country. The Yankees did not believe he had any money after having been robbed twice and put no faith in his offer. The boy's father in turn said he would give thirty ounces of gold that he had if they would let him take his son out of California. The Yankees asked him whether he had that much gold. He answered, yes; he had it in a secret pocket that had escaped the searching. The Americans took it, then told him he could not be let go but they would give the gold to his son. The poor boy no more got the gold than he was ever to see his father again—except in the next world.

Terán was infuriated at seeing what was happening and said in a low voice to his companions, "Give me a knife and, by God, if I have to die I will kill three or four of those devils and die fighting." No one answered him. The other Chileans were afraid the Yankees might have heard him and would take some special vengeance on all of them because of his attitude. Terán repeated his request two or three times. He felt that even they were abandoning him. But what could they do? What he wanted was impossible; no one had any weapons. When the Americans came to tie him, Terán turned to them and said, "Give me a dagger and then you can kill me any way you choose." Some were annoyed, others paid no heed, and all went on with their work. Terán, seeing he was going to die, then asked for a pencil and paper so he could write a few words to his family. One of the Yankees dug a piece of paper out of his pack and gave it to him along with a pencil. Terán wrote on both sides of the sheet, and the Yankee promised to give the letter to the other Chileans when they were released. I am afraid the letter no more reached his family than the gold did the boy. No one knew what he had written, but his friends said he had wanted to leave his property to his brother, and earlier had told them he would like to make his will.

Finally Terán, Damián Ursúa, and Francisco Cárdenas were tied to oak trees. It is sad to write this; they had wanted to go back to their country and see their native soil, their families, and friends once more, but they had only a few minutes of life left. Death was to be their whole future. The most pathetic thing of all was the death of the boy's father. He embraced his son with tears and many words of tenderness and sorrow. But not even this most hallowed and solemn grief affected the Yankees. They separated the two and began the execution. They shot from a distance of fifty feet, not all at once but one after another. This intensified the suspense because some bullets struck and others missed, and firing successively that way only strung out the agony. But I will not prolong the harrowing of the sensibilities of their parents and fellow countrymen by dwelling upon the details of their suffering. Let me only add that the Chileans who had to bury the men found fifteen bullet holes in Terán and about the same number in the other two.

The Chilean workers were held for several weeks and made to cook for the Americans. The orphaned boy they kept permanently as a slave. The whipped and mutilated Chileans were free to leave, but for several days not one of them could move.

These tragic events took place three years ago. Coller is today a rich and respected American citizen and holds the legitimate title of a judge in Double Springs. Nickleson, or "Four Eyes," is a licensed doctor of medicine in Marysville. The area where this happened is populated today by farming families from New Orleans. A traveler who goes past the camp at Mokelumne toward Melones will find the ruins of the Chilean buildings in Chile Gulch on the Calaveras. A mile farther on he will see three crosses that the pious survivors erected in the names of their fallen countrymen.[3] There is an inscription: "Say the Our Father and a Hail Mary for the souls of the Chileans who were killed here on January 1, 1850." There is no other memorial, and in years to come, when the crosses have crumbled away, these men will exist only in legend.

3. There is a bronze plaque at Chile Gulch today.

Escena de California
Dibujo de Vicente Pérez Rosales

California Scene

PEDRO ISIDORO COMBET
1816-1867

Very little information is available on Combet, a surprising fact in view of a genius for comedy that strongly recalls Mark Twain. He was born in France, probably in Normandy if one can rely on allusions in his writing. When he came to Chile is uncertain, but he resided for many years in Santiago, where he operated a book store and a bindery. He also, at some period, managed a food store in the capital.

In 1850 he came to Valparaíso, the port of Santiago, with the intention of sailing to California to take advantage of the opportunities offered by the Gold Rush. In this he was merely doing what many of his Chilean countrymen also were doing. His luck in the mines seems to have been no better than theirs, and he returned to Chile in 1851, having spent a little more than a year in California.

He is described as a portly gentleman with a smiling and genial expression. A caricature of Combet was used to advertise a gourmet eating house in Santiago. His manner is said to have been frank and engaging, a characterization that the reader will find entirely believable.

His sketches of California were published in El Museo of Santiago in 1853.

MEMORIES OF CALIFORNIA

Views of the Placers

There were twelve of us, all miners or, better yet, washers of gold, gathered around the tent of Rondeau (a hunter from the forests of Canada) on one of those beautiful summer nights that are among the prodigies of California.

We were there to remind him of the promise he had made several days before that he would tell us about a bear hunt in which he had just managed to save his skin.

We were all sitting on the ground around a big fire of oak logs, and had a kettle, full of water for tea, set on a grating of three iron bars. At one side, in a sailor's tool bag that had once been white, was some discolored sugar; on the other was a tray full of hardtack each of us had contributed, and which therefore represented the products of many nations. They were so dry and soiled, though, that Lucullus would never have served them at one of his better banquets.

The fire, shining on faces more or less covered with dust and grime, gave us a reddish diabolical appearance such as makeup men give to actors in such operas as Robin Hood or Robert the Devil. Though we tried to speak correctly, most of us (with the exception of Law and myself) said "knot" when we meant to say "tie," or "stop" instead of "it's enough." Someone said "The kettle boils, I believe," and got back the reply, "It does not boil." They were all good men, but their jargon did suggest that none of them had ever served as a secretary of a school or an embassy.[1]

"Papa" Rondeau, with his family grouped around him, dominated the meeting. He was seated on an empty box that had once, long before, held twelve bottles of brandy, and he seemed to be concentrating and probing his memory to recall the story he had promised us. He was a man of about fifty, rather tall, and you could see in him that balance of nervous energy and physical

---

1. Unfortunately the point of this comment is lost in translation.

[153]

strength that marks a man of courage, and which must have served
him well in the calling he had followed before the Gold Rush.
His black eyes, under heavy eyebrows, had a determined expression;
and when he used them to emphasize his points they flashed with
a vitality that caught your attention. You could recognize in him
a man whose entire life in the woods had been a victorious war
against the animals of the forest, the kind of man Fenimore Cooper
sketched so well in *The Prairie* and *The Last of the Mohicans*.
Shrewdness, will power, and strength showed in his expressions.
His speech betrayed his Norman ancestry. He was a man of the
eighteenth century, with all the superstitions of that period, like
all French Canadians today who were cut off from the mother
country. They have trouble pronouncing the name of Napoleon
and those of his famous victories. Their flag is still the white banner
of the Lilies, and their motto remains "Religion, King and Law"—
an anachronism they give voice to with the same sincerity as their
fathers. They put the King before the Law—poor Canadians!

Rondeau had left Canada some five years before and come to
California overland with a hunting party. He was working for an
American company, gathering furs—beaver, marten, otter, and
fox—for which a good market existed in Europe. He had been
traveling five months amid numberless dangers and in all weathers,
sleeping on the ground, going without food, and braving savage
tribes such as the Sampiche, Cheyenne, Sioux, Enervos, and Black-
feet, peoples who did not have a shirt to cover their hides. When
his party reached the area of the placers they found tribes whose
customs were peaceful, and they settled down among them. He
had stayed there four years and collected a good deal of fine fur.
One day Rondeau had seen a young maiden being chased by a
wolf on the wooded banks of one of the branches of the Mokelumne
River. Quick as thought he had taken aim at the fierce beast and
killed it with one shot. The Indians were so grateful to him that
the chief gave him the girl in marriage. Today he is the father
of six children, half white, half Indian, who mumble in a French
that L'Homond and the forty sages would have some difficulty in
understanding.[2]

Madame Rondeau (whose name, Yathue, means Sky) is one of
the most piquant representatives of her race—but by our standards

2. Abbé Charles-Francois L'Hommond, author of *Grammaire Latine*.

she is a bit of a monster. She is short and fat, a build no age has
ever thought flattering. The expression on her face is somewhat
stolid, her mouth is frightfully large, and her lower lip resembles
the cornice of a Doric temple. Her chin looks as though it were
proud of its overhang. She wears a man's boots, and mounts a horse
like a man; but, I am told, she is a good mother and a faithful
wife.

"Excuse me, Papa Rondeau, but for a quarter of an hour you
have acted like the captain who wanted to lecture his passengers
when they asked for good bread instead of the bad they'd been
given."

This remark by Lafaye reminded Papa Rondeau that we were
all waiting to hear from him. He shook his head twice as though
to clear his throat for a long tale. He then related his story in
a Canadian style that I will try to convey to the reader, with only
such changes as are absolutely necessary to make it intelligible:

"In 1839, on a rainy January day, our party had made camp
on the banks of the Merced River (at a spot Mexican miners today
call the Arroyo Seco) to wait for a change in the weather to bring
an end to our discomfort. We had been enduring the rains for two
months—that is, ever since we had reached California.

"The rain had been nearly continuous, except for very brief intervals. As a result, my brave friends and I were in a pitiable state.
Our food was spoiled and the country too boggy for travel. As we
had no hope of being able to work (that is, to hunt) for fox and
other animals, we had decided to pitch our tent there, to repair
our carts and to rest our animals, until better weather would permit
us to go on to the Sacramento River. There was a Russian (fur)
company there that we planned to join so we could work together.[3]

"The first nights we spent there would have been unendurable
for men less experienced than we were. In the shriek of the wind
that whistled through the pines there were mingled the howling
of wolves, the yapping of jackals, and the growl of bears who
seemed to be angry at our invasion of their territories. However,
a few gunshots in the direction where they were loudest and the
barking of our hunting dogs kept them away from our camp.

"On the fourth day the rain stopped. The sun rose radiant. It
gilded the green crests of the mountains, and its luminous rays

---

3. This is an error. The Russians were at Fort Ross on the California coast.

fell through the trees upon our tent. Happiness then was reborn in the men of our party. It had been three weeks since we had seen the sun, and we were feeling as gloomy as the weather. After we had strung up some ropes and hung our equipment out to dry, I said to Touret:

" 'Tell me, Touret, wouldn't you like to go pay a visit to our hosts in the woods? I've had my gun loaded for three days and I don't want to leave it that way.'

" 'Let's go, Rondeau, but on one condition, or rather three: we won't go before breakfast; we'll go alone; we'll take only our rifles and shoot only bears.'

The tobacco chewer (Lafaye) interrupted, "What a man Touret must have been! Caramba! I'd certainly like to take a drink with a man like that."

I spoke up at once, "Come on now, Lafaye. Be quiet, and let Papa Rondeau go on." We shoved the log further into the fire, and the old hunter took up the story again, after having accepted a glass of brandy one of us offered him.

"So I said, 'I agree, Touret,' and I held out my hand. 'I am not afraid, but if you want to test my courage, that's fine with me. You'll see.'

"After we shook hands we both got ready for our expedition against the bears.

"Touret was a good hunter, the bravest of the brave. He could recognize his prey at a great distance. He had a sure eye and he knew the tracks and the habits of all the animals. He could point out to you and identify for you the spoor of an animal on a path, tell you what variety it was, whether it was traveling fast or slowly, whether it was wounded, and even how old it was. If the spoor disappeared from the path, he would point out where it had left by showing you where the animal had left an almost imperceptible footprint and where branches had been pushed apart at its passing. All of these things were certain and positive signs. He could look at the kinds of trees, shrubs, and plants, and tell you what animal frequented which places because it was used to feeding on the seeds or fruits. Casting a knowing eye over the terrain of hills and woods, he would indicate the spot where the animal was apt to be—and he was rarely wrong!

"So, after we had eaten our salt meat and biscuit, we filled our flasks with brandy to the degree each preferred and shouldered our guns. We set out toward a ridge covered with oaks that stretched off to our left about two miles from camp.

"It was noon when we reached the foot of the slope. The sun was gone behind large grey clouds that had gathered around the crest. A stiff cold wind was violently shaking the branches, still wet, of the huge and lugubrious conifers, stripping them of foliage. And in the stentorian sounds of nature there were mingled now and then the mournful howl of hungry wolves and the discordant yapping of jackals (or coyotes, as they call them in California). Everything indicated that the rain was about to start again.

"I said to Touret, 'Let's go back to camp.'

" 'No, by the Virgin of Montreal! Now that we've come this far we should go on up the hill. I want to dine on the ham of one of those long-haired gentlemen. We have,' he said, casting an eye on the state of the sky, 'more than an hour before the rain starts, and I think that's enough time for us to finish our business.'

"We began climbing slowly because the sogginess of the ground made it difficult. Now and again we slipped, and the noise we made set rabbits to scurrying away. As you know, they are not scarce. Touret, though, had a bear in mind; and I would not have shot at any other animal than a bear for anything in the world.

"Nevertheless, as we pushed on up into the thickness of the woods I don't know what kind of vague uneasiness began to come over me. The wind kept on screaming, but the cawing of crows who darted about in the treetops was the only thing that disturbed the solitude. As for me, this was my introduction to the hunt, and I knew no more about it than I had learned from listening to my comrades. I was a soldier in battle for the first time. I was not really afraid, but I couldn't explain the feeling I had.

"We had just finished crossing with great difficulty a little grove of young conifers when Touret stopped me by taking me by the arm, putting his finger to his lips to tell me I mustn't speak. Then, with an avid glance in all directions, he indicated some bushes of wild cherry about a hundred feet away, and taking his hand from my arm he pointed to the cherries and said in a low voice:

" 'Do you see, Rondeau?'

" 'See what?'

" 'Over there.'

"Holy Virgin! Following the direct line his arm indicated I saw a she-bear with two cubs.

" 'Well, Rondeau, didn't I tell you we were going to get some ham from those gentlemen?' he said in a low voice. 'But there is a problem. The fact that the father of those cubs is not with his better half makes me nervous. But she indicates he is not far away. I want you to stay here so he won't catch me by surprise. One of us is enough to start the affair. Get ready for action.'

"I knew by his words that the slight pallor the sight of those three monsters had given me had been the reason for his decision. 'No, a thousand times no!' I said, 'my place is beside you. If you think because the view of those three monsters startled me for a moment I am not a brave hunter, you're mistaken, Touret.'

"I had spoken out vigorously in spite of the signals of my good friend that I should keep my voice low. That was why the she-bear, having heard the sounds, began to dart uneasy and ferocious looks in our direction. 'You see, Rondeau, your voice and movements are going to make us lose the finest prize I've ever seen in all my years as a bear hunter in Canada.' And pressing my arm fiercely with his nervous hand he made me crouch down lower behind the only thicket close to us. It was a very sensible move when you consider that, because of the nature of the ground, the bears were masters; and they could easily have seen us without this precaution.

"Then we arranged, but now in a low voice, that Touret would go on ahead to begin the attack, and I would follow him about fifty feet to the rear in case the male bear, which we imagined was not far away, saw that his mate and offspring were being attacked, and came to their rescue.[4] Touret moved off and began to use the skillful tactics that had served him in a hundred previous hunts. He slipped along cautiously from tree to tree, sometimes dragging himself along the ground, in such a way that he raised no suspicion of his nearness. When he was about forty feet from the she-bear he vanished in a thick clump of bushes.

"Suddenly the she-bear stood up on her hind feet, and then bounded toward Touret. I heard his gun go off but I couldn't see anything. The bushes were too dense. The two cubs, after a momen-

---

4. A he-bear does not guard his family. Quite the contrary, he is a menace to them and is driven away by the mother if he approaches.

tary paralysis, ran to help their mother. At that moment I had a moment of dizziness. A cold sweat ran down my cheeks, and my heart was beating as though it would break out right through my chest. I was horrified at what was happening when I heard a cry, 'Help me, Rondeau. Hurry!' I ran at once to the spot from which these cries of alarm came.

"As I rounded the bushes I heard the deafening sounds of the struggle, and a few steps farther on I glimpsed through the branches three red figures rolling on the ground together. I felt sure that my companion was as good as dead. Then the feeling came on me I have always had when hunting in moments of danger. I became brave. I ran boldly up to the animal, and seeing my friend stretched on the ground with no sign of life, I shot the she-bear, which had poor Touret between her feet, and left her dead on the spot. I would have shot the cubs, too, but I could think of nothing but trying to save my friend if there was still a chance; the shouts I gave when I saw their mother fall had sent them scooting off up the mountain.

"The wind was increasing and a few drops of cold rain began to fall.

"I ran to my companion, found him stretched out, face down, and covered with blood. His leather clothing also was bloody, and I could see the deep marks of the bear's claws on his neck. I thought him dead, but when I got down to him he was still breathing. I called out to him, 'Touret, Touret, I'm your friend, Rondeau, the one you called.' He did not answer, but I took out my flask, turned him over onto his back, and let him smell the brandy. It seemed to do him good, because he began to breathe more freely. Seeing this I put the bottle to his mouth and let him swallow a few drops.

"I was paler than he was and kept saying to myself, 'What a fine mess you made, Rondeau. If you hadn't suggested this damned hunt I would never have thought of it.' My friends, as God is my witness, I was crying like a baby.

"While I was letting my liquor fall drop by drop into his mouth, though, I saw color returning to his face. His lips seemed to be trying to articulate some words. I spoke to him again then, and he answered by squeezing my hand and heaving a deep sigh.

"I had not noticed before that he had a wide gash on his chest. I took out my handkerchief, wet it in the rain that was coming down in torrents, then doused it with brandy and spread it on the wound. I did the same thing with his handkerchief. I used a neck cloth to cover the wound on the back of his neck.

"The body of the she-bear was lying beside me. I sat down on it and raised my friend's head to my knees. The rain had not stopped and the cold wet wind chilled me to the bone. 'Now, now, Touret. Now my good friend, courage.' At that he opened his eyes and said in a weak and faltering voice, 'Courage and I are old comrades, my brave Rondeau; but I have lost a lot of blood. The bear was too much for me. Get me over to that oak tree so we can rest till the rain stops.' He got up and, hanging on to my arms, managed to reach the tree whose spreading branches gave us a little protection.

" 'Those damned bears, how they clawed at me,' he said as he began to come back to himself, 'They knew you were close by so they wanted to tear my chest open.'

"It was very foolish of us to try to attack a she-bear with two half-grown cubs. They are so hungry that time of year that they would have eaten Touret if I had not got there so fast.

" 'It's all right,' I said, 'We'll talk about it later.'

" 'Oh this is nothing. Apart from a little sting I feel in my wounds and some weakness, it doesn't hurt at all. Meanwhile the quicker we get back to camp, the better—I'm very cold, Rondau, and I'm all soaked with blood and water.'

"Fifteen minutes later we left the victorious battlefield which had cost us so much. The crows were going to take advantage of it, to judge by the number that had assembled over our heads in the little while we had remained there.

"Next day Touret was better, and, under pressure from all the men of our party whose own lives were filled with interesting incidents of this sort, he told us what follows:

" 'After I'd got fifty feet ahead of Rondeau I went on with the greatest possible caution toward the spot where the bears were. The she-bear was very restless and kept looking around in all directions. No doubt she had sensed our presence. Nevertheless I went on because I had only two charges in my gun and I didn't want to miss. At thirty feet I was crouched behind some bushes, where Rondeau found me later, and there with the utmost care I took my aim. I pulled the trigger, but the gun did not fire because the charge had got wet. Quick as lightning I got the gun reloaded, worried by the fact the first had not fired. But the bear had heard and came charging down on me. Then we started to battle, one to one. She was up on her hind legs with her paws stretched out, but she was so excited and angry that I managed with my usual dexterity to keep away from her. I felt vainly for my hunting knife, but Rondeau and I had agreed not to carry any. So I had to use the stock of my gun to fend her off while I took advantage of the chance to call for Rondeau to help me. Then one of the cubs charged me, and, trying to avoid it I stumbled on the branches of the brambles and fell down. God and Rondeau alone know what happened next.'

"A cry for a war of vengeance against the bears went up from all the hunters. We all started out to find the she-bear—to the chagrin of the crows who had eaten a good part already. And we made a jacket of the fur for the gallant Touret.

"Two months later, when we started out for Sacramento, we had seventy-eight bear skins piled in our carts."

One of our listeners then spoke up, "And Touret, did he make a contribution to this campaign of destruction?"

Rondeau replied, "So much so that half of the bears, at least, had been shot by him; only he took good care when he went hunting that he had his hunting knife along."

It had grown late, and as we were in the habit of rising early to get to work—once the day heated up, work was impossible until about four in the afternoon—I rose hurriedly because Triplon, an ex-whaler, had begun to speak. "There are extraordinary things that happen when you are fishing as well as when hunting," he said, "but all you need is courage. Those who don't have it can't do anything. Now, one fine day like this—"

I said goodnight to the group, shook the hand of the ex-hunter, bowed to the lady with the architectonic lip, and retired to my tent to sleep. Despite the fascination the tale of Papa Rondeau had exerted, I was suddenly transported in thought to Chile, and memories of it flooded back with extraordinary sweetness. And that very night I made up my mind to return to that dear land and to my relatives and friends.

We will search in vain the annals of all the nations of the earth to find deeds so odd and peculiar as those that happened in California during the immense migration from all parts of the world to that area between the years 1849 and 1850.

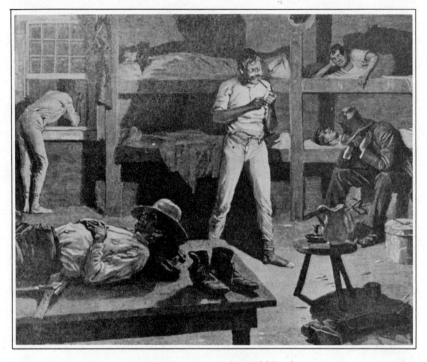

Boarding House in the Gold Rush

The truth is, no country has ever offered such a great fountain of wealth (a powerful force that always attracts immigrants), which was at the same time so easy to exploit, as this new El Dorado. That is why all neighboring countries envied her.

Nevertheless, in the epoch of which we speak, those who were found there were for the most part Americans, Mexicans, Chileans, and Frenchmen. These last came mainly from South America, as did the other Europeans who were represented there in small numbers. Europe itself was left behind in this mass migration because it was so far away and the cost of travel was so great.

After San Francisco, the new city of San José was the focal point of all the miners who had become disillusioned because they had not found in the mines, even after from four to six months, the ten-thousand pounds of gold the newspapers had promised they would. Marquet and I were among this number, and that is why we came to San José.

It was a Sunday. Our entry was anything but a triumphal procession. My costume was a red wool undershirt of the kind worn by
those who say "port side" instead of "left," and Chilean underpants
appropriate to those who say "nyo" for "señor." I was wearing
a Mexican sombrero as big as an umbrella and capable of shading
a hay wagon. Marquet had on the same kind of costume, but with
one little touch of elegance unknown there—a necktie!

Oh Marquet, luxury will be the ruin of you!

It was time for Mass when we reached the plaza, and the bells
were calling the faithful to church. We had a chance, therefore,
to see many Californios of both sexes, a people we had hardly seen
at all upon our arrival at San Francisco. Everything seemed to
radiate a feeling of happiness. The people here had become rich
by selling building lots at the rate of one-thousand pesos a block;
before the coming of the Americans that amount of land would
have brought only six pesos. The men dressed like the Mexicans,
except that their sarapes or mantles hung down to their feet and
were of velvet adorned with wide, gold-lace embroidery. But what
most caught our attention, naturally, were the women, who, if not
usually very pretty, nevertheless had all the grace of Andalusian
women. Their clothing showed very clearly that fashion magazines
had not yet arrived in San José, because all you could see were
dresses of yellow, green, or white silk. Furthermore, on their tiny
shoes they had designs of birds, flaming hearts, or flowers—some
with initials in the center. These were gifts of very loving husbands,
no doubt, because it is unlikely that anyone but a husband would
dare to put a flaming heart on shoes. I must tell you, dear reader
(this is a new style: to call your reader your friend; it is an indirect
way to flatter him without having him hiss back at you)—to repeat,
I must tell you that all Californios are shoemakers. They had to
be because, before the mines were discovered, only two or three
ships a year stopped at San Francisco. You must not, therefore,
think this a curious kind of gift.

They wore the classic mantilla the women of Spain and Lima
still wear, and with the same grace and coquetry.

Marquet had run into one of his friends, so I left him because
I wanted to go to Mass. With this in mind I went around to the
rear of the church where I had seen a little pond. There I washed
my face and cleaned my shoes. I turned my shirt inside out, ran
my fingers through my hair, and, setting on my head my monumen-

tal hat whose brim must have been a cubit wide, I made my way toward the sacred edifice.

It was a High Mass and the subchanters were three of my compatriots, whose clothing was certainly not much better than mine. A fourth man, who was accompanying them on a bass viol, I recognized at once; he was Adolfo de Beauvoison. I had met him in the mines and we used to play music and sing every evening after work was over for the day. He was a young man whose musical education left nothing to be desired. He had just spotted me, and at his signal I took my stand in front of the choir stand and lent my voice to the celebration of the Mass.

The intervals between the singing were filled in by six Mexican musicians. Their instruments were harps, flutes, guitars and violoncellos, and they harmonized perfectly.

Nothing could have been more impressive and picturesque than this gathering of the faithful of all Catholic nations: the types and manners all mixed together. America was represented by the South Americans and Europe by Frenchmen, Italians, Spaniards, and Irishmen.

This assembly of men of many races, wearing the same kind of clothes (wool shirts), and worshipping the same God, all of this did affect me deeply and inspired philosophical ideas in me that the nature and style of these pages do not permit me to dwell on as I should like to do—a descendant of the Normans rubbing elbows with an Indian from Sonora.

The priest gave us in Spanish a sermon that showed he knew very well his parishioners had not read Bossuet, Massilon, or Bourdaloue. He did not speak in high-flown phrases as do priests of little experience dealing with an unlearned flock. Instead he talked of love for religion in clear and simple terms, giving them a glimpse of the temptations and seductions they were going to be exposed to because of the coming of the Americans and Protestantism. He advised them that devotion to work was the true source of wealth, and a sure remedy against vice, and he recommended to them, finally, a tolerance such as the very Americans themselves practiced.

After Mass, Adolfo de Beauvoison introduced me to the priest, who thanked me for having sung the divine office. When Adolfo told him I had sung in the cathedral at Santiago, he proposed that I stay in San José. Accommodations could be found for me during the day, and in the evenings, if I wished, I could teach seven or eight boys to sing. He would give me twenty dollars a week, and I would also be paid for helping out in church services.

I hesitated for a moment, because it is difficult to teach what you hardly know yourself. But on reflection I decided that passing on a part of the knowledge the good Don Bernardo Alcedo had taken the pains to teach me would occupy the boys no more than six months; and then I could give my post to someone with more ability. So I expressed my thanks and accepted. On the following day I was made chapel master and first tenor in the church of San José.

God must have inspired me to go to Mass, for to this act of devotion I owe the reunion with my friend, Adolfo, and meeting the priest whose kindnesses to me were of great importance during my difficulties in California. This worthy ecclesiastic was an enlightened man. He understood the human heart and he was a wise apostle of Christianity. In everything he was frank, ingenuous, and trustful. A man of goodness himself, he could not believe any man would choose to do wrong by his own will and without being forced to it. His generosity was proverbial in San José. He was tolerant without fawning, an ardent defender of his religion and his rights as a minister of the altar in confronting the American authorities; and he was respected by them. The French were his best friends. He had spent three or four years in Paris, enough to familiarize himself with our customs and to learn to speak French with few mistakes. Whenever I read the story of a good priest, the name of don José Pinero comes to mind.

I had twenty dollars a week as chapel master—I was much taken with the title—and furthermore my assistance in ceremonials brought in half again as much. This was not enough, though, for food and minor expenses took all of my regular salary. I was due back in Chile with a fortune by this time (*El Mercurio* of Valparaíso had promised I'd have one). I put my intellectual faculties to work to see whether I could find an honorable way to make some money.

A man's industrial knowledge had the fullest scope there [in California]. Everything was still to be done. This society was not like the sluggish and decrepit ones we had left behind in other countries, in which half the population lives on the sweat of the other half, where you have only to put a pair of glasses on your nose to have people point to you and say, "There is a wise man." In California they do not look at a young man with a pale bald forehead and say, "This is a poet." Instead they would say, "There is a poor fellow who ought to be in the hospital. Why didn't he stay at home in his own country?" A bad journalist or magazine writer who put the pompous words, "Literary Man," on his calling cards would die of hunger. Why?

The reason is that society does not recognize any kind of competence except the practical, industrial sort. If one went to them with a beautiful translation of Homer or Virgil in one's hand they would say, "Those were good men, no doubt, but they must have been stupid to waste all that time writing. We need some cabbage; have you got any to sell?" What can a man with an education say to that? What he had better do is plant cabbage and carrots. That is how I got to meet, on several occasions, some very distinguished writers for the French or Chilean press: buying lettuce or parsley.

The gentleman who brought peons from Mexico or Chile had to call them "my boys," and see to it that they got plenty of suet and chili in their food; otherwise they might have abandoned him— and he would have been helpless if he had to handle a pick and shovel himself. Merchants in California were not very different from miners; they wore the same wool shirts, were friendly and amiable with their customers, and offered a glass of brandy to workers and sailors when they came in to buy (and paid them very well in addition).

You did not see there that businessman's pose of self-importance that makes them come out of their houses holding an open letter in front of their faces (which of course they are not reading), or induces them to walk along with hand to forehead as if engaged in such deep thought they cannot interrupt it to greet anyone, not even important persons. Such merchants are simply as churlish as they are vain. In California they would make fun of them. None are more insolent to such gentry than people who do not depend on them. There are aspects of this that do not lack spiritual significance.

Such was the society in which I found myself mingling in San José. I had to forget about writing books in a land where a mention of Homer brought the reply, "carrots." I had to ask myself, "What can you do?" After reflecting a while and making an exhaustive list of my various abilities, I ended by agreeing that I was capable of nothing. Meeting a Mr. Napoleon Charpin that night rescued me from this embarrassing plight. When I described to him the dilemma I found myself in, so far as choosing an art or profession in San José, he said to me, "If you want manual labor I am going to build an adobe house and the count of Narbonne will lay the adobes. You can help him to mix the mud, and I'll give you five dollars a day and board at my house."

Oh Napoleon, name twice great, I bless you!

I accepted.

The following morning at dawn I had my trousers rolled up above the knees and was treading the mud mixture, singing the cavatina from Romeo and Juliet: *"la tremenda ultrice spada. . . ."*

At breakfast my boss complimented me and said he was satisfied with my work because I had reduced the mud to the consistency of butter. This showed there were great hopes that I could make my fortune in this line of work. "Many an adobe layer has begun by mixing mud," he told me confidentially. I do not know why I agreed mechanically that many a marshal of France has risen, knapsack on back.[5]

I couldn't sleep that night. I dreamed I was on a scaffold, a master adobe brick layer, fitting adobes to the top of an edifice I had just finished. Oh, noble ambition! Open to all generous hearts! Source of such great hopes and misfortunes! How beautiful that night seemed in which, muddy as I was, and sleeping on a mat of mangy furs, you deigned to visit me!

Eight days later I went to thank Mr. Carpin. Then I took a stroll down the streets of San José with a ruler in my hand. I dreamed the night before that I was an adobe builder making twelve dollars a day. Such builders were scarce then, and I had gone only a little way when a French gentleman came up to me and asked me if I were one. I did not even pale. "As you can see," I replied, "I am carrying a plane and ruler." "Well," he said, "that doesn't make it as obvious as that two and two are four. However, you have a figure that shows well enough it must be your trade. What would you charge to build me two bedrooms and a kitchen at the back of my store?" "Well," I said in turn, "that depends. I'll have to see the ground you want to build on and know the size of the rooms."

"Good, let's go and take a look."

"Let's go."

---

5. The reference is to Napoleon's famous remark that a common French soldier carried a marshal's baton in his knapsack.

I figured the length of the two rooms and kitchen at 148 feet. They would be 10 feet wide and 7 feet high.

Next day I tried to find a mud mixer to help me in the job—which had begun to look somewhat difficult. All who applied, though, spoke with such elegance of diction and had such aristocratic manners I was afraid they would resent the kind of work I had for them. Then a Chilean youth showed up whom I had seen as an officer in the civic guard at Santiago. He was one of the sort who never shirked required exercises at the Pampilla so he could take a pleasure stroll down the Alameda; and whose calves tingled with anticipation of the following day when he would take part in the parade at the Plaza de Independencia with the Corpus Christi procession. He said to me with an humble air, "Oh Musiú Combet, I know you, I remember when you lived on Calle Ahumada. You bound a book for me: *The Law of Nations*, by Bello. If you want me to, I can mix mud for you; I know how to do it. I did that kind of work in San Francisco before going to the damned mines."

"You know how to do it?" I expostulated. "What do you mean by that? Do you think you can become a master craftsman by simply pouring water on a mix, and then treading on it for fifteen minutes without real interest? Are you then entitled to exclaim, with your face raised to the sky and all streaked with dirt and sweat, 'I know how to mix mud!' You have to put a lot of study and hard work into this craft to learn how to reduce mud to the consistency of butter. Believe me, Señor Bello is a man I venerate. I bow before him as I would before any man whose talent rises so far above the ordinary level. Nevertheless, even if you knew as much as our holy father, the pope, about his *Law of Nations*, his *Principles of International Law*, his *Castillian Grammar*, and his beautiful verses on the burning of the Compañía—all of that would not make you a true craftsman in mixing mud. Abandon this vanity, which can only injure your case, and, instead, ask me to initiate you in the art of building."

He was hungry, so he submitted. Next morning he was dancing on Chilean cement, and showing a considerable interest and ability in the work. I was worn out trying to look calm when my employer looked at me, and to maintain an air of confidence worthy of a better job. The first row of adobes went down well enough; the second row was off level by an inch; the third row by two inches; and so it went from then on. At the fifth tier I found I'd formed a cornice. I told myself I could fill in the low spots with the mud my assistant was mixing and so cover up the defects. Four days later I demanded in a loud voice that a carpenter be brought to set the lintels of the doors and windows so I could finish the job.

The carpenter came. He knew his business, so he turned to me and said, "You must have been called in to redo this work. The man who put these walls up was certainly no builder. Nothing here is plumb. It will all fall in and bury the people who live here. I'm certainly not going to put any carpentry into these buildings if they are going to stay this way."

"How can it be, my friend, that you are not familiar with this method of building? Have you never been in Chile or other countries where they have earthquakes?"

"No."

"Well, in Chile they don't build any other way." (I humbly beg pardon from Juan, Pedro, and all Chilean builders—blame it on *El Mercurio de Valparaíso* for making those promises.) "This was all carefully planned. Now you seem to me an intelligent man, so I will explain to you the reason why we build this way. We used to build on the plumb, but found it a bad method. The least tremor knocked walls out of plumb—like these. But we found that if you build them out of plumb to begin with, the shaking straightens them up."

"That seems odd. But you must have noticed we don't have any earthquakes in California, so far as I know."

"That's true, my good carpenter, but we ought to take every precaution. If it doesn't happen today, it could tomorrow. Moreover, just between us, my worthy craftsman, if you refuse to set in these lintels you'll do me a lot of damage because nobody will want to hire me from then on. Where are you from?"

"Rouen."

"That's a beautiful city, by my faith. Those are good people. Which wine do you like best, Bordeaux or Burgundy?"

The carpenter could not resist an argument so eloquent, and told me he preferred Bordeaux. So we went to have a bottle at a cafe nearby. There he told me about his birthplace, which I had never seen, and about the *gre-e-a-at* Napoleon.

The following day he did the work.

I was on the scaffolding, happy and satisfied as I watched the good carpenter set the lintels—while he cursed the unevenness of the walls. I was singing at the top of my voice, *"Lorsque mon coeur à fait un choix à moi la belle doit se rendre,"* from Zampa, when I heard these words below me, "What a fine voice, Mister Dare-Devil. We could use him if he were willing." "Admirable," said another voice, "I've never heard better." I turned at once and saw two men looking up at me with an interested expression. Then one of them said, "Aren't you the man who sings in church?"

"I am; and, if it's not too bold of me, I would like to know why you ask."

The other man spoke up. "The reason, my dear sir, is this. When we heard you singing a moment ago I said to my friend, Mister Dare-Devil—whom I would like to present to you—'It can't be; it is not possible that you could be the same person who, last Sunday in church sang the beautiful *Gloria* by an unknown composer which we enjoyed so much. My friend said, 'I'm certain it's him.' 'You're mistaken. The singer last Sunday had a fine voice, but this one is superb. Didn't you hear that low C-flat, so clear and vibrant, the purity of his low register, and how fresh and accented the notes are in his middle range! What a shame! If it only were he,' I said. Mister Dare-Devil, though, was sure you were the same. I wanted to find out for sure, so that is why we came nearer to listen and to ask you."

"Now I can die."

Oh vanity, the weakness of man! A defect found in some women but in all artists. You must believe, my most wise and amiable reader, that in spite of my being a builder, and, even more, in spite of my knowing by heart the fable of the fox and the crow, I opened my wide beak to reply to them in grateful accents. "It is your indulgence toward me that makes you use such words. I'm afraid you would have a hard time convincing me that I possess the artistic qualities that you are trying to apply to me. I repeat to you, I am convinced that these compliments are due simply to excessive kindness on your part, because my musical studies were so brief!"

"So much modesty joined to such great talent does you even more credit. But you should be told that we are artists and capable, therefore, to judge outstanding singers like yourself. You must have heard of O and B, traveling under the pseudonyms of Dare-Devil and Dare-Nothing, whose talents have been recognized throughout France and Portugal. So, well, we have the honor of greeting you, and, if we can be completely frank, we want to tell you that it gives us great distress to see you working as a builder. Your place is not on top of a mason's scaffold but on that of an artist, drunk with applause and triumph after he has held a discerning audience suspended between delirium and frenzy—and—and—."

"You're thirsty, Dare-Nothing," said Dare-Devil when he saw his friend was hung up in the middle of his labyrinthine description of artistic glory.

I was beginning to stiffen with the clay on my cheeks and all over my face. My assistant a few paces away was singing *"a la resbalosa y Zamba"* as he worked. He had almost achieved perfection, thanks to my instructions. He had not understood our conversation on music, however, because he did not know a word of French.

Taking up where he left off, Mr. Dare-Devil said to me, "Shall we have the honor of seeing you after work tonight for two or three hours? We have a project we'd like to lay before you."

"Where?"

"At Mercier's, the best cafe."

"Fine, I'll be there."

"Till tonight then."

"Till tonight."

I returned to work but the adobes seemed heavier than before. I was silent and thoughtful. I had talent! And I owed its discovery solely to the presence of two artists who had admired me for a moment, and who by their frankness had made me blush for the work I was doing.

I wondered how many unknown talents existed in garrets and workshops because they lacked a little support, kindness, and well-being that would make it possible for them to shine in living splendor among men of letters (the great ones). I thought of all the famous names: Galileo, Raphael, Newton, Montgolfier, Bonaparte, etc. Then in sudden retrospection I remembered the ingratitude shown to Columbus; Camoens and the painter, Guibert, dying in the poor house; Robespierre; Saint Helena! Poor humanity. Aretino, despite his bad epigrams, celebrated, praised, and enriched by the great dukes of Italy and by the pope, and winning the homage of Francis I. The apostate, Talleyrand, hypocrite and coward all his life, a man of talent but not genius, nevertheless dying as a man should die!

I, dripping mud, exlaimed, "Poor humanity!"

It must be true that I had talent. I obviously beieved it, standing there thinking about glory and its vicissitudes.

My assistant was working harder and better. I do not know what he was thinking about at that moment—perhaps about some past procession or review. But he glanced up and noticed that I looked sad and pensive. "Don't you feel well, Musiú Combet?" he said. "Perhaps you ought to take a rest. Your health is more important than all the gold of California."

I agreed, so I told him he could stop. We would not work any more that day.

Talent! What a pleasant sound that had in my shameless ears. It was the first time anyone had said that about me.

When night came I went to the Mercier Cafe. There was a dense cloud of smoke that came from the cigarettes of the Mexicans and the Chileans, and from the cigars and pipes of the Americans, Frenchmen, and Germans, so it was difficult to recognize the people who were there. An orchestra in which a cornet and trombone played the chief roles, and which was more sound than music, seemed to stir the crowds gathered at the gaming tables. The only voices you could hear were those of the dealers; if they were French, it was: *"Faites votre jeu, Messieurs,"* and if Americans, "Come along, let us play." The Mexicans and Chileans were the only ones silent. They played only *monte,* and you could lose in one night the fruit of five or six months of hard work in the mines. Pistol shots were not a rarity, for the Yankees killed a man for a mere "yes," or "no," in perfectly cold blood—which is certainly not to their credit.

For several minutes I circulated round the tables looking for Mr. Dare-Devil or Mr. Dare-Nothing. Then I heard coming from a corner a voice I could not help but recognize. It was saying loudly, "Yes sir, I am an artist from head to foot. To your health, dear colleagues." I knew it immediately to be the voice of Mr. Dare-Nothing, and I steered myself toward the spot from which it came.

When he saw me he rose from the table where he was sitting with three or four other individuals and rushed with great enthusiasm to take my hand and invite me to have a drink from two bottles of wine that he ordered from the waiter in a loud voice.

My friend, Adolfo, was there, along with a Señor Baudoin, a self-styled musician who played the bass viol even worse than our artist, Pereira, in Santiago. The presence of Adolfo and the bass

viol player surprised me a great deal, but they explained that the
same two gentlemen had invited them to a meeting at the cafe
that night to talk over a matter that concerned them. "No doubt
we were all here for the same reason," I replied, "for I also had
been asked to come for the same purpose."

"Yes, gentlemen, the same purpose," said Mr. Dare-Devil, "and
I want to—"

"Shut up, my dear friend," Mr. Dare-Nothing interrupted. "You
are a great artisit, a favorite of Apollo, but you will have to agree
with me that you do not have the skill in elocution needed to
explain worthily to these gentlemen the object of our meeting."

Without being disconcerted in the least, Mr. Dare-Devil took
a glass, filled it to overflowing, and said as he handed it to me,
"First do us the kindness of having a drink with us."

This manner of negotiating by drinking a glass of wine at each
dot and comma of the conversation seemed a little odd to me for
such great artists as they declared themselves to be. Still I did
not dare to say a word nor to doubt their talents, for I had both
read and seen that many celebrated artists drew their inspiration
from this nectar: Horace and Apelles, for example. Emile Debreaux

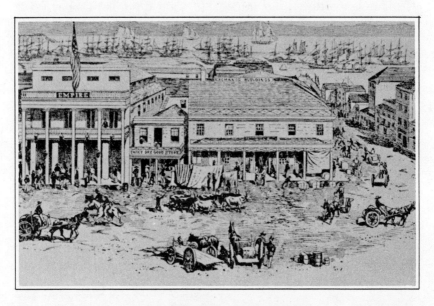

Corner of the Plaza, February 1850

produced divine poetry only on the day following inebriation. Fré-
dérick Lemaître and Roucourt, the two famous dramatic artists,
were inimitable in a scene when they had had four or five glasses
of wine. A friend of mine used to give beautiful commentaries on
Montesquieu's *L'Esprit des Lois* when he had enjoyed two or three
drinks of wormwood.[6] So I kept still and waited.

After drinking, Mr. Dare-Nothing took the floor and spoke, "Dear
colleagues, the purpose of our meeting is to arrange a concert that
Mr. Dare-Devil and I plan to give in San José, with your help.
But, before joining in the venture you may wish to know who we
are and how it happens that artists such as we are should have
left France, the cradle of the arts. That is what I am going to
explain to you."

"Surely you have heard us spoken of in all of France and in
Portugal—"

"And Brazil," added Dare-Devil.

"Shut up," said Dare-Nothing warningly; then he went on, "After
we had toured those two countries and received an infinite number
of crowns and applaudings, we went back to Paris. Then I said
to Dare-Devil, 'Old friend, we still have Italy and Germany to
win laurels worthy of our talent; but I am tired of Europe. What
we need is a new land. I want to test a philosophy of art. I want
to study the reactions of men in the new world to the melodic
chords of a disciple of Pythagoras. If you are willing, we will go
to California and make our names famous to the antipodes."

The bass viol player said, "I had the same—"

"Pardon me, sir. Let me continue. You can speak later," Mr.
Dare-Nothing answered him.

**The account of the travels of these two from Europe to California
is omitted.**

"Finally, to conclude, I want to tell you we reached San Francisco eight days ago, but we were unable to give a concert there
because of the apparent lack of a site. Therefore we have come
to San José, where we have had the honor of meeting with
you.

"Waiter, two bottles of wine," shouted Mr. Dare-Devil.

---

6. Absinthe.

"Now, dear brothers of Apollo, we must confess we find ourselves a bit short of *cum quibus*,[7] and eager for glory in this part of the new world. We can satisfy both these needs with the help of your various talents and through our names famous in France as well as Portugal.

"What are you going to decide?"

The bass viol player spoke up strongly, "I am in favor of it." Adolfo submitted in a murmur, and I coughed violently so as not to give my consent.

"I see," remarked Mr. Dare-Nothing, "you are all in favor. Now all we have to do is find a suitable hall, set up a program for a first performance, and make the placards. I'll take charge of the placards with the best will in the world if you will allow me."

At a signal of approval from us he went on, "Mister Combet will sing two pieces, whichever he pleases. Dare-Devil could sing too, but he has a cold, poor fellow, and it would be better if he plays the clarinet. Mister Adolfo will play the piano to accompany the singers; and in the overture we commence with he will play second violin. The bass viol has his part to play in all the symphonic pieces; and we can get some of the Mexicans who play in the church. That will give us a respectable orchestra."

"How does that arrangement suit you?"

"Perfectly."

"Then tomorrow noon we'll decide on the concert program so each one can study his part. After that we'll look for a hall and the other things we'll need. So, then, until tomorrow."

"Till tomorrow," we answered in chorus.

We separated then, but not until we had another glass of wine at the invitation of Mr. Dare-Devil, who wanted to drink another toast to his colleagues before we broke up.

When I had crawled into my tent, made of three blankets sewed together, and let myself fall on the one old pelt that served me as a bed, I started to reflect on the vicissitudes of human life: upon the ceaseless hunger for acquisition that is innate in man, so that neither home nor family nor friends are enough to keep him from the career of a vagabond when opposed to the dreams of his inexperienced mind! What a warning! "The son of a family," as they say in Santiago, a young man who is one of the most distinguished

---

7. The wherewithal: funds.

in the land, known by his elegance on the Alameda, and at Tamajar, reduced to selling cookies made by his partner, a peon. Other men whose articles had achieved great success in various periodicals of the capital were selling salad vegetables they had gathered in the countryside. A captain of the national guard at Santiago, a man of martial bearing, was selling *empanadas*[8] at the door of his tent in San José. A foreign baron whom we all knew in Chile for his eccentricities was shouting, "Oranges, four dollars a dozen!" in almost a scream. The count of Narbonne was an adobe mason, etc. These reflections forced me finally to admit that in this unique land each man had to do whatever his physical strength and capacity equipped him to do.

I knew a few notes of music, therefore I should sing, all the more so because this might help me to amass the fortune *El Mercurio* had promised I would. Still I confess that presenting myself for the first time before the public as a singer was not the least of my worries. But audacity is found also in great hearts, they say; and how could a man survive in California without audacity? On the following morning I went to visit a Chilean lady who had come with her husband and who had brought an excellent piano and a choice selection of cavatinas, duets, trios, etc., which she was kind enough to put at my disposition. I chose two pieces (and here I humbly beg pardon on my knees from Madame Panatelli and from my friend, Lanza). They were the finale of *Lucia de Lammermoor,* and the drinking song from *Lucrezia Borgia.*

At the hour set I went to the house of my colleagues with my two masterworks under my arm. They were all there. Mr. Dare-Nothing had recruited three Mexican guitar players and two Frenchmen, one of whom played the flute and the other the violoncello. Misters Dare-Nothing and Dare-Devil had decided not to play in the orchestral pieces. The first said his work on the variations of *Colonna* had worn him out, and the second said the same thing about his potpourri.

After a short discussion it was decided that the concert would take place the following Tuesday. Adolfo de Beauvoison would gladly do the transcribing necessary to adapt violin music for guitars, and he would act as the director of the orchestra. The bass viol man and I were commissioned to find a hall where we could hold the concert, and finally Mr. Dare-Devil and Mr. Dare-Nothing were

8. A Chilean pasty or small meat pie.

to do the programs and placards by hand, for lack of a printer. Adolfo and I both asked that pseudonyms be used instead of our names.

We were to practice daily up to the time of the concert as soon as a hall had been found. Dare-Devil and Dare-Nothing would not take part in these practice sessions because their musical talents did not require it for the pieces they were to play.

I found a suitable hall next day. It belonged to a Chilean who intended to put a restaurant in it. It was a good-sized room, fifty-two by twenty-eight feet, well carpeted, and in the center of town. The arrangement I made was that he was to get one-fourth of the receipts, and would furnish the lights, the chairs, and a stage twenty-six feet square at one end of the hall on which we could show off our artistic talents. He kept the right, too, to sell liquor and food during the concert.

When everything was settled we began our rehearsals.

The orchestra was made up in this fashion: three guitars, a second violin, a flute, a violoncello, a bass viol, and a drum to be played by a brother of the proprietor. It produced a formidable sound in the middle and lower range. However, to please the public, we had the solos that the two great artists, Mr. Dare-Devil and Mr. Dare-Nothing[9], were to present; so we were sure of a successful presentation.

Nothing else was talked about in San José but the great concert to be given the following Tuesday. The members of California's legislature, which was then in session in the city, were happy to come as a rest from their parliamentary labors. The French, Mexicans, and Chileans would be there to safeguard the artists and fellow countrymen. The Italians would come for the love of art and to hear in this half-savage land the immortal music of Donizetti.

By Thursday, after working without a stop, and thanks to the lady who lent me her piano and music, and to Adolfo who rehearsed me four of five time a day, I felt I was ready to sing my two selections. During the rehearsal on the morning of the concert, Mr. Dare-Nothing threw his arms around me and said, "My sublime friend, you have a fortune in your voice. Eight or ten concerts like the one we are going to give and I'll send you off to Italy to complete your training."

---

9. The names Dare-Devil and Dare-Nothing are attempts to reproduce in English the French pseudonyms, Risquetout and Risquerien.

No one had heard our two great artists play up to that time. Whenever we asked them, they refused. But this did not surprise us in the least because we knew great artists always did that so they could produce a greater effect.

On the following morning, very early, I found the following placard, in French, English, and Spanish, pinned to the wall of my tent. [See pp. 180–81 for this art.]

I could not but blush at such shamelessness, at least so far as concerned me, and I immediately decided to complain about the ridiculous titles applied to me. I pulled down the placard and made up my mind to do the same with every one I found on the walls and tents, and force them to put up more modest placards. To get this under way I started out for their residence. Oh madness! There was not a wall, a tent, or a piece of wood anywhere that did not have pinned to it one of those damnable placards. Between my tent and their residence there were by my count forty-two of them.

When I entered their home the two infamous characters were sleeping the sleep of the just. They had worked all night painting and distributing the program of which I was so ashamed. The noise I made on entry awakened them, and I began to throw in their faces their idiocy in thinking they could fool the public by such ridiculous titles and ranks. I told them that most of the Frenchmen and Chileans in San José had known me in Chile, and consequently they knew very well I was not the first tenor in Santiago but only a student of the chapel master, and furthermore Curicó was a small town that didn't have anything remotely resembling an academy of music. They had probably intended to make fun of me, but they had made a mistake in that because I would not sing at all if they did not get rid of those placards.

At this, they both began laughing. Then Mr. Dare-Nothing said with the utmost seriousness, "What a baby you are! You take offense at something everyone does. It is obvious you are just beginning an artistic career, which I planned to open for you. My God! Where would artists be if they didn't mix a little fakery in along with their talent? How little you know about the public! Don't fool yourself, an unknown talent will get nowhere with people. Believe me, if any artist, no matter how eminent he is, was not advertised in the papers and by placards, he would not have any audience at the concerts he gave. You've got to take the world as you find

it and stop fretting yourself over something that all artists do. The
public likes to be fooled. Do you follow me? Believe me, that saying
is not sophistry. Furthermore," he added, crossing his arms and
looking me right in the eye, "do you think I would have been
this modest if I'd come to any other town than San José? Certainly
not! I would have done all the other things artistic celebrities do.
I would have gone to the editor of the daily paper in town and
come to a friendly understanding with him; and next day something
like this would appear in the daily paper: 'The whole world is
talking about the departure of the celebrated Dare-Nothing for this
or that city. His loss will be keenly felt by all true lovers of art,
and it will be difficult to replace him. We cannot but congratulate
the directory of the N. Theater upon the acquisition they are about
to obtain. Mr. Dare-Nothing may rest assured that our sympathies
are with him wherever he happens to go.'

"Two days later the same paper would announce: 'The arts had
almost suffered an irreparable loss in the person of Mr. Dare-Nothing. On leaving the coach in the small city of B., this eminent
artist felt himself stricken with a nausea and vomiting that put
his life in danger. All the medical resources of the city were called
upon to lavish their care upon the illustrious patient. They do not
dare yet to declare him out of danger.'

"The next day it would announce: 'Mr. Dare-Nothing has been
declared out of danger and has continued his journey to the city
of N., where he is awaited with impatience, etc.' That would go
on until I arrived at my destination, where another editor fulsomely
announced my coming and the date of my first concert.

"Now don't you see how this kind of publicity is bound to be
more productive for an artist of talent, real or not, than arriving
incognito? Be reasonable and leave the placards the way they are."

At that moment the bass viol player came in. "What are you
talking about?" he said.

Mr. Dare-Nothing told him about my excess of delicacy and
shame at seeing myself honored with so many titles on the program.

"Oh," he said, laughing and turning to me, "Where have you
been, my friend? It seems you've never been vaccinated. I wish
they had put on the placard that I was the Sultan Mohammed
before I turned artist. That way I might have made a dollar more."

Mr. Dare-Devil, who had remained silent during the conversation,
then lifted his head and said to me, "Come, come, be reasonable.

AT THE CHILEAN HOUSE
FACING CITY HALL
A GREAT INSTRUMENTAL AND VOCAL
CONCERT

Mr. Dare-Devil and Mr. Dare-Nothing, so well known in France and Portugal and visitors to this city, unable to deny pleas made to them by so many inhabitants of this city that they offer a concert, have the honor to announce that they have gathered four or five local artists of the first rank, with whom they will present the following program, worthy in all respects of a public as respectable as it is illustrious.

PART ONE

Overture of *The White Lady* by the whole orchestra. Piano accompanied by flute, violoncello, bass viol, featuring Mr. Vasontout, first flautist in the Chapel of the Prince of Mónaco, corresponding member of the Academies of Music of Pezenas, Saint-Brieux, and Cauderot.

Mr. Giflard, first violocello in the Theater of Saint-Ménèhould, with license in San José.

Mr. Filomeno Rosignol, first bass viol in the chapel of His Imperial Majesty, Faustino I, Emperor of Haiti, and member of numerous Academies of Music.

The piano will be played by the celebrated Mr. Clavier, disciple of the great professors Litz and Hertz, and whose talent is equally known through the waltzes and rondeaux he offers on the accordion.

After the Overture, the celebrated Mr. Dare-Devil, decorated by all the kings of Europe, will offer the great

POTPOURRI OF HAYDEN

2: Final aria of *Lucia de Lammermoor* (music by Donizetti) sung, with piano accompaniment, by Mr. Maigrot, former first tenor of the Cathedral of Santiago, chapel master of the Church of San José, and corresponding member of the Academies of Music of Curicó (Chile) and Saint Petersburg.

3: Beethoven *Symphony* by Mr. Clavier.

4: Great Air with variations of *La Colonna* played on the flute by Mr. Dare-Nothing, honorary member of all existing Academies.

PART TWO

Overture executed by all the artists. *The Great Caravan of Cairo.*

The Rain of Emeralds (music by the late Tal) written for the oboe and played on the clarinet by the celebrated Mr. Dare-Devil.

"Drinking Song" from *Lucrezia Borgia,* with piano accompaniment, sung by Mr. Maigrot.

Famous variations on *The Swollen Foot* (music by the incomparable Tulou).

Price of Admission .... Three Dollars.
Soldiers in uniform and small children, half price.

Stage lighting and decorating by Mr. José Puisard (known as the Star of Savoy!).

Two special lights have been added to the ordinary lighting.

Special announcement by the owner of the establishment: for Chilean gentlemen, the refreshment stand at the rear will offer fried fish, national jerky, and milk punch with brandy.

[181]

Let's have a glass of wine if necessary, and be an artist for once in your life."

I refused, to his great surprise. He could not understand how anybody could refuse a glass of wine. I went away, half-convinced of what they had said about the way things really were. Still, I could not understand why, to be an artist, it was necessary to fool the public and adopt such a routine of customs and attitudes.

Tuesday finally came, and that morning we set up the hall. A semicircle was formed of the cafe tables, with tablecloths that fell to the floor. The piano was set against a side wall, with two rows of seats facing the audience for the musicians to occupy. The entrance area was filled with counters supported by chairs here and there, and behind these was a large case filled with liquor that the landlord intended to sell for his own profit during the concert.

We had held our last rehearsal, with which our great artists were well satisfied, and we separated with the agreement that we would meet at seven that evening.

At the hour set all were assembled, decked out in the strangest costumes. Each had tried to fix himself up for so respectable a public as decently as he could. Mr. Dare-Devil and Mr. Dare-Nothing were the only ones who could show the remnants of a good wardrobe, thanks to their recent arrival in this country. The bass viol player wore pants of a somewhat doubtful whiteness, without a necktie, but with a cloak over his shoulders. Adolfo de Beauvoison wore an army cloak, and I had on a huge California sarape profusely ornamented with gold, which gave me the appearance of a priest dressed in a cope rather than that of *Edgar* in the Italian opera. The rest of the performers were more or less the same.

The hall was filling little by little. By eight o'clock we counted about one hundred fifty people seated and some twenty more drinking at the rear, among them some Chileans of low extraction. One of them began to shout in the tone of one half-inebriated, "How long, pal? When do you begin your *treater* and your comedy?" Our entry silenced him.

Mr. Dare-Devil and Mr. Dare-Nothing led the way and the rest of us followed with instruments in hand. I brought up the rear— which gave me the air of the parish priest closing a procession, thanks to my huge sarape.

Following a maneuver Mr. Dare-Nothing had taught us, we formed a line on the stage, advanced three paces, and bowed to the respectable public. Then we divided, half going to the right, half to the left, to take the seats reserved for us. I swear on my honor I did not laugh during this marching about that seemed more military than artistic. Then we began the overture of the *White Lady*.

The Americans applauded enthusiastically.

After that was over, Mr. Dare-Nothing arose, and, taking Mr. Dare-Devil by the hand, led him toward the public and introduced him, amidst the applause, in three languages as: Sir Dare-Devil, Señor Dare-Devil, and Monsieur Dare-Devil. When these strange introductions were over, Mr. Dare-Devil put his instrument to his lips and began to play his great potpourri, which he said was of Haydn. The infamous imposter! It was rather his own conglomeration. No blind man who ever played an instrument in the streets of Santiago had offended my ears as much as this drunkard did that night. I was red with rage.

The Italians were grumbling.

Then it was my turn. Mr. Dare-Nothing turned to me, taking me by the hand, and said, "Before you go to the piano I want to present you to the public." "No," I said. "But it makes a good impression—" I didn't give him time for it, and, at a signal from me, Adolfo went to the piano and I followed.

Because it was set against the wall, Adolfo did not face the public. That was a good thing for me because I was shaking from head to foot and was scarcely able to bow. Mr. Dare-Nothing noticed that and said, "Cough, my friend, cough. That prepares the public to feel sorry for you. Many artists do that before they sing. Don't be afraid. Brave it out." Adolfo had begun the introduction to that sublime masterpiece, the finale of *Lucia* that I was to sing, and I no longer heard anything; I was transported to another world, intoxicated by the delicious music; I didn't even think about the audience. I sang as if I were all alone. I cannot say I did well, but the crowd showed great kindness and lavished their applause on me with a good deal of clapping.

Then it was Adolfo's turn. He arose and bowed with that modesty that becomes him so well, then launched into the Beethoven *Symphony* and executed it with unusual art and grace. That gained for him many manifestations of pleasure and approval on the part of the public.

A low murmur such as is always heard at the appearance of a famous artist ran through the hall. Dare-Nothing had just finished presenting himself to the audience.

I was finally going to hear a distinguished artist on the flute.

It made me recall the comrade of my boyhood, Remusat, already famous at the age of fourteen on this instrument. I settled myself as comfortably as I could, gave my attention, and waited. Mr. Dare-Devil gave his companion the same embellished greetings and introductions in three languages. When that was over, the variations on an air from *La Colonna* was begun.

The infamous charlatan had scarcely begun when I recognized that the supposed variations were nothing more than a patriotic song by Emile Debreaux. It was given in the most discordant tones. The theme started on E-major; the variations were in F-natural, the ending in A-flat. The barbarian no doubt thought that true variations consisted in rearranging the notes so they would have no relationship any more. But he paid dearly for his audacity because the Italians, Chileans, and French hissed and shouted loudly—all of which he took with his usual calmness (What practice can achieve!). Others applauded.

So that was all there was to the talent of these great artists who had made me abandon my career as a builder, only to involve me in their infamous fraud and audacity. It was plain those two wretches had used us to get the money they needed to go to the mines. But take care, you thief Dare-Nothing, and Dare-Devil, you drunkard, I foresee a bad end for you; you will perish in a fusillade of rotten apples and oranges, and on your deathbeds you will remember the shameless tricks you played. May God forgive you!

The second part of the concert was better than the first. I insisted strongly that Dare-Devil not play again, and Adolfo offered in place of the pompous title, *The Rain of Emeralds,* a more modest *Variations* of Chalet, executed on the piano. I sang with some confidence the "Drinking Song" from *Lucrezia;* and as the public expressed respect and deference, I had no cause to complain.

The bold Dare-Nothing ended the affair with one of those twists so common to rascals like himself. After having announced with great fuss that he would play the famous variations (there were plenty of those in our concert) on *The Swollen Foot,* he had the shamelessness to say to the audience that many persons had come to him and asked him instead for the great and celebrated revolutionary hymn, *La Marseillaise,* so popular the world over, and especially in France and Portugal; and that, acceding to their wishes, he was going to do this for them. And, in effect, he played it immediately to the great satisfaction of the French and the Americans, who left the hall with continuous shouts of "Vive la France!" "Long live the United States!" "Long live Washington!" and "Long live Lafayette!"

Well, should we call Dare-Nothing a brute? No, he was only a charlatan and a rascal. I take oath with hand to my breast—

We divided the proceeds after the concert and each went his own way. I wanted to revenge myself on those two foxes, in spite of the fact I had been the crow. Adolfo was more prudent and told me to put the idea out of my head, "If you want to teach a lesson to all the dare-devils and dare-nothings there are in California, you will never have time to amass that wealth *El Mercurio* promised you." So, for that reason we withdrew quietly without deigning to reply to Mr. Dare-Devil, who invited us to raise a glass to the fraternity of artists.

Next morning Adolfo and I were twenty feet down in the ground, cleaning out a well. We ought to have stayed down there out of shame for having taken part in the concert of the previous evening, and for having been the playthings of those two miserable fakes.

Oh, California!

Dibujo de Jorge Délano Fredrik (Coke)

Benjamín Vicuña MacKenna

BENJAMÍN VICUÑA MACKENNA
1831-1886

Historian, economist, educator, and statesman, Vicuña Mackenna is regarded as one of the greatest men Chile has produced. He was born in Santiago. His father, Pedro Félix Vicuña, was involved in the failure of an attempted revolution, and Benjamín, at the age of twenty, was forced to leave Chile in 1852. From November of that year until October of 1855, he devoted himself to world travel.

His first port of call was San Francisco. The frenzies of the Gold Rush had by that time subsided, but he was in a position to note the phenomenal growth of California in that early period. Fortunately, he had decided to keep a running account of his experiences in a diary. This work was published by the press of the journal, Ferrocarril, at Santiago in 1862. It was titled Páginas de mi Diario durante tres Años de Viaje, and ran to 454 pages. It is one of the classics in the literature of Chile.

Upon his return home, he launched a newspaper, and succeeded so well that he was named editor of the leading Santiago journal, El Mercurio. He also served as foreign correspondent for that paper in Europe. Concerned with the education of his countrymen, he accepted a chair in the faculties of Philosophy and the Humanities at the National University. Very fittingly, that university has republished his collected works.

In his later years he was called upon to serve the Republic of Chile in various capacities, and ended his career, amid universal acclaim, in the national Senate.

The text that follows forms the first section of his diary. It covers the story of his voyage to California and his experiences there.

PAGES FROM THE DIARY
OF MY TRAVELS

On November 26, 1852, I set sail from the harbor of Valparaíso on the Chilean brig *Francisco Ramón Vicuña*. Those were days so full of alarms and distresses that it was almost a relief to leave my native soil. I envisioned far-off lands beyond the sea where I might find a new sphere of activity and a future that destiny had denied to me in my fatherland. The wind filling our sails made the ship fairly fly along, and soon the vast stretch of Valparaíso housing looked like a mass of white rocks strewn along the base of the hills. Viewed in the last light of day, the Chilean coast had never looked so full of color, and yet so sad. It seemed to be echoing our goodbye. Only one leaving home for the first time will know in his heart what I mean.

During those moments the full moon appeared. It was like a star of consolation glimpsed through castellated feudal ruins the dark clouds seemed to form in the sky; and as I leaned on the poop railing and watched the ship slice through the waves—with my mind, my soul, and all my senses absorbed in the novelty of the sight—I knew I was at last a traveler on the high road of the ocean.

At dawn the following morning we were in sight of the lofty peak of Papudo, the last of Chile I was to see, and a place I knew well. One of the unique features of the sloping formation of the Chilean landscape is that from its coastline the whole country can be seen as an amphitheater across its valleys and secondary mountinas to the peaks of the Andes. So a Chilean voyager on the high seas can think of himself as still being in the places that are near and dear to him. When the land had disappeared completely, a line of light clouds still marked the direction of the coast; but the noon breezes, that other precious gift of nature and of our topography, blew them into the interior and we could see them no more.

Our course to San Francisco compelled us to take a westward tack out upon the high seas where we ought to find the prevailing southerlies. We were heading west, therefore, with a slight inclina-

[189]

tion toward the north by our compass. After five days sailing, however, the sky began to lose its brilliant blue color, the nights were less starry, and by afternoon the horizon showed a yellowish haze. The wind was no longer cool and moist. This was a sign that we had passed the latitude that separates Chile from the desert of Atacama. That same night we saw by the light of the moon the barren islands of San Félix, looking in the distance like two shadows. We were to see so little land on our route that the shadowy outline of those rocks brought us a genuine pleasure.

From then on we lived the life of a sailor in all its fullness. Our only diversion was the view of the ocean; and it, except for a few blustery days, was very calm. At times the days dawned with a strange beauty that was quite new to me. It was so exotic that it did not seem to have any relationship to me or to the wonderful sky under which I was born. In place of the horizons of the zone behind us, we now had a sun enveloped in thin and colorless haze, heavens dark and windless, and hot nights without any stars; and although it did have a peculiar beauty, I had trouble trying to recognize such a world. As nature offered little in the way of diversions, I sought them in my surroundings; but the small ship with its crew of twelve constantly busy maneuvering the sails had no novelties to present. Captain Cavassa was a good man, from Genoa as were all the sailors. Several times he told of his forays in the Mediterranean, and at other times he played on an old guitar, offering fanciful arrangements of favorite songs from Cerro Alegre; of these he like the *zamacueca* best. The crew stayed pretty much to themselves. I had hired the ship, so I was its only passenger.

I do not know why, but you acquire a habit of silence and meditation on the high seas; perhaps you reflect the stillness and the immensity of space in which you are sailing. This may be why it became my solitary pleasure to rest against the gunwale, or, seated on a yard of the bowsprit, to watch the prow of the ship cut the waves and raise a garland of white foam which renewed itself endlessly. You may wish for things to happen on a ship, but they never do; to seek them is dangerous. So we had to content ourselves with the meager things of interest the bridge of the brig could offer: the seamen going about their work, the two dogs we had on board who were constantly romping around and who seemed the only happy beings around us. An occasional fish was caught on the hooks we trailed from the poop. Sea swallows circled endlessly at a respectful distance from the ship, as if they feared to come within range of the rusty rifles we carried in the cabin. These were the only colors that varied the monotony of that canvas of blue sea and sky we were crossing. One afternoon we saw two large birds, spotted with red and white, land on the masts. Perhaps they were wandering pilgrims like me, seeking another nest in a strange land. They came back again for two or three days, and seemed to be headed in the same direction we were—but finally they disappeared.

The changelessness of the ocean, with day following day, made me lose all sense of time. All the hours were the same, and the days like the hours. Time seemed to me a thing as formless and immense as the ocean. It could be cut into any lengths, according to wish or fancy, but any one of these would still seem too long to me. This weariness, however, never grew any worse, at least while a favorable wind was blowing—such winds were always welcomed by us as friends—but, the captain often exclaimed, Satan, not God, was the lord of the winds.

In the fifty days we were at sea there was only once when we had a stir of what might be called excitement; the rest of the voyage all of us felt thoroughly bored. On that one occasion, which seemed so serious then but is comical now, a rat gnawed a hole in the ship's keel just under the ladder and precisely at the waterline. But as the ship was taking the wind upon its port side, it was sailing slightly heeled over to starboard and so only a little water got in: enough to ruin twenty-five sacks of flour. The captain felt sure that, otherwise, we would have taken on enough water in one night to have foundered. From that moment a vicious war was declared on the rat and the sailors hunted it through the hold like a furry pirate. The bo'sun who was in charge of the hold swore that he would sacrifice it and eat it in a stew as soon as it was caught, because once under another captain he had not escaped (he said colorfully, as sailors and Genoese do) "from a most damnable beating even by climbing to the top of the mainmast!" Finally the cat caught the culprit and it was thrown into the sea, to the great excitement of the crew, the dogs, and the cat. We escaped, but had to throw overboard the twenty-five sacks and some thirty boxes of vermicelli belonging to the captain. It was made in Valparaíso, though the boxes said clearly it was from Genoa. The captain was remarkably good-natured that day; his old guitar never sounded so lively and melodious. These men of the ocean possess nothing—but how much does such a man need as he rides a wooden horse around the world?

The classic and unique day of boredom was the one when we were completely becalmed. The ship, trapped in a sea without waves or even ruffles of water, balancing itself like a dead mass, its sails drooping, fluttering a little when a slight breeze struck it from any direction, was like a huge swan that had been wounded and was unable to lift its wings. The captain and his officers cursed as usual, but I was enjoying the strange phenomenon. We had been in a bad storm at night; now I wanted to see the ocean at peace for the sake of contrast. It was twelve o'clock noon when the calm settled in completely. The sea was motionless and there was not even the smallest cloud in the sky. Only a light blue line showed where sky and ocean met. If it had not been for the motion of the sun, and the little sparkles the water gave now and then as a puff of wind made its stiff face break into a momentary smile, we could not have told where we were; the sails flapping above might have been the canvas of a balloon suspended there, or the sails of a ship magically immobilized in some strange repose of nature. The ocean was in fact like a sleeping giant, letting himself be caressed by languid breezes. The sun was reflected in all his majesty on the motionless sea. The storm winds were chained at the poles of the earth, or had been sent high into the heavens to sweep away the tiniest cloud, mist, or shadow that could mar the face of nature on this festive day.

On December 19 we crossed the equator, twenty-two days out of Valparaíso. We were at least one thousand leagues from the nearest coast. The heat was quite intense. But I escaped the Baptism of Neptune the sailors had planned for me. It was not that they respected me as an employer—the laws of the sea are inexorable about that; it was that the captain had bought them off with a promise of a double wine ration at Easter, a feast they observe joyfully. The heat lasted two weeks. Ten days after crossing the equator I had to change from slippers into heavy boots.

We spent New Year's Day casually off the point of that name on the coast of Mexico. On January 8 we saw the first ship we had a chance to hail. It was the brig *Mathius Saar*, bound from San Francisco to the Sandwich Isles for oranges and bananas. We communicated by writing questions and answers on slates. We synchronized our chronometers. The captain rechecked his calculations, and four days later we were in view of land at the entrance of the Golden Gate. Our voyage had lasted forty-seven days.

An official pilot boat met us, and, making a graceful curve by our prow, put a pilot on board. I wanted to get ashore that afternoon in the pilot boat. Its captain received me with the most complete indifference, as if his rowers had brought a carton of textiles. He was the first stranger in a strange land. I decided to imitate him, and so I also adopted an air of quiet indifference—until I saw that the pilot boat, instead of going back to the harbor, was heading out to sea. I asked the captain then if we were to get back that night. He replied that he did not know, but he invited me to the cabin and offered me tea without sugar in a tin cup. Resigned to what had happened, I lay down on a cot and went to sleep.

At about three o'clock in the morning I felt myself being shaken by a strong arm to wake me up. Half-asleep, and by the light of a little cabin lantern, I saw a husky young man in a yellow overcoat with a note book in his hand. Without any preliminaries he asked me where I came from, what cargo I brought, etc. I told him, he made some notes, and left. I knew by this rough introduction that we were anchored at San Francisco; and that the Sacramento River was not the Seine, nor its inhabitants Parisians. Later I found my interrogator was not a customs officer but a reporter from one of the newspapers. Learning of my arrival by telegraph, he wanted advance news that would affect the market.

At dawn I went up on deck. The city, strewn over the hills, was silent. A gas lamp still burned in the lighthouse, but in a little while the sun dimmed its flame and the city began to stir. The steamships fired up their boilers and wagons began to arrive at the docks. I was thinking about this curious new world at whose gates I stood. Four years ago this broad bay was only a lonely lake, disturbed occasionally by keels of small fishing barks. Now I saw a lighthouse and a telegraph line, and heard the sharp hiss of steam. All the great discoveries of the age were in use here. I looked at the tranquil bay, my view obstructed by piers lined with ships. The city is the most beautiful in the Pacific. It rises on hills where yesterday tents were set up, and where the day before that there were the huts of fishermen. I recalled cities I had seen that were more than three hundred years old and compared them with this child of yesterday. They seemed old without ever having been young.

At six o'clock the captain went ashore in his boat; I went with him. When we got to the pier he mounted the steps without saying goodbye or even giving me a glance. I wanted to thank him for his services, but when I did he seemed surprised that I thought he had done me a service; he just smiled and shook hands. I had paid eighty dollars for a harbor pilot, and that was all that was expected from me; it did not matter to the captain whether I came ashore in my boat or his, and I did not owe him any more money for that, nor even any thanks. An oarsman I talked to a little later did not have that attitude, though. When I asked what he would charge me to row me out to my ship, which was coming in about a half-mile away, he lifted his oar just the way a knight of old might have clasped hand to sword, and replied, "Ten dollars!"

Lying alongside the pier where I disembarked was the frigate *Magellan*, which had left Valparaíso the same afternoon we did, loaded not with flour and blankets but with three hundred French republicans deported by Louis Napoleon. They had arrived recently, each one carrying the scanty gear of an exile. Many of these poor men I recognized later shining shoes on the streets of the city for a quarter a pair. Sad twist of fortune.

I did not know anyone in San Francisco, but I hoped to spot some Chilean features on the streets so I set out on a walk in mud up to my ankles. San Francisco seemed to me the oddest and most extraordinary city in the world. It is as unique in the world as Venice is in Europe; it *is* a Venice built of pine instead of marble. It is a city of ships, piers, and tides. Large ships with railings, a good distance from the beach, served as residences, stores, and restaurants. I saw places where the tide had flowed down the street, turning the interior of houses into lakes. The whole central part of the city swayed noticeably because it was built on piles the size of ship's masts driven down into the mud. The men all seemed to be running, and they spoke in monosyllables as if using only half of the word for the sake of economy. Everywhere I looked there was noise and bustle. Wagons rolled by, pulled by great draft horses who made the piers shake with their hooves. Ships, the largest I had ever seen, were unloading merchandise from all over the world: Chinese silks, timber from Norway, flour from Talcahuano, and articles from Paris. A bundle could scarely fall on the dock before a worker hoisted it onto a wagon and the driver set off at a gallop.

Those places where there were no men running or horses going at a trot had machinery doing the work of man and animal both. The unloading of the ships was done by a machine about the size and shape of a stove, and it could lift a box of considerable size. In other places a steam hammer was driving whole Oregon pines down into the ground as piles. A mill for polishing rice from China stupified one in the center of the city with its mechanical squeals. I saw an apparatus run by steam being used for land levelling, and it worked with as much precision as human labor could have done. It had a big ugly biter armed with iron teeth, and a big iron stomach. The biter opened its jaws and dug its teeth into the earth one, two, or three times on the side of a hill it intended to remove; and when its stomach was full it turned its neck around and vomited into a wagon. A man then gave the wagon a push and it rode down the slope on iron rails for about a mile and dumped itself into the bay. The contractor was thus improving two sites in one operation. Never anywhere since have I seen steam applied to so many uses or worked so constantly as in San Francisco; because nowhere else in the world has there ever been brought together more power and industrial skill; and also because here manual labor is the most expensive kind.

After I had lived in San Francisco a month I saw other aspects of it, but they only made it even more unique. I went through Chinatown, the Mexican area, and Little Chile (or Chilecito, the same name given to the women's section in Valparaíso). All of it had a strange and odd character. It is a hodge-podge of cities, a tower of Babel of all nationalities. You can hear all the languages on earth in its streets: Chinese, Norwegian, Russian, and Polynesian. You can see the garb of all the nationalities, and find any kind of tailor you want. There are Chinese with belted black pantaloons and blue blouses, with pigtails down to their knees; a Mexican with his sarape or blanket; the Chilean in his poncho; a Parisian in his smock; an Irishman with torn coat and crushed felt hat; and the Yankee, lord of all, in his red flannel shirt, heavy boots, and trousers belted at the waist.

These were the men who in four years had improvised a state and had rebuilt the city of San Francisco three times from its ashes. They were citizens of a special sort and with a special sense of law. They proved this when they organized the secret vigilance committee and set up a most unique inquisition to protect the city from the ravages of repeated fires. They had broken into a jail, pistol in hand, to hang two confessed incendiaries who were escaping punishment through complicity of the authorities. This is one of the most striking deeds in the phenomenal era in which we live: the people themselves carrying out the work of justice, inflicting with their own hands the punishment that only executioners can conduct legally. Leading businessmen, respectable fathers of families held the ropes and pushed the convicted felons off the gallows plank. How different from the spectacle in other countries where firing squads of infantry carry out the sentence, to the sorrow of all the people. Arsonists in San Francisco were justly feared, for they were organized in secret societies. This did not help them, though, when lynch law became the supreme code in California. At that period a Dutchman failed to show due respect to the corpse of a beautiful woman in Sacramento. A jury of transients, made up of carpenters, shoe shiners, and a clergyman, held a meeting and found the Dutchman guilty. Eight wanted to hang him, but the whole twelve finally decided on two hundred lashes—and two hundred lashes he got, one by one, across his back! One day in the town of Calaveras an Italian was killed at dawn. The jury's verdict was: "If the victim is Italian, the murderer must have been Italian"; so all Italians were ordered to leave within twenty-four hours.

I never saw a church in San Francisco, except perhaps a Protestant chapel roofed with shakes—and it was out in a suburb as though they were ashamed of it. In the center of the town, though, there were gaudy saloons like the Bella Union, El Dorado, or Polka, where you could have found five hundred men at a time with money staked on the same card, or wrapped up in the same frantic and delirious game, their minds intoxicated by the music, by the liquor (which flowed in bucketfuls at the expense of the house), and by the seductiveness of the ladies who took and paid off bets at the tables or equally fascinating painted ladies whose pictures hung on the walls. All of this was meant to drug the senses while the soul was being gnawed by feverish greed. Gambling houses, open day and night, were the actual churches of San Francisco, and gold was the only God worshipped. People say they even called customers with bells, though the punctual attendance of the faithful makes that seem needless. I have seen Mexicans in shirt sleeves with piles of gold they could hardly get their arms around; they make up the majority of the gamblers, especially at El Dorado, which is the oldest California "church." They have sworn to me that, in private rooms at Bella Union, eighty thousand dollars has changed hands on the turn of a card.

The most common game, though, is roulette. It is incredible how the blind passion of gambling can make a man trust the fairness of those mechanisms installed by authorized house bandits with official approval. Although the owners do pay off, keep a well-supplied and inexpensive stock of refreshments for customers, and provide magnificent rooms free, everyone knows they make hundreds of thousands of dollars a year. That is a contribution to them from human credulity and weakness.

I cannot describe San Francisco in detail because I was there only a month, not nearly long enough to understand so peculiar a city; and I was engaged on another matter. I visited the theaters; there were nine of them, all small. I had to pay five dollars just to hear an aria sung by La Biscaccianti. It cost me the same to hear Catalina Hayes one other night, and they said that was cheaper than in Santiago. Everything seems to cost five dollars here, even to ride a block in one of the magnificent coaches of San Francisco, or to enter a French cafe to watch the dancing for half an hour. There is a French theater, and also a Chinese theater—the latter outside of town. I went to the French theater one Sunday night and almost found myself on the barricades with everyone singing the *Marseillaise*. It was in the house of a Miss Nelson, the Rachel of San Francisco, a great favorite of the public; but not of the company, which wanted to fire her. The audience was angry and demanded loudly that she reappear. The company refused, and a battle of Trafalgar was about to break out fought with chairs when an inspired voice cried out from the women's gallery: "The *Marseillaise*, citizens." The orchestra entoned the hymn, and the two factions joined in as true sons of the fatherland.

To go to the Chinese theater required one to take a long walk around one of the hills of the city. The theater was a dark wooden flophouse, but reasonably clean. There was a small audience of sixty; I counted eighty actors. Here the situation was the reverse of that in the French theater: the spectators were calm but the actors were violent. The whole drama—it lasted three hours—was crude, bloody, and shrieking combat. If there was only one actor on the stage, he made up for the lack of opponents on whom to

vent his truculence by clawing at his own face and yanking at
his huge false beard. Hardly had two other actors appeared on
stage, after a good deal of yowling (for there is nothing you can
compare Chinese declamation to except hellish cat yowling), than
they started giving each other the most furious blows. After some
mutual battering, it seemed that a man of peace arrived and was
to serve as judge, but he soon got into the fight, backed up by
others, until the stage was full of battlers, a king and queen among
them, joined in unequal combat in which all except the king and
his consort were slain by a warrior who wielded a lance with his
bare arm. But their majesties did not escape earthly punishment,
for the conqueror forced them to stretch out on their bellies and
beat them with the largest staves I ever saw; or at least they appeared so. That was the only pleasant scene in the play. There
was not a single scene with feeling, nor any amorous rendezvous;
all was mock fighting and blows. It is strange that such a timid
and effeminate people enjoy only bellicose farces, and should be
so ferocious in war as recent events[1] show. Another peculiarity
of the show was the orchestra made up of six musicians; one of
them played on an old metal tub and another drummed with light
sticks on a table. Of course there was not the least harmony, but
what was really odd was that they abandoned their instruments
whenever they felt like it, and took time out for a smoke.

I had a chance to watch the Chinese on another occasion. I
was in a gambling hall in Chinatown. It was a room with three
large tables of rough timber. Some men were standing around the
tables. The one who led the game was in the center. He tossed
handsful of copper money on the tablecloth; each coin had a hole
in its center. Then he raked them back in with a stick by twos.
I gathered that the game was "even or odd," and after the usual
salutation of *chin chin*, which means "How are you?" and its response, *chau chau*, or "At your service," I put a peseta on the
table to try my luck with the manipulations of these supposedly
untrustworthy sons of heaven. The Chinese at the first and second
tables refused to let me play, but at the third I was in luck and
won the stakes at first throw. I then left, guarding carefully that
money, resulting from the great generosity of the sons of the celes-
tial empire. I must add that the Chinese were very reasonable and
courteous in their stores. They usually spoke good English. Some

---

1. The Tai-ping Rebellion broke out in China in 1850.

PIONEER DAYS IN SAN FRANCISCO.

The Road to Mission Dolores, San Francisco

of them were well-to-do; they are said to be gifted with special talent as bankers and money changers. I do not know why, but looking at this race with its brunet complexion, its prominent cheekbones, its narrowed eyes and their black color, it appeared to me an absolute fact that American Indians had the same ancestry. They present the same features with some differences attributable to climate. When I saw the North American Indians later, my opinion was strengthened. These mysteries are beyond solution as yet, though.

Another peculiar spectacle in San Francisco was that offered by the companies of singers and musicians that are so popular in the United States.[2] They are disguised as Negroes, and this disguise is the essence of their performance. They also parody well-known operas, and even if they are not artistically very satisfying, the originality of the improvisations makes one smile. I saw, for exam-

---

2. Minstrel shows.

ple, a parody of Romeo and Juliet. Juliet was a man in a Negro
makeup, and Romeo was another *Fascico*.[3] They sang in good harmony the duet *Al fin son tuo*, and at the most ecstatically amorous
and pathetic moment, Juliet gave Romeo a mighty kick and he
let out a bray. These improvisations were very much to the taste
of the Americans. Their greatest pleasure seems to be the physical
act of laughing; that may be why there are companies of this sort
in every city of the Union, as well as traveling ones that perform
on the streets.

One afternoon I set out on foot for the little town of *Misiones*,[4]
a league from San Francisco. The road was paved with wood, and
was used by citizens of San Francisco when they wanted to take
a stroll. On both sides of the road I saw rustic houses set off with
sentimental signs such as "Al Feliz Reposo" with subtitles like
"Milk and Water Punch," or some other similar means of producing
sweet repose. Wealthy businessmen of San Francisco drove past
in their swift buggies at a speed of at least fifteen miles an hour;
others were walking. I turned off the road to one side toward some
sandy hills that overlooked the bay. Under some bushy shrubs I
found one hundred or so scattered stones in disorder, most of them
with a cover of wood. The site and the epitaphs on each stone
conveyed a terrible lesson for those who visited there. The gravedigger had written the history of California: the murders, ship-
wrecks, deaths from starvation and grief, vows of vengeance written
over the immolated body of a man by his brother—such was the
tale told by the epitaphs. Most of the dead were between twenty
and thirty years of age.[5]

Somewhere there must rest the remains of the Chilean Rear
Admiral Carlos Wooster, rival and successor of Lord Cochrane,
who died at Sacramento in 1849. He had asked in his will that
his shroud be made of the Chilean and the American flags sewn
together, and that a headstone should mark his grave for his friends
to see. But the dead have no friends in San Francisco, and the
only memorial of him that remains are the medals given him for
the capture of the *Isabel* and of Chiloé. These medals had been

3. A Chilean entertainer popular at the time.

4. Mission Dolores.

5. This was in Yerba Buena cemetery, between what are now Larkin, Market, and
McAllister Streets.

pawned in a jewelry store. They were redeemed by the noble and patriotic gesture of the Chilean consul, Don Felipe Fierro.[6]

The sad site recalled to my mind another person linked to Chile more by feeling than fame, a modest youth few knew by name, but one who had in him all that is noblest in Chilean character. He died here in the earliest days of a career he was undertaking with energy and determination. He may have been the first Chilean to die in this land so unfriendly to our nation. He drowned in the bay. Others died of cholera and plague, under the guns of the "Hounds," by treacherous dagger stroke, or with dagger in hand defending their lives and property. The name of my friend, whom none who knew him can ever forget, was Rafael Martínez.

I had come to San Francisco with two thousand sacks of Chilean wheat as a cargo. My consignee sold them all in a few hours at twenty-nine and a half dollars a sack. They had cost only eight dollars in Valparaíso, so that made us a profit of thirty-five thousand dollars. But I, who thought I knew so much about San Francisco, discovered I knew nothing. In the first place, the pilot lost two of my anchors in the mouth of the bay and made me pay eighty dollars, or five cents a day for each unit of the ship's tonnage. The towing of the ship two or three miles cost fifty dollars more. When I got finally tied up to one of the hundreds of public or private piers on the bay, the owner, a butcher, told me there would be no charge provided I bought all the meat for the crew from him. The ship was unloaded, but the bill for about a month came to two hundred forty-nine dollars, or about five cents a day for each ton of the ship's total tonnage of two hundred fifty.

When we got moored at the pier, the customs service sent on board an inspector whom we had to feed as well as paying six dollars a day. After the cargo was sold, other men came to make an official quality inspection. Every sack was marked as good, bad, or very bad, according to the amount of damage each sack showed. One ounce of damaged flour got the whole sack stamped as bad; but our official, a man of the highest rank in the service, marked a large part of the cargo as very bad, and there was an eight dollar difference in price between that and the good. He had obviously been bribed by the purchaser—as had happened in the case of

---

6. For Wooster's career, see López, *Historia de La Marina de Chile*, pages 136–53. Wooster was from the United States.

the ship *Castor*, which arrived when flour was selling at forty dollars a sack; not one was found to be good. The stamping of the sacks dropped the value of my cargo six thousand dollars. I wanted to make some comments, but the officials would not listen. I raised my voice, but they remained unmoved.

What was I to do? I knew that one of the legal tricks in vogue then in California was to provoke someone to strike you. That carried a fine of ten thousand dollars; and the court orders were so strict that a man's ship was legally attached at once if he was found guilty, and he was subjected to other harassment—except that of being sent to jail, because there they would have to feed him, and that cost too much! My venture was going onto the rocks in every sense. The price of flour fell in eight days from thirty dollars to nine dollars, and the purchaser refused to accept the second half of the flour. I had to be patient. How was I to lodge a complaint against an American merchant? Could a lawyer help me? I remembered that one day I had gone with my consignee, Señor Lorca, to confer with a lawyer about some lots he had to reclaim in the town of Benicia. We met the lawyer coming down the stairs, hat on head and with a book under his arm. He waited two minutes while I explained my situation; but when I tried to give a fuller explanation, my friend, Lorca took my arm and said goodbye for us. "Don't you realize," he told me, "that if you held him up three minutes longer he would have sent you a bill for fifty dollars for a stairway conference?" The final upshot was that I lost twenty thousand dollars of my original gain. Even that, comparatively, was a marvelous result.

My first original purchaser, Mr. Osborne, bought the rest of my cargo at nine dollars a sack, when he had paid twenty-nine and a half dollars for the first lot. The thing that surprised me most, though, was that he gave the same calculating and close attention to the last purchase, which was his ruin, as he had to the first when he had hoped to strike it rich. That is the way North Americans are: no matter whether the affair is great or small, it is still business, and they have the same zest and interest in every instance. They may go bankrupt ten times, but just as often they start with nothing and make a fortune. Half of San Francisco burned down one night, but next day gangs of workers were all over the area, hauling away rubbish and bringing in new materials. They even swear that at the height of the fire the owners were calmly negotiating contracts with carpenters and masons to start in rebuilding next day.

They have done the wildest kinds of business you can imagine in San Francisco, such as auctioning off women in the public square. I got there when matters had settled down somewhat: a ship arrived with sixty French women; none of them had paid her passage, so they offered a girl to anyone who would pay what she owed. Next day they did not have a single one left. The strangest thing I saw, though, was a shop offering coffins of all sizes either on cash or credit, with the price dependent on the size. It was so common an occurrence in California to die or be dead that already the all-pervasiveness of death made it a profitable enterprise to gamble with the fates. One morning my attention was caught by a noisy group on one of the piers. Everyone who went by was laughing. I went down there and saw a drowned man floating in the water, fully dressed, and with a noose around his neck. In San Francisco a man earned four dollars a day; but if dead he earned nothing. He didn't count as a man any more; he was not a man in anyone's eyes. Daily spectacles such as these did not predispose the mind to very agreeable thoughts.

Before I left San Francisco I wanted to see the Sacramento River, which had been described to me as very beautiful. At four o'clock one afternoon I went down to the pier where the steamers were and boarded the *Senator*, the oldest and most luxurious of those that sailed on California waters. There were four other steamers there with boilers going. Each one was ringing its bell to call passengers, and all together they made a strange sound like a lugubrious echo of farewell; and for many it was, because they were on their way to the mines in the interior. Finally we set out, with two steamers ahead and two beside us. It was pleasant to think of the wealth these ships were going to distribute to the towns along the riverbanks, for each one was destined to be a town that had yesterday been empty countryside: San José, Stockton, Sacramento, Marysville, and the mining districts. In the center of the bay each ship turned off on its own course, and we went on toward Sacramento with other ships ahead of us. It was already dark. At about ten we tied up to the pier at Benicia for a few moments to debark and embark passengers. When we started on up the river we were completely alone. The rapid and narrow stream scarcely gave us enough room. The pilots, standing alert at the helm, avoid a bank

Sacramento in the 1850s

here, a channel there, or perhaps another steamer coming down the river like a streak of lightning, or perhaps a small sailing ship tied up at the foot of a tree from whose branches it seemed to be suspended. It was a scene full of magnificence and novelty. Our powerful ship plowed on through a dense forest like a grey nocturnal bird surveying its dominions. There was solitude around us and silence on board.

All the passengers had gone to sleep in the large cabin, which was ringed with sofas of crimson velvet and warmed by a central stove. The sight in the cabin made a most amusing contrast with the view of the night as seen from the empty deck. As there were more passengers than sofas, the passengers were all piled in together forming groups worthy of an expert caricaturist. I remember one of the gold seekers was sleeping on top of another so that one of his big boots lay on the stomach of his companion and the other on his nose in a grotesque tangle of arms and legs. There was a general snoring, with figures of these conquerors of labor stretched out everywhere. There was only one detail of this California dormitory that had a certain sweetness: it was a mother who had gone to sleep looking at her baby, her half-bare bosom just above his lips. Both were asleep, but they seemed to be looking at each other.

At midnight I went down to the 'tweendeck cabin where you could rent a mattress for two dollars. I had barely stretched out when the ship turned until it was almost sailing on its side. A frightful alarm broke out and everyone ran for the stairs where, some climbing and some falling, they formed a Gordian knot. But at the height of the excitement a guffaw from the deck restored calm. The ship had hit a tree on the bank. The boat that was lashed to the rails was smashed into smithereens. Because this ship drew so little water it would have been easy for it to have turned completely over, in which case we would, no doubt, have had some aquatic visitors with us in the hold.

Before dawn an enormous ship's bell began to ring, sending echoes all through the ship. It announced that we had arrived and everyone had to disembark. If you wanted to catch a few more winks of sleep it would have to be at the expense of your ears, because that insistent bell resounded at the head of each bed like a reveille suitable to this land of gold and of barbarism.

Descending to shore I visited Sacramento, a great city in embryo. It was divided by three great streets running from the river toward the Sierra Nevada whose shining peaks were visible, far away across the plains. These streets were named for the letters of the alphabet: A, B, and so on, and those crossing them were numbers: 1, 2, 3, and so on. To locate a house by this excellent system was wonderfully easy; the address gave you not only the street but the block where it was to be found, for example, 3 C Street. This pithiness is characteristically Yankee, as infallible as a rifle shot. Sacramento, through its location in the middle of California and half-way up the river is certain to have a great future. When I was there it had just gone through a great fire, followed by a flood in which street traffic was by boat. To protect the city they were building a levee of earth and timber; I saw some wretched Chinese working on it. They were living in a hollow spot with water up to their ankles, confined there by the prejudice of the Americans. The Chinese seem unfitted for any but domestic service. That is why they are laundrymen in California. I saw them ironing clothes in San

Francisco with a stew pan filled with hot coals. Unfortunately, their immigration, which is curbed in California by laws, is flooding over onto our beaches and those of Peru. I do not see what benefit these beings, trained to eat rice and to dry tea leaves, can bring to our agriculture. I know a bit about ten of these colonies working on public projects in the district of Quillota, and the administrator told me the only thing they were good for was catching rats in the pasture. They make a stew with them in big pots, just as they do with dogs and foxes—although they like the latter animals better roasted. These unhappy people are, furthermore, subjected to forced contracts running for from eight to ten years; and this is a positive slavery that the laws do not authorize.

At two o'clock in the afternoon of the same day I arrived in Sacramento, February 12, 1853, I went down the river again in a swift steamer that left before the *Senator* did. On entering the cabin I was surrounded by a flock of sheep who were using it as a sheepfold. They were being taken to San Francisco. Another broad, rounded ship also was on its way down, with a herd of mules. Because I was making this voyage by daylight I was able to admire the extent and richness of these plains that the river bathes for more than fifty leagues between the Sierra Nevada and the coast. The development of this land, once it is peopled by a youthful and energetic race, is bound to be swift and sure; it possesses natural resources on a large scale: the climate, the mines, the fertility of the soil, the mountains of the interior, and navigable rivers. In terms of production it will be, beyond dispute, a formidable rival for Chile, which lies in a comparable southern latitude and produces the same things. However, if this competition serves as a stimulus and a lesson, it may not be a bad thing for us in the long run. They have already introduced all sorts of farm machinery here, and the soil is so fertile that they did not bother to harvest a large crop of barley they raised in the summer of 1853 because they had already oversupplied the market and driven prices too low. Señor don J. Manuel Ramírez, who owns a rich farm near Marysville, assured me that in a wagon load of watermelons he sent to the agricultural fair at Sacramento there was not one that weighed less than an arroba, that is, fifty pounds.

On February 15, 1853, at eight o'clock in the morning, I boarded the steamship *Panamá*. It cut through San Francisco Bay not as though impelled by a gentle breeze but with all the force of its steam, like a true Yankee. It brushed aside the other ships it passed here and there, until, finally, it collided with a brig and knocked off a piece of its prow as well as the lifeboat that was hanging over its side. It seemed to me a bad omen, but the captain and my fellow passengers merely laughed.

I was wondering about my prospects for good and ill in the long visit I was beginning to the United States in view of the strange kind of people around me, when suddenly two brawny Yankees interrupted my thoughts by asking me if they could get by. They were carrying a very sick man whom they placed on one of the three beds in my stateroom. This was the second ill-omened thing to happen on the trip, but I knew I must resign myself to it like a good Christian. The sick man was about fifty and he was in the last stages of tuberculosis. His name was Carpenter, and he was traveling alone. He lasted five days, and they were an agony for me because my bed was only a half-yard above his. All I could hear at night was his harsh and agonizing snoring, and when he asked for something he took my hand in his, which was covered with an icy sweat. On the fourth day I decided this was intolerable and I demanded that the steward give me another bed; which he finally did. The third passenger in the stateroom did not feel the way I did. He was an American whaling captain who had been in Talcahuano, and still sighed for a Panchita he had known there. Finally the poor fellow died, stretched on a mattress on the floor of the room. The only person who was with him at that moment, reading to him selections from the Bible, was a young man who stood out in the crowd of travelers because of his modesty. All of the others simply passed by with complete indifference, even the ship's doctor. There was some excuse for him because he told me twenty-five or thirty passengers always died on the voyage from Panamá to San Francisco. When Mr. Carpenter had breathed his last, two sailors wrapped his body in an American flag, and, placing him on a plank, pushed him into the sea. No one even noticed this California funeral unless they happened to hear the splash as the body hit the water. What seemed most odd to me was that the patient had wanted to go in this ship that was bound for the disease-ridden climate of Panamá. Perhaps he wanted to avoid the cost of a land funeral; if so, he succeeded completely, for I have never seen a burial cheaper and more simple than the one given him.

Our trip to Acapulco lasted eight days. We touched at Monterey during the night, and the discharge of a cannon brought some passengers on board. The only thing I saw of this port was the mountain that gave its name to it.[7] Lights were shining through the trees, and the place looked primitive and romantic. On the eighteenth day, after having passed through the Santa Bárbara Channel, we made another stop at San Diego, a California village, as primitive as a Jesuit mission. I counted twenty houses scattered over a hill. However, in the distance one could see what they call New Town, an American settlement already of some importance. When we left the bay the steamer *Golden Gate* passed by. This is the largest ship sailing the Pacific up to the present. It carried one thousand five hundred passengers. About as many of them were standing on the deck as it would hold, and they gave us a "Hurrah!" in a thunderous sound that we returned. I do not know whether it was an expression of pleasure or simply a custom in this area. There must have been some sobs mingled in that shout, because we learned later that in the eight days between Panamá and Acapulco they had fourteen sea burials. On the twenty-second, at breakfast time, we finally anchored in the beautiful roads off Acapulco.

7. This is an error. Monterey was named by Vizcaíno in honor of the viceroy, Gasparde Zúñiga y Acevedo, Count of Monterey.

LETTERS FROM CALIFORNIA
APPEARING IN
EL MERCURIO

selected from
LOS CHILENOS EN
SAN FRANCISCO DE CALIFORNIA

BY
ROBERTO HERNANDEZ CORNEJO

San Francisco
February 16, 1849

We arrived on January 23, and as soon as we got on shore our first concern was to find a place to live. This was difficult because of the shortage of housing.

My dear friend, I have so much to tell you that it all is piled up in my mind. There just would not be enough space to write it all out in detail. Everything is so very strange in this country. There is no curb on the people. They are everything. They give all the rules and orders. There is absolutely no authority. Not long ago a man, looking like a parrot on a stick, announced he was the customs collector. He knew so little that he declared domestic production was subject to duty. He was one of the many curiosities of this land. Three days later, he and his clerks went on a terrible drinking spree, and on the following day they all resigned. The official said he was tired of the job; the clerks complained they were paid only six dollars a day. So we had to do without a customs house for four days until another man came and took over the money box and the books.

The people behave remarkably well. This is more than anyone had a right to hope for, considering that we have three thousand people following no law but their own will. Actually, I am inclined to say that this is the best of all governments—if it is a government.

There is a group called The Twenty, who settle disputes. They summon the parties, call in some bystanders who act as a court

San Francisco Street

San Francisco Post Office

of justice. The complaint and the reply are heard, and then they
vote. The man found guilty pays a fine. If he is a murderer he
is sentenced to be hanged; he is arraigned before the group for
robbery and murder and, if convicted, is sent to the gallows. The
proceedings take very little time. All of this surprised me, and I
marvelled at the way these men carry out the task and then report
to the people what they have done.

As I said, there are about three thousand people here. Seven
months ago there were fewer than one thousand inhabitants in all.
There were but ninety houses; now there are three hundred, not
counting those being constructed. Other towns are in proportion
except the town of Sutter, where three thousand Mexicans are reported to have arrived; but as for the twenty thousand North Americans they said we would find here, none has reached California
as yet.

This port will need a lot of Chilean food for some time to come:
mainly flour, barley, beans, nuts, cheese, jerky, and brandy. Please
ship me these things. The market for them is very good, and they
will be most useful. I think that the amount may come to some
fifty thousand pesos but we can settle that here.

❊   ❊   ❊

San Francisco
February 21, 1849

We reached this place on January 23. This is a land where Divine
Providence opened its treasury so each man could win wealth he
would have no rights to on the basis of a just distribution. Everything
is gold now; they talk of nothing else. If a man does not make
a fortune in this area it would have to be because he is physically
incapacitated or because the devil has tied his hands.

I am getting ready to go to a recently discovered placer where
no gold pan is needed because the gold is found in nuggets of from
thirty to fifty ounces. I need some twenty thousand of these, so
I want to take plenty of time to get the best ones.

To the present we have an extreme form of democracy here,
if it is government at all. The people gather in the public square

and anyone who wishes to may talk. Accusations are made and judgments given as well as in the best courts. If there is a suspect he is arrested, tried, and hanged, and the business is taken care of promptly.

No one can be a property owner here unless he is a citizen, so I have to make purchases under the name of someone else; but I have made up my mind to remain a citizen of Chile.

The population is made up of men from all over the world; but in spite of the fact that there are many Chileans, Chile is the only country that does not have a warship in the bay nor a consul in the city to protect its citizens. This is very bad.

* * *

San Francisco
February 28, 1849

I am still stunned by all the confusion I've witnessed since the moment of landing. Gold is so common they toss it around. All who come back from the interior have it—so they play *monte*.

Many Chileans are jacks of all trades. On February 12 . . . they held a meeting to find some way to set up a government. But their resolves remained only on paper; they couldn't put them into effect. Another meeting just a few days ago was more important. It was made up of all the recent arrivals and declared itself highly opposed to admitting slavery and in favor of free labor in California. A Chilean also spoke in the meeting. He had been given a vote as a member of the council.

There is a great deal of insecurity here now. The authorities offer no protection. One is at a great disadvantage without a knowledge of English. One day a comrade turned to me in a desperate frame of mind: "Why," he asked, "are we the only ones who cannot understand English? I saw a gringo on the street talking to a mule and the mule understood him! A driver spoke to his oxen in English and they obeyed him! Why can't we understand this damned gibberish if mules and oxen can do it?" At least, his lamentations restored our good humor.

* * *

San Francisco
May 1, 1849

My friend: I promised to give you the news when we reached this port. I now have the pleasure of fulfilling this debt of friendship. I'll begin by telling you that from all I have been able to learn the wealth of gold is beyond all doubt. But to get the gold you have to overcome a mountain of difficulties.

Chilean expeditions to California have been organized in exactly the wrong way. We should bring many more peons; machines are useless here. Just to carry a machine up to the mines costs two-thousand to three thousand pesos, at the least. The price of everything here varies, as the saying goes, with the customer. There is an enormous variety of prices. One person will sell a bottle of wine for one peso, while someone else is asking three pesos; and both will sell all they have.

Later on, it is feared, Chileans will be forbidden in the mines, but there is not enough strength to enforce this as yet, and I think that for a couple of years at least there will be nothing to worry about.

This country is very rich. It has been so backward only because it was in the hands of the Spaniards.

They charge eight to ten pesos to wash a dozen shirts, but for seven pesos you can buy a dozen white cotton ones. So dirty clothing is discarded in the streets.

Apart from robbery, you can do whatever you please. The only thing I dislike about San Francisco is that it is always windy and cold. Its beautiful bay, though, must be one of the best to be found anywhere. It could hold all the navies of the world. The powerful currents and the strong winds, however, make disembarking difficult.

The city offers no diversions. Men are uninterested in anything but making money. They never seem to rest. Here you can certainly apply the English saying, "time is money," for it is the only thing they think about from morning until night. Society is something God must provide, for women are very scarce; and you cannot have society without this most precious part of nature.

All the men want to marry, and if there were two hundred women, they would all find husbands. Men here are not bothered by little difficulties that can be brushed aside. A number of Chilean

women from the red light district of Valparaíso have married here
and even enjoyed the luxury of choosing among their suitors.

※　※　※

San Francisco
May 15, 1849

As I told you in my earlier letters, we arrived on February 13
without any trouble. I had a thousand difficulties about getting
a permit to disembark, and over the arbitrary custom duties. These
ended only today. The captain sent all the sailors to the mines,
so there were only four men to unload one thousand two hundred
tons of cargo. I had to make trips back and forth so as to supervise
things, and work harder than a peon in the storeroom. I had to
make a list of what is yours and mine, make sure it got there all
right, and was not damaged. The launch charged me forty pesos
more or less for each load; and when there was less than a full
load, the charge was fifty cents a bundle. I did not want to hire
private launches to carry the cargo because, as there is no authority
to appeal to, it would be a stupid thing to do that. There is an
alcalde but he will not hear complaints, and so we have a headless
government in effect. The only judge in the city is now relieved
of his duties by the military governor and called upon himself to
answer an accusation. This place, my brother, is a prison, especially
for us Chileans who, for what reason I do not know, are looked
upon with great disfavor.

The reports of the mines you hear in this city are contradictory,
and you may have more dependable news in Valparaíso than we
have here. I can tell you I have not missed a single returning miner.
I've interviewed them and learned what I could about the mines.
Some say they found gold; some say they found only a little; and
some found none. Because of this uncertainty, and not wanting
to do the wrong thing, I have thought about giving up mining and
finding a way to get back to Chile; but I have heard so much
about the washings that I've finally decided to go and try my luck
for both our sakes. I have to make many difficult preparations for
such a venture and freight charges by sea and river are very high.
The danger to be overcome is serious, too. Food is a problem now,
even though it is more plentiful and cheaper here than in Chile.
The peons are a third cause for anxiety, though they are all still
with me at present.

PEDRO RUIZ ALDEA
1830–1870

—————◆◉◆—————

The birthplace of Ruiz Aldea was probably Concepción, Chile. His life was a short and stormy one. In 1851, at the age of twenty-one, he took part in the revolution against Montt, and, at its failure, he was forced to leave his native land temporarily. In 1859 he was involved in a second revolution, which also failed. This time, though, he was captured, tried, and condemned to death. The sentence of execution was first commuted to life imprisonment, and then to a second exile. He left Chile in 1860.

It was during this enforced absence from Chile that he came to California. The journey and the experiences in California he describes are in marked contrast to those of his fellow countrymen of a decade earlier. His account helps, therefore, to underline the exceptional nature of the hardships, antagonisms, and violence the first Chileans had faced.

In 1861, because of the proclamation of an amnesty, he returned to Chile. In the following year he founded a journal, La Tarántula, in Concepción. In 1864 he moved to Los Angeles, a small city to the southeast of Concepción, and there established another journal, El Guia del Arauco; his was the first periodical and the first printing press in that area. At the time of his death he was editing a third journal, El Meteoro. All of these show a strong interest in reform. He also contributed articles, mainly of a humorous nature, to Ferrocarril.

The selection that follows appeared in La Tarántula in 1862.

LETTERS OF AN OUTLAW

At seven o'clock in the morning they came to wake me up so I could get ready for breakfast. I did not feel like eating, though, and the heat made me drowsy; so I slept on until eight.

At that time I went up on deck for a breath of air. There I noticed for the first time what a large group of people we had on board. The men were reading, writing, or sketching. The children were playing. The ladies were talking together or sewing. It was all like a miniature republic in which each person could follow the interests or amusements of his choice.

Freedom really reigned on these ships. A man could take his coat off if he felt uncomfortable. He could sit down anywhere he chose, even on the deck. If the lounging chairs were all occupied he could lie down on the deck and go to sleep there. Nobody would bother him. The deck flooring was covered with a thick carpet, and there were two deck stewards constantly going about sweeping up even the least trash. In addition there were two receptacles for waste material. The decks were almost excessively clean.

I went down into the steerage compartment, which also carried passengers. I found these were given the same care and attention that we were. I noticed there were fifteen head of cattle, a sty for swine, and pens for every kind of fowl.

They tell me that on this ship, as well as on all the ships of this company, there is a hospital area reserved for persons who become ill. There is a drug shop in the charge of a doctor; and there is also a shop where they sell liquor and refeshments. During the morning hours there tends to be such a throng of customers that it is all two Yankees can do to wait on them. What they mainly order is lemonade, sarsaparilla (not the medical sort), and a marvelous ice cream soda.

At twelve, a bell tells us it is time for us to go down to lunch. Each passenger is assigned a seat at the table by a numbered card; mine placed me with four ladies. This caused me some embarrassment: they asked me to pass the bread and I handed them the

[219]

sugar. At that, my seat companions, knowing I did not speak English, adopted the custom of helping themselves.

At five o'clock in the afternoon they ring the bell again for dinner. At this meal, as at breakfast, they serve either tea or coffee, whichever you prefer, after the main course. Children get a special breakfast at six in the morning.

In the evening there is a party. Some pair off and dance to the sound of a violin. The violinist, as he plays, calls out to the dancers the movements they are to execute.

On other nights there are concerts of violin, guitar, flute, and accordion, but they never play all together. The violinist plays only solos. Afterward some of the ladies get together and sing, either by themselves or accompanied by gentlemen.

These concerts are not without charm. The throngs seated or moving about make a striking picture; the moon sheds rays of gentle light; the waves murmur, and the breezes play with the candles. All of this helps build up a poetic atmosphere at these affairs. These deck parties go on until the first light of morning. By that time the overwarm air of the cabins has become cool, and the people begin to retire to them. The lamp keeps on burning in the salon, and the waiters remain watchful. At the first bell, while it is still night (that is, at four o'clock) and the moon still rules the arch of heaven, the sailors go about waking up the passengers still sleeping on the poop deck so they can clean it.

In spite of the fact that we have been sailing three days and that the ship goes at the rate of twelve miles an hour, the temperature has not varied an iota. Today, June 2, I awake, wilted with the heat. My first interest is getting a glass of water, and a second later I am ready to eat.

The fourth day dawns cloudy, and the north wind restores our exhausted strength very nicely. On this day, a Sunday, while I am reading on deck, I hear a voice in the salon raised in a tone of warning; it goes on growing louder and louder. Finally it arouses my curiosity. At first I thought it was some kind of argument, but since there is only one voice, stern and solemn, and because of the unusual silence, I go down to find out what is going on. All the ladies and gentlemen, except those of a different religion, are gathered in the salon listening with religious attention to an orator. This orator stands at the head of the group; on a table is a jug of water and a book that he touches from time to time as though

to affirm with it what he has said, and he pronounces the name
of Saint Paul. Later he stops speaking, and another man takes his
place. This one speaks in a low voice, in the tone one uses in
praying, and with his eyes closed. Then the first one speaks a few
more words, holds out his arms to the crowd, and they all stand
up. This is the way the Yankees celebrate Sunday.

On the night of the fifth, after the singing and dancing were
over, I remained as usual to sleep on the deck, watching the light
of the moon as it danced on the water producing phosphorescent
effects. I had been asleep about an hour in a feverish dream when
some imperious shouts and the clangor of a bell woke me up. I
looked around and saw we were sailing between two coasts. It
was one o'clock in the morning; we were entering the port of
Acapulco. The town was spread confusedly about the base of some
mountains. A smoky torch was burning on a ship, and we veered
to the left toward it. At some of the houses along the beach we
could hear dogs barking.

We anchored and began to take on water and coal. Mexicans
came selling oranges, lemons, cigars, bananas, pineapples, enchila-
das, and some very pretty bouquets of flowers made from shell-
fish—this was a curiosity very much admired. At six that morning
when the loading was finished the ship got under way, leaving
the port, and we went back to resume our sleep. At eleven o'clock
that same day the steamer stopped at the port of Manzanillo to
debark a few passengers bound for Mazatlán. The passenger boat
left the ship as we stood crowded upon the deck watching it appear
and disappear in the rolling waves; then it circled around behind
some rocks and we did not see it any more.

In those two days the weather had changed completely. One
no longer felt the oppressive heat of the previous night, nor the
constant thirst for water that tormented us. Summer clothing now
gave way to the sort that gave more protection; and the parties
on deck were now held in the salon. Last night I tried to sleep
on deck, but at one o'clock the cold awakened me and I went
down to my cabin.

Now the nights were spent in reading, playing, or conversing
around the tables, but there was such a crowd that one had to
be alert to find a chair or a place on a sofa.

This morning a Yankee started to play a saraband on the violin.
Everyone standing around no sooner heard it than they started

dancing it, and even the Negroes going around making the beds joined in. Yesterday on the forward deck I saw two passengers executing this devilish dance with a truly unusual vigor and grace.

Some days afterward a confused roaring of voices was raised, and we all left our seats to go and see what it was: it was a whale that was passing. Later it was a troop of tortoises, and later still a school of fishes. Later yet the same clamor came again; this time it was just the sun going down in the ocean.

Today, June 13, I awoke at five in the morning. The weather was stormy. The sea was tossing in fearful confusion. The steamer was creaking and quivering, and the passengers sitting on the rails so as not to fall down. From time to time they would look up to see the mountains of water that came roaring to break against the side of the ship and flood the deck. The waiters were setting the tables, the cups of tea rocked, the plates rolled and crashed on the floor. The bell called us to come for breakfast, but it was impossible to eat in comfort. How we bumped and stumbled into one another!

After breakfast they passed out the lists of hotels, inns, and other establishments. At ten I went to my berth to gather up my loose articles. More than once I had to stop doing this, either because the ship was heeling over or because the water rose above my port hole and cut off the light. The stewards were rolling up the bedding, and in one room they were taking down cots they had set up. The ladies were donning their finer clothing. The weather was moderating little by little.

At one o'clock in the afternoon, standing on deck, I could make out a misty coast, and farming land on the slopes of some of the hills. Later the horizon became clearer and things began to emerge more sharply. We were heading toward land, the sun was breaking through the clouds. Four banners were hoisted; we saw houses and cattle, then a fortress, and then, around a bend of the coast—San Francisco, city of romance.

At three-thirty we are approaching a dock structure where coaches are waiting for us. How well dressed these people look! All of them are handing us cards and handbills and offering us hotels and their carriages. What a confusion of sounds! What a babble of tongues! Has the last trumpet sounded?

The port of San Francisco is vast. There are streets, elegant buildings, spacious stores. The bay is as calm as a lake. You can see a ship with masts, a dense cloud of smoke given off by steamers of every size, piles of lumber, bundles, boxes, barrels, a multitude of freight handlers who come and go like ants. There are carts drawn by powerful Percheron horses, carriages crammed with passengers, men hawking cigars, oranges, and newspapers, an army of Chinese with long pigtails, parrots speaking English they have been taught, and an infinity of things baffling description.

At four o'clock I take a coach for the California Hotel where Spanish is spoken as well as English and French. At the same hour, the newspapers are announcing the arrival of the *Golden Gate*, and one of them has a list of the passengers who total 803. The French daily paper puts the number at 1,000.

Here is an odd coincidence: I left Valparaíso on Thursday, got off in Panamá on Thursday, reembarked for this port on a Thursday, and arrived here in San Francisco on Thursday.

TRAVEL ALONG THE COAST

Some days later I undertook an excursion along the coast. At eight in the morning, in the *San Antonio*, I crossed the bay that divides San Francisco from O'Kland. As the steamer pulled out I went up on the deck to take in the view of the bay. From my position I could see to left and right a confused forest of masts and the immense residential area of San Francisco climbing up and down the hills. Before me through the morning fog I saw the town of O'Kland and a forest of oaks. The sea and coast stretched off to the north of the town; to the south there was something I could not make out. They told me later it was the town of San Antonio.

The crossing took a half-hour, and cost a quarter. We approach a pier and I get off. There are four coaches there to take people to various places farther on.

O'Kland has one main street, wide and sandy, and at the far end there are some isolated oaks. The town is full of inns, shops, hotels, and cafes or restaurants. Like all the towns of California, it is linked to the outside world by telegraph, steamship, stagecoach, the press, and other facilities.

In California, if it is a question of establishing a post office, they do not ask, as we do in Chile, how big the town is, but simply where it is. They do not say, as someone said in our Senate when it was proposed to build a railroad between Concepción and Talca-huano: "Why do those boobs want a railroad? To amuse themselves?"

In California it does not happen, as it does with us, that when some miserable little facility is built we talk about it with delight and bless our government officials—we are so used to them never doing anything!

I remember in Santiago how the people crowded around gaping at the sight when telegraph poles were set up to connect with Valparaíso, and in their delusions cried out: "How clear it is that we are in the Age of Miracles!"

When it was explained to them later that the telegraph system could not carry letters the way the post office did, the crowd exclaimed in disappointment, "Fiddlesticks, it's good for nothing but conversation!"

Why set up the telegraph in Concepción if it is good for nothing but conversation? Why have a railroad if the boobs are interested only in amusing themselves? Why have a post office? A stagecoach line? A printing press? A library? Why any of these if the people are not in a condition to appreciate them?

But let us leave these domestic problems and return to those in California.

In the group of stagecoaches that wait for passengers at the dock, there is one whose driver calls out in English, "Going to San Pablo!" I get into this conveyance and we set out. The vegetation has a luxuriant charm. The most intoxicating scents perfume the air. The sky is clear, and the air soft and agreeable. On one side the sea appears like a great emerald; on the other a row of hills stretches; and in the center lies a most lovely valley, sown with wheat and barley that is just beginning to head. Why do these beautiful fields bring back to my memory those of Chile? In everything my eyes see there is reflected the adored vision of my faraway fatherland.

I arrive at a place called The Quail, and alight from the coach. The field hands keep on with their work without paying any attention to who is arriving or leaving. It is all so different from Chile: there we look when anyone goes by; we talk about it and drop our work to find out who it is, where he has come from, where he is going, and why.

From The Quail I start out for San Pablo on horseback with a Chilean. It was hot, but luckily we soon reach the town and dismount at a Chilean hotel.

Who is this Madame Serwood, the Mammoth Lady, whose picture I have been seeing everywhere for days? This Madame Serwood is an Irish woman of an extraordinary size. She weighs 643 pounds, and displays herself in hotels for an entrance fee of fifty cents. One day the Yankees wanted to make her strip and get weighed while they watched, but the good madame would not accept the challenge.

From San Pablo to Pinol and from there to San Joaquín, everywhere I saw the same panorama with some slight changes of terrain. I saw ships pass on their way to Sacramento and other towns. I also saw Vallejo, and farther on, behind some hills to our right, I saw Martínez.

In spite of being among Chileans, a good part of the talk was over my head because they used Mexican words whose meaning I did not know. Here are some of them with their respective translations:

Milpas	Chácaras	Cornfields
Chícaros	Arvejas	Vetch
Elotes	Choclos	Young maize
Hijotes	Frejoles	Beans
Pinol	Harina	Flour
Sacate	Pasto	Pasture
Rancho	Fundo	Farm
Reata	Lazo	Lariat
Mecate	Soga	Halter
Chirrión	Chicote	Rope handle
Jalar	Tirar	Pull
Persogar	Amarrar un Caballo	Tie a Horse
Pillar hijotes	Arrancar porotos	Harvest beans
Envolver tamales	Hacer humitas	Make tamales

Many of these words give rise to laughable mistakes. One day when I was traveling by stage from Martínez, a passenger from that town said to me: "When are you going to rent yourself?" [¿Cuando se arrienda usted?] What he meant to ask was: "When are you coming back?"

Chileans enjoy more rights and advantages in California than in Chile. That is the reason why they emigrate to that country.

The Chilean is the most sought-after of all South Americans for agricultural work. The reason is that he understands this kind of work and he can compete with the Yankee in physical strength. The Chilean is not thought of as a day laborer but as a steady hired hand on the farms. He lives in a room, sleeps on a bed, eats in a dining room, earns from one to two dollars on a farm, and three or four in the mines. He eats fresh meat, vegetables, fish, white bread, butter; and at certain times takes tea or coffee if he feels like it. He dresses with more or less care and decency according to his means. He travels on steamships and on stage-coaches. He stays at first-class hotels, and goes to the theater. In short, he is welcome anywhere, and no one shows any hostility to him unless he gives them due cause for it. In California, if he is bankrupt they do not put him in jail, as they do so savagely here in Chile. If he does not want to work for wages, he buys whatever land he wants. If he wants to get married, he pays the fee that seems proper to him, and the marriage ceremony is the same for everyone.

The conditions that face our peons and tenants here [in Chile] are certainly very different. How do they treat them on our haciendas?—like raw Negro slaves, subject to the voice and whip of a master. They sleep in the open fields, in haystacks, or in the kitchen. They eat a ration of badly cooked beans, with a flour gruel when they can get it. They earn a miserable daily wage, dress shabbily, and find themselves frequently in the police stations, in jail, or some dive. How can we hope that our *huasos* [cowboys] become civilized if we regard them as a race of outlaws, if we profit from their sweat to increase our fortunes, if we exclude them from participation in public affairs, and only take them into account when they stage revolts?

Our field hands do not get a single day of rest all year long. They work all week for their patrón and then are at the call of a judge or commandant. What does the judge want? He wants to send a letter to the lower haciendas. He wants them to arrest certain neighbors whom he dislikes. He wants them to patrol at night. And they must perform these services gratis, without any pay, on their own horses, and at their own expense, under threat of a fine or the gallows.

Why, and in virtue of what law, are citizens obliged to take on the duty of patrolling? The only legitimate reason would be public security—but that security is the responsibility of public agencies, not of individuals.

Compulsory patrol service by citizens is a new obligation, and we do not recognize any right or authority in the executive branch to demand it. Only Congress can impose such duties; this is expressly stated in the Constitution.

To force citizens to undertake duties as watchmen all night and thus incapacitate them for work next day is both burdensome and damaging to them. Meanwhile the soldier is sleeping in the barracks, receiving his pay every month, rising in rank and receiving awards without fighting. The farm hands do not have any of these prerogatives.

Our workers do not even get Sunday off, because the commandant is waiting for them in the field to teach them something. What?—how to handle a lance!

And when they are not undergoing these instructions for the commandant, they are working for nothing in his harvest fields, hunting for animals he has let stray—is there anything more odious than these personal services exacted from our field hands by militia underlings or commandants? This is why military men are so fond of frontier assignments.

The poor never escape their lot because they have no time to work for themselves; they do not have enough even to care for their own families. So, having nothing and constantly in debt, they go to jail, or they turn to crime, or they uproot themselves from their own country and flee to live among the Araucanians in immorality and licentiousness.

To escape the poverty that burdens them, the judges and militia commandants who tyrannize over them, the priest who will not marry them unless they pay him a fee greater than they can earn in a month or two, they leave their country and go to a foreign land.

And they are right! They will find among the Araucanians and the Yankees more opportunity, more liberty, better pay, and less slavery. Among us they find ignominy, chains, and the gallows!

BIBLIOGRAPHY

Ayers, James J. *Gold and Sunshine: Reminiscences of Early California.* Boston, 1922.

Bancroft, Hubert Howe. *California inter Pocula.* San Francisco, 1888.

———. *History of California,* vols. 5–6. San Francisco, 1888–89.

———. *Popular Tribunals,* 2 vols. San Francisco, 1887.

Barros Arana, Juan. *Un decenio de la Historia de Chile,* 2 vols. Santiago, 1913.

Bowman, Alan P. *Index to the 1850 Census of California.* Baltimore, 1972.

Bunster, Enrique. *Chilenos en California.* Santiago, 1954.

Caughey, John W. *Gold is the Cornerstone.* Berkeley, 1948.

Clappe, Louise. *The Shirley Letters from the California Mines.* New York, 1949.

Colección de artículos noticias y capítulos de cartas con respecto a California publicados por la prensa sobre el descubrimiento de los lavaderos de San Francisco. Santiago, 1849.

Combet, Pedro Isidoro. "Recuerdos de California." *El Museo,* I (1853).

Davis, William H. *Seventy-five Years in California.* San Francisco, 1929.

Faugstead, George E. *The Chileans in the California Gold Rush.* Palo Alto, 1974.

Feliú Cruz, Guillermo. 'Vicente Pérez, escritor." *Boletín de la Biblioteca Nacional* 5 (1933).

Giacobbi, Stephen. *Chile and Her Argonauts in the Gold Rush.* Palo Alto, 1974.

Henry Varonius, F.S.C. "Chilean Forty-niners." *Academy Scrapbook* 5 (1968).

Hernández Cornejo, Roberto. *Los Chilenos en San Francisco de California.* 2 vols. Valparaíso, 1930.

Ishams, George S. *Guide to California and the Mines.* New York, 1950.

[230] Bibliography

Jackson, Joseph F. *Bad Company*. New York, 1949.

Johnson, John J. "Talcahuano and Concepción as seen by the Forty-niners." *Hispanic American Historical Review*, 26 (1950).

López, Carlos U. *Chilenos in California*. Palo alto, 1973.

———. "El Asalto a Chilecito." *El Mercurio* (1973).

———. *Episodios chilenos en California*. Valparaíso, 1975.

———. *Historia de la Marina de Chile*. Santiago, 1969.

Monaghan, Jay. *Chile, Peru and the California Gold Rush*. Berkeley, 1973.

Nadeau, Remi. *Ghost Towns and Mining Camps of California*. Los Angeles, 1965.

Nasatir, Abraham. "Chileans in California during the Gold Rush." California Historical Quarterly 3 (1934).

Navarro, Jil. "Los chilenos en California." *El Correo del Sur* 3 (1853–54).

Pereira Salas, Eugenio. *Bibliografía chilena sobre el Gold Rush en California*. Washington, n.d.

Pérez Rosales, Vicente. *A California Adventure*. San Francisco, 1947.

———. *Diario de un Viaje a California*. Buenos Aires, 1971.

———. *Recuerdos del Pasado*. Santiago, 1882.

———. "Viaje a California." *Revista Chilena* 10 (1878).

Perkins, William. *El Campo de los Sonoraenses: Tres años de residencia en California, 1849–1851*. Buenos Aires, 1937.

Pitt, Leonard. *The Decline of the Californios*. Berkeley, 1966.

Rassmussen, Louis J. *San Francisco Ship Passenger Lists*. San Bruno, 1958.

Ruiz Aldea, Pedro. "La Cartera de un Proscrito." *La Tarántula* 1 (1862).

Véliz, Claudio. *Historia de la Marina Mercante de Chile*. Santiago, 1961.

Vicuña Mackenna, Benjamín. *Páginas de mi Diario de Viaje*. Santiago, 1862.

———. *Páginas de mi Diario durante tres años de viajes*. Santiago, 1936.

Wood, Richard C. *Calaveras: The Land of the Skulls*. Sonora, 1950.